Riding the Biscuit Highway

James Wilson

An extraordinary tale of three friends who attempt to bicycle 15,000 miles down the Americas

Published 2008 by arima publishing

www.arimapublishing.com

ISBN 978 1 84549 306 6

© James Wilson 2008

All rights reserved

This book is copyright. Subject to statutory exception and to provisions of relevant collective licensing agreements, no part of this publication may be reproduced, stored in a retrieval system, or transmitted in any form or by any means, without the prior written permission of the author.

Printed and bound in the United Kingdom

Typeset in Garamond 11/14

This book is sold subject to the conditions that it shall not, by way of trade or otherwise, be lent, re-sold, hired out, or otherwise circulated without the publisher's prior consent in any form of binding or cover other than that which it is published and without a similar condition including this condition being imposed on the subsequent purchaser.

Photography by Anthony Arnold, James Wilson and Martin Green
Sketches by Simon Eardley (www.simoneardleyart.piczo.com)

Swirl is an imprint of arima publishing.

arima publishing
ASK House, Northgate Avenue
Bury St Edmunds, Suffolk IP32 6BB
t: (+44) 01284 700321

www.arimapublishing.com

Front Cover Photo; Descending from Puente del Inca, Mendoza, Argentina
Rear Cover Photo; Approaching the Atigun Pass, Brooks Range, Alaska

Contents

Foreword		5
Preface		7
Acknowledgements		9
Prologue		13
Chapter 1	"There's a flippin' Caribou on the runway!"	17
Chapter 2	"You guys are stallions!"	29
Chapter 3	"I've been looking for you guys for 150 miles!"	39
Chapter 4	Room 118	49
Chapter 5	"Bye Jeanette!"	57
Chapter 6	"You never listen to a thing I say!"	67
Chapter 7	"It's the boonies down there"	77
Chapter 8	Punctures, Diarrhoea and Paralysis	85
Chapter 9	Pink Flamingos	91
Chapter 10	Mud huts and Casinos	99
Chapter 11	"Smelly, dirty and full of death"	113
Chapter 12	The Children of Chalatenango	123
Chapter 13	"This might sting a little"	133
Chapter 14	Carlos and Alonso	145
Chapter 15	Chicken and Rice	157
Chapter 16	"Pull your shorts down"	167
Chapter 17	A touch of Stardom	177
Chapter 18	Patagonia	187
Epilogue		199
Plan International		201
Statistics		203
Kit List		205
Route & Chapter Guide		207

Foreword

The romantic ideal of escaping the rat race is something that many aspire to, but the reality of walking away from security and comfort into a world of risk, challenge and uncertainty is often far harder than it seems.

One of the great paradoxes of expedition life is that living with friends on the open road (or desert dune, Arctic plateau or Himalayan valley) can often be intensely claustrophobic; that the seemingly carefree pursuit of an arbitrary goal can often lead to intense pressure, to bitter disagreement and to an inescapable exposure of all aspects of human nature.

This book is a frank and brutally honest account of a 347-day, 15,000-mile odyssey that is in many ways a journey of self-discovery, a story of the fripperies of modern life being stripped away as three friends struggle to achieve a seemingly impossible challenge against mounting odds.

I cannot recall a single day of any of my own expeditions that has been "ok" or "not too bad", and James' experience echoes my own. This is a story of soaring highs and crushing lows, a tale of perspiration, desperation and inspiration that will, I hope, encourage others to seek out their own adventures, not as a decadent escape from a 9-5 existence, but as an opportunity to delve deep into themselves; to experience a life stripped bare and to test themselves, and the bonds that hold we humans together, to their very limits.

Ben Saunders, *Polar Explorer.*

Preface

Like the trip, writing this book became a passion. Ultimately, I thought the experience worth telling and sharing with those who also dream of trying something different, along a path where the unknown is reason enough. I didn't want feelings and emotions to disappear completely, to be left only with some photos and a grubby diary when the year was like no other, a year that revealed many strengths and just as many weaknesses.

Bear in mind that this is *my* take on our journey. Unearthing deeper feelings was painful but they reveal the swirling mess inside my head. I could never sculpt a hopeless tale like some travel writers, who'd have you believe the natives are waiting to pounce because their backup GPS has gone on the blink. This is more an open examination, a show all account of the monotonous and unglamorous. It focuses on the attitudes that led to loss of direction and appreciation of the bigger picture; a result of the mind-blowing frustration and an inescapable duty to continue. Although there were countless side-splitting moments and episodes of real wonder, being together for so long came at a price. On many occasions I wanted to walk away from my friends, from the bike and in a strange way even from myself.

James Wilson.

Acknowledgements

I am extremely grateful to Anthony and Martin for their contributions. Their passages give the book more balance and bring a refreshing insight into the more pertinent episodes on the road.

To Tim Garratt, a man who knows a great deal about cycle touring and writing about it. For his undying enthusiasm when I needed guidance and encouragement, Tim has been a great source of advice and information regarding story telling.

Finally, a word of thanks to Simon Eardley for the numerous sketches of life on the road.

*To Anthony, Martin
&
The Children of Chalatenango*

Prologue

Location: Bullards Beach, USA. Mile: 3,210. 3rd November.

'What are you doing mate?' I heard Martin say.

'I am getting out of here' snapped Paps.

Poking my head out from my warm sleeping bag, I shouted beyond the walls of my tent. 'What's going on?'

There was no response so I put my shoes and jacket back on and stepped out into the squall. Zipping up my tent door I felt the cold, unforgiving wind that had been tracking our every move for the past week and wondered over to where the action was. I huddled next to Stu, watching him boil up a pan of water and began listening to the argument that was now in full flow.

'You never listen to a thing I say!' screamed Paps. 'I've been telling you and Wils for a week that my knee hurts but we keep doing 50-mile days!'

'We did 36 miles yesterday and got a hotel because it was raining and your knee hurt.'

'Yesterday I had to get off and push! I can't keep going on like this.'

'Well, what do you want us to do about it? We did four days to Canon Beach and then took a day's rest. Then we've done five days to get here.'

'Canon Beach wasn't a day off 'cos we cycled from Seaside.'

'That was because we didn't want to pay US$45 for a hostel!'

'Yeah, but it's not a day off.'

'OK, but it was only nine miles,' insisted Martin. 'Why are you leaving now?'

'What choice do I have? You and Wils just talk like nothing is happening to me! If we are gonna do the miles I have to leave now and do it bit by bit.'

'If your knee is that bad, let's talk about it, don't just walk off!'

'I do try to talk about it! You and Wils aren't listening to what I am saying! It's fucking painful! Sometimes I am two or three miles behind. When you stop, I catch up, you ask me how I am and then ride off again. I am fed up spending all day on my own! You two don't seem to get it!'

I had never seen Paps so angry yet he seemed to have the appetite for more. The argument had caused my heart to race and my tongue to fall silent but suddenly I felt compelled to get involved.

'Hang on a minute!' I cried. 'You've hardly said a word to Martin and I in two days! All we get are grunts and you being in a mardy! Bottling it up will get us nowhere. What are we meant to do, be in a bad mood too?'

'It feels like I am all alone out here.'

'Mate, yesterday we got to Reedsport and got a hotel room. I went and did the laundry and I bought some beer. Martin cooked a great meal but none of it had any effect whatsoever! We got no response from you. How do you think that makes us feel?'

'I appreciated it, believe me,' said Paps, attaching his tent to the top of his trailer.

'Maybe Wils and I *do* need to listen more but that's only possible if you talk to us,' said Martin, taking over. 'You aren't alone. There's no point in doing a half day now. You know what everyone thinks of them, they're rubbish. Everyone gets wet and sweaty and we still have to take the tents down and put them back up again. Come on mate, put your tent back up and let's get out of the rain.'

'I can't see I have any choice.'

'Yes you do. If you go now we will have failed. We are stronger than this.'

Paps remained motionless, head bowed with both gloved hands clasping the handlebar of his bike. The rain was unrelenting, swirling around on a vicious wind that shook the tall mature trees surrounding us. Raindrops exploded in my ears as they hit the hood of my anorak. It was dark, cold and I felt strangely removed yet the significance of the next few moments was huge.

13 weeks earlier...

Chapter 1

'There's a flippin' caribou on the runway!'

>*'A goal without a plan is just a wish.'*
>Antoine de Saint-Exupery
>Born France, 1900

Start Point: Deadhorse, USA. Mile: 0. 4th August.

We peered out through the window of the reconfigured Boeing 737 jet as it swept in over the runway.

'Did you see that?' asked Martin. 'There's a flippin' caribou on the runway!'

Martin, Anthony and I had been studying the landscape intensely as the pilot made his final approach. There were no snowy peaks or thick carpet of pine trees. It was just tundra and in the distance a shimmering Arctic Ocean. I kept thinking, "Shit, this is it…this is it." We hit the deck hard and taxied to a stop opposite a tiny terminal building the size of a large bungalow. A rush of goose bumps flew up my back and down my arms as I unclipped my seatbelt and followed Martin out of the aircraft and onto the tarmac. Drawing in a deep lungful of warm August air I stole a quick glance at Anthony. "This really is it…" The other passengers strode meaningfully toward the terminal without a care in the world. No matter that we were 300 miles north of the Arctic Circle, this was their place of work, a testosterone-filled world where biting mosquitoes, marauding grizzly and polar bears and temperatures of -40°C were all part of the deal. This was Deadhorse, a minute outpost on the shores of Prudhoe Bay where a couple of porta-cabin hotels and a number of sheds marked the edge of civilisation and the location of Alaska's largest oil field. Beyond the buildings was nothing but thousands of square miles of Arctic tundra known as the North Slope.

Before too long we had picked up six heavily strapped cardboard boxes and I had cut my hand on a sharp piece of fencing as nerves continued to devour me. A lady working in the terminal came over to see what we were up to as I sucked blood from my finger.

'How far are you going?' she asked, studying our partly built bikes and trailers.

'All the way I'm afraid, all the way to Argentina,' replied Anthony.

'Well be careful,' she said, without blinking. 'There's a grizzly in the complex somewhere.'

'You're joking right?' said Anthony.

'They're looking for food ya know, scavenging, being nearly autumn and all. Do ya need anything?'

'We were just wondering where the Arctic Caribou Hotel is?' asked Martin.

Security within the oil fields was tight. It wasn't possible to start our journey from the shores of the Arctic Ocean so we hooked up with Bob, who ran a licensed outfit operating out of the hotel. Bob was a quiet middle-aged man who gave you the impression he'd seen it all before. He took us out to the coast in his van, to a pebble beach scattered with large amounts of driftwood. The water was a near perfect mirror with icebergs marking the distant horizon. The whole scene made me stop and reflect, to wonder if the south Atlantic would look the same as this.

I returned to my friends, stripped off my shoes and socks and stood in the freezing water still reeling from the slightly crazy sensation our remote location afforded us. Martin had the video camera running.

'So, we are at the edge of the Arctic Ocean and about to start cycling,' he said by way of setting the scene for future viewers. 'How do you feel?'

'Nervous!' I replied. 'Let's get pedalling!'

Back at the hotel things got even wackier when a group of British motorcyclists rolled in from Argentina. Their 15,000-mile journey was over. They and their bikes were covered in dust and splattered with mud, their panniers decked out with dozens of stickers denoting months on the road. Through the grime, their faces told a story. All of them looked mightily proud, almost euphoric but there was also a feeling of relief etched across their brows. As they stood around, hugging each other and regaling the final chapter, I found myself gawking like a third-form pupil watching the sixth-form football team. Their powerful, wide-bodied machines towered above our skinny pushbikes. The examination we had set ourselves was now clear for all to see.

What have we got ourselves involved in? I barely know how to change a tyre...

My rising distress was broken by a request to get one of us on camera. The bikers had hired a professional film crew to document their journey and the director was keen on an interview. Without much prompting Anthony stepped forward. Anthony, or *Paps* as he was known - having been born in Papua New Guinea – was a very confident, personable and annoyingly charismatic character.

'Hi guys, you're just starting right?' encouraged the director, as the cameraman swung around to get Martin and I in the shot.

'Ahh, yes we are, and thanks for reminding us just how far it is to Argentina!' quipped Paps, dressing up his home-counties accent just a fraction. 'Let me show you our bikes and kit. As you can see we're *cycling* it, not sitting on powerful motorbikes like yourselves...'

His teasing caused the muscles in my face to contort. In truth though, I was struggling. We were minutes from starting something that had to be finished. It just had to be. What made it worse was that we were here of our own doing. We'd constructed the whole damn thing out of ideas, jest and bravado. The planning stage had come and gone and now the challenge of a lifetime awaited. Terror status was only being held at bay because two close friends were in the same boat. I had them to lean on, to drag me through but what were they thinking? What was about to happen to us? Would we even make it to the nearest settlement 240 miles away? Would we run out of food? Would we succumb to a grizzly? Right at that moment, the enormity engulfed me. The road into the unknown was waiting.

Paps's briefing came to an end and the group went indoors, presumably for a shower and something to eat. Then all went quiet. The lowly noise of a truck driver striking his tyres with a wooden baton rang out across the gravel yard. We were almost ready. Just a litre or two of petrol for the stove and we'd be set. We headed west a few hundred metres to a fuel station, the weight of my trailer making the bike slightly awkward to ride.

'There's no-one here,' I said, pulling up opposite one of the fuel pumps.

Just then an Engineer drove by in a huge 4x4, closely followed by an even bigger dust trail. Paps gesticulated with a fuel bottle. "Help yourselves!" came his signal.

Brilliant sunshine reflected off the white dusty gravel as everyone straddled their ride. 'This is it boys!' stated Martin, with a masochistic grin on his face.

He got no response from Paps or I. We headed out to the start of the Dalton highway, our companion for the next 400 miles and the only way out. Looking back the whole business was a strange anticlimax. Crunching our way along the wide gravel road, the first few rotations of the pedals got me thinking again…

- *Martin is right, this is it. I can't believe it.*
- *Well you've got your challenge.*
- *I know but I'm going home if it gets too tough.*
- *No you're not. You're too stubborn and you've told too many people.*
- *Yes but I've never done more than a 3-day trip before.*
- *That's your fault. Too late now.*

The horizon was perfectly flat in all directions, save for the odd oil well and the disappearing skyline of Deadhorse behind us. We rode three abreast using the Dalton's width, its edges marked by two-metre high metal stakes, guides to drivers during heavy snowfall. It was warm and mosquitoes began flooding in from the surrounding heather, hovering ominously above our heads. We were on our way.

*

Paps, Martin and I had formed our friendship at Bangor University in North Wales. Ten years later the idea for a big challenge had grown past the proverbial bullshit stage and entered full commitment. We wanted to escape before marriage and children threatened to put a stop on things. I was also bored with the conformity of everyday life and the contemplation of forty more years of the same. I couldn't have cared less about forging my way up the career ladder and was hacked off with sitting in traffic and succumbing to suburban banality. Surely the stuff worth exploring was buried beneath years of material world creature comforts? I mean, how well did we really know ourselves? What would happen if we changed the boundaries for a while and exposed ourselves to a world we knew nothing of and had little control over?

There could be no half measures. The challenge had to strip away timescales and distances that we understood and it had to be done in a way that removed any real reliance on others. The scale had to be obscene. The form of the challenge centred on all of us enjoying sport and physical exertion. Martin was a chisel-jawed good-looking sod, agile and strong as an ox, his body conditioned by years of fitness and strength training. He'd had a myriad of jobs after University and then settled into the fitness industry, eventually passing a series of exams and qualifying as a personal trainer. His company was flourishing but he was desperate to rip free and "disappear," as he put it. Paps was another pretty boy, blessed with plenty of sporting ability. He'd spent years living all over the place, moving to Australia with his family in 1982 and then on to the UK in '88 staying until after University, when he then worked in Singapore, the UK and back in Australia gaining a teaching qualification in Perth. Then there was me, Wils. Only my family or work colleagues called me by my Christian name. I had eked out a career in Environmental Engineering but was desperate to break free. What drew me most was the chance to team up with two close friends on a crazy project. I needed something tangible to hang my hat on, something to take me away from the ocean of pessimism and regret that would await in future years because I knew great things were possible. I knew something was lurking inside me that needed fulfilling and this was my chance.

The idea of a cycle ride made sense to all of us even though none of us had done any cycling. Its simplicity meant we didn't have to go off and learn a whole bunch of new skills. Skills that you need to attempt a Himalayan peak or Channel swim, for example. Yet by racking up the timescales and distances, the ride might enter the same realms of audacity. Eight hours in the saddle, carrying 30kgs of gear sounded tough; tougher still the mental fatigue. Here was where the temptation to quit would be just as great as the will needed to carry on. We took this embryonic idea forward and looked for a route. Martin favoured a crack at London to Sydney but Paps and I were discouraged by the extended stretches of open water. Instead, we preferred an equally ambitious trail, the famed Pan-Americana. This was a legendary road amongst the cycling and motorcycling fraternity which snaked its way down the Americas through 14 countries and seven time zones ending in Tierra del Fuego, Argentina. It had everything. There was Arctic tundra, mountain passes, jungle and desert. Our thirst for self-examination had grown beyond all rationale and the Pan-Americana sat at the heart of it. Paps recalls…

Of course, one has to be in a position to actually get away with doing such a thing if the opportunity arises. In other words, you are willing to walk away from your job and any domestic commitments. For me it also involved other notions such as wanting to run away from life and its responsibilities. The fact that the trip came about through banter over email and phone didn't lessen its importance or seriousness. This time the scale was so much grander. Looking back I don't remember how the conversations went exactly but it is a question often asked of me. We certainly didn't know that we were about to embark on an adventure that would take over much of the next 3 years of our lives and that during that time, we would be stretched to our limits mentally, physically, financially and emotionally.

I dared not tell anyone at first because the details were still emerging and it sounded so bloody pretentious. "Look at us! We're going to cycle 15,000 miles and do so living out of a tent, carrying our own gear!" Even I wanted to say, "Piss off you twat!" This shyness was well founded because scepticism would come from many quarters. "Yeah, of course you are," or "Really? Umm, anyway what you drinkin'?" The doubters galvanised our resolve, gave weight to the project and confirmed how utterly inconceivable it would be to pull off so we pushed on with the planning, managing by phone and email. Paps was living in Australia and Martin in Surrey. I, on the other hand, was spread between work in Essex and an MSc course in Cardiff so the project took shape slowly. We had landed on a simple, repetitive exercise but knew little of what came with it. I knew nothing about bike parts or their maintenance. We knew nothing of what kit we needed, when to begin, what our living costs would be. Nor did we know anything of half the countries we would pass through, the political situations and risk to our safety, nor the terrain or weather. Everyone took on assigned responsibilities for the route, for items of kit and once a week Paps and I reported back to each other using phone cards.

'The first four to five hundred miles are on gravel, there isn't a building for 240 miles and by day four we need to climb a pass higher than Ben Nevis,' stated Paps, 10,000 miles away in Perth.

'What?'

Hyping up the scale of everything suited Paps and I but Martin was so laid back about the whole thing, I wondered if he was reading from a different trip brief. "It'll be a blast!" he would reply. I remain adamant he saw the whole thing as a spot of cycling with plenty of adventures in-between. My fear allowed only more occasional escapism. I couldn't help wonder what it would feel like to be so together, so alone, so tired, so elated. I craved what I couldn't predict and that felt exciting. The weeks went by and my trip file got bigger and bigger. I held aspirations of clinching a deal with Channel 4 or the BBC with a video diary that viewers could connect with from the comfort of their armchairs. On the back of this, sponsorship from kit manufacturers would become a doddle and we might even get a bit of cash to go toward food, inoculations, flights and insurance. Yet all our efforts went nowhere. I scratched my head and rethought our approach but the media companies still didn't bite and we were forced to concede that funding would largely come from our own pockets. Then a decision was made that took everything to a completely new level.

Plan International was a relatively modest but high impact, children's charity with a proven record in impoverished communities throughout Africa, Asia and Latin America. Our idea was to use the trip to build a project alongside them, in one of the countries along our route. After all, how could we cycle through thousands of miles of poverty and raise money for someone back home? This way, we'd meet the community and see the results of our fundraising. Plan's approach compared favourably to the bigger charities we spoke to. At the first meeting in London, they had staff covering finance, planning, strategy, marketing and fundraising and within weeks we'd agreed to finance a number of community projects in Chalatenango, a mountainous region of El Salvador cut off from much of the meagre government support. Investment was needed to train teachers, provide books and computers, as well as refurbish classrooms, build a pre-school and cultivate the children's interest and knowledge in agriculture through development of vegetable plots within the school grounds. There would also be funds to teach parents on the importance of their children's education and to develop and train children as young as four on methods of disaster relief, a perpetual problem in El Salvador. Crucially, Plan agreed to cover project administration costs thus ensuring 100% of the cash reached the community. The onus was on us now. Martin recalls...

We wrote and spoke to hundreds of businesses, contacts and friends but our fundraising efforts had to be imaginative and unique as people were hard to break down and quite frankly sceptical about our intentions. So we started formulating a number of higher profile, "in your face" style events. Each one proved to be a standalone project in its own right. Whenever the public were involved we needed insurance, permission and declarations. In public places we had to submit accounts of how much money was raised and often advertise our intentions weeks in advance. Handouts and posters had to be printed, all this while trying to plan the trip itself, research equipment and run my newly-formed gym and have a life of some sort. One of our biggest problems was getting people to understand what we were going to do. During the spin-a-thons people assumed that we were merely simulating the 15,000 miles on static bikes. When we explained that it was just a promotional appearance and that we were flying to Alaska at the beginning of August very few could picture the scale. People seemed unable to grasp the enormity. In fact, according to my family, I was going on a holiday that included some cycling!

In the end it was Shaun and Liz, some good friends of mine, who really got the ball rolling for us, Shaun being the kind of guy who thrives on a challenge and actively encourages others to do the same. He also appreciates initiative and has a great attitude towards anything a little outrageous. One Sunday morning we had a conversation that went something like this.

'What if I buy you guys the bikes?' said Shaun.

'Pardon?'

'How much do you need for the bikes?'

'About two grand,' I said, not quite believing what I had heard.

'Will you promise to use them as leverage?'

I enjoyed telling the other two that I had secured the bikes and made it sound like I had entered into a huge business deal that required me to be an astute and ruthless businessman. With the bikes in hand things did seem a little easier. We showed them off at our public appearances. You could almost hear friends and family thinking, 'Bloody hell, they're serious.'

The two biggest events took weeks of preparation, the first being a non-stop 55-hour spin-a-thon in my home town of Shrewsbury, utilising two static gym bikes Martin brought up from London. We picked 55 hours, a logical if not ambitious choice after our trip name, '*55 Degrees South*' – the latitude of Ushuaia, Tierra del Fuego. With one of us turning the pedals and the other two out front summer shoppers were intrigued enough to pause on their way past. We spoke about our ride and the projects and invariably got a few pennies or even notes dropped into the bucket. Courteously, two police officers paid us a visit late in the afternoon when shoppers were being replaced by weekend revellers.

'You'll have some attention tonight once this lot has had a few beers!' said one of them, with a heavy amount of glee in his voice.

Nightfall descended and they weren't wrong. Witty remarks were flung our way as a steady flow of inebriated Salopians made their way between pubs along the street behind us. 'You're not getting very far on that bike, mate!' shouted one chap much to the amusement of his mates.

At 2.20am another jovial character past by giving us and a small group of college leavers who had seemingly taken up residence in our cause, an interlude from the boredom. 'Hey up, what have we got here?' he quizzed, as we came into focus. 'What the bloody hell are you lot doing? No, hang on don't tell me, you're cycling for charity. I remember now, you were here at 3 o'clock when I was doing my shopping. Good god, you've got some stamina, I'll give you that! D'ya want one of my chips, mate?' he enquired finally, turning to Martin who was on the bike and thus unable to escape his attention.

'No, I'm fine thanks.'

'Come on, you need the energy!'

'No, honestly, I'm fine, you eat them,' continued Martin, playing along.

'What about if I just rub one along your lip, like that?' he said, sticking out his hand and rubbing a chip along Martin's bottom lip. Martin retracted straight away as we all fell about in laughter. 'Do you know what else I've got in here?' continued the drunk, in reference to the pile of food in his right hand.

'I have no idea!'

'Chicken…laced with Speed,' came the reply. 'Fancy some of that?'

On and on into the night we went, one hour staring at the town clock then two hours of respite and a little sleep. From 3am onwards it was like a graveyard. Rain started to fall and Martin and I joined Paps under the canopy. We sat there, the three of us all alone, watching the rain, talking quietly about our imminent departure to Alaska. It was thought-provoking stuff.

The two night spin-a-thon proved a good money-spinner but we had an even grander event planned in London a month later. The idea was the brainchild of Paps's sister, Tishara, who luckily for us worked at an Investment Bank in the City. Tishara thought her colleagues would be willing to part with a portion of their sizeable bonuses if we tempted them with otherwise inaccessible prizes given by generous friends, family and contacts. Items ranged from Premiership football tickets, Wimbledon tickets, and even a week's stay at a private ski lodge in the French Alps. We also had track racing, a hotel package and a round of golf with the Pro at Sunningdale up for grabs. We booked a posh bar in London's West End and laid on a load of champagne, cocktails and canapés to grease the wheels and it worked a treat. Never realising he was an art buff, a friend of mine bid £300 for two paintings from Australia after standing too close to the champagne stand! We were just two days away from leaving and many people were involved in our venture now. They had donated money as well as convinced others to do so, thereby staking their reputations on us. I remember that level of trust weighing heavily on my shoulders as I packed my bike box the following day. Excitement morphed into dread and then fear. Did I have what it took to get to Canada never mind Ushuaia?

*

Getting to Prudhoe wasn't exactly straightforward. It meant taking four flights, the first being London to New York. I arrived with my sister, Lucy, on the back of concessions from her employer, British Airways and with a couple of days to kill before the connecting flights to Alaska we strolled around the city and met some friends for lunch. Then the boys arrived. Martin recalls...

The first time I actually sat and contemplated the trip as a whole it was already too late to back out. The planning had taken over my thoughts and now I was sitting in a bar in New York. My girlfriend, Sam, had gone home and I had no idea when I would see her again. There was no more planning to do, no more choosing equipment and I didn't have to juggle work. The only thing to think about was the impending ride. I would love to say that I was excited or even scared. To be honest I have no idea what I was feeling. My mind became a kaleidoscope of emotions, tumbling and tossing back and forth. Sometimes I smiled inside thinking 'brilliant we are here, about to go.' Then the fear would well up as the enormity and unknown overtook me. I lay on the floor of the hotel room trying to grab a handle on my feelings. Only one thing was for certain, I wasn't going home until I had cycled to the Antarctic Ocean.

We said farewell to my sister and flew to Seattle on the west coast. From there we connected to Anchorage in southern Alaska and endured a tiresome 10-hour wait for our flight to Deadhorse, a further 800 miles to the north. We used the time to leave the airport and head for a supermarket.

'Come on, it's 240 miles to Coldfoot on gravel and we have to get over the Brooks,' I said, with some concern. 'Let's chuck in another few packs of biscuits and some more porridge.'

'I know but the trailers are going to weigh a tonne!' replied Martin.

We spent US$70 in that store, a lot of money considering our budget and it didn't go unnoticed by the staff. 'Where you off to then?' enquired the middle-aged checkout lady zapping our food.

'We're flying up to Prudhoe and then cycling south,' answered Martin, never one to dramatise.

'You're leaving it a bit late aren't ya?'

'I'm sure we'll be alright.'

Truth be told, it was late in the season. The beginning of August signalled the end of summer in northern Alaska and it left us vulnerable to Arctic winds and snowfall. Even more worrying was the prospect of being in Canada in October. Our late start was deliberate though, an intentional effort to accommodate a fourth member, Marke. Marke was also a close friend from Uni days and the only cyclist of all of us yet tragically he had failed to complete his Doctorate in time and was forced to pull out when we were already committed to the August start date. Although he wasn't riding, Marke had taken on management of the website which he would update with photos and reports we sent from the road and also deal with all the left over administration.

*

Rolling out of Deadhorse conversation eventually started flowing. 2 miles done, 14,998 miles remaining.
'How does everyone feel?'
'Is your bike ok?'
'Anyone hungry yet?'
The plan was to get clear of Deadhorse and then find a place to camp, as we hadn't slept properly for two days. Unsurprisingly, a suitable pitch site soon presented itself to our left, next to the small River Sag. We dragged the bikes and trailers some 200 yards across the heather and began making camp. Within seconds hundreds of mosquitoes swarmed in, attacking exposed skin that we quickly covered in repellent. I was more concerned with the black and grizzly bears, a fear we'd have for the next 4000 miles. Rightly or wrongly we had decided against purchasing pepper sprays or any other form of defence, as the idea of being close enough to use them seemed to defeat the object all together. Our only defence would be good camp etiquette and making ourselves heard to avoid startling one out scavenging. In the evenings it meant carting all our food, cooking and eating equipment a distance from the tents to eat. All this gear would then be washed and hoisted up into a tree to deter the bears from raiding camp. Whilst on the North Slope where there were no trees or even a bush greater than knee height, we would leave the gear in any hollow we could find. We also knew that making ourselves look big by huddling together or waving our arms around whilst slowly retreating could discourage an attack. Yet, if we were attacked, we didn't really have any plan at all. We had read that it was sometimes best to play dead and that other times it was important to fight back but these responses weren't specific to a particular species and besides, who knows what you are going to do when a dinner plate-sized paw is being swung in your direction? Having a plan was all well and good but we had zero experience in dealing with bears, either first hand or through anecdotal references. We later heard some horrific stories, which we first thought were designed to scare silly little English folk but were later corroborated more than once, of trekkers and cyclists alike being mauled or worse by grizzly and black bears out on the trails and road.

Hovering over the stove, Paps replaced the pot of cooked rice for sizzling strips of beef. I had visions of every bear within a 10-mile radius honing in on our location. The marauding mosquitoes added to the angst, forcing us to gulp down our food by sliding the bowls between our faces and head nets. Very quickly the chores were done and we were in our tents listening to the pitter-patter of mosquitoes dive-bombing the flysheet. When I went for a pee at midnight it was still light enough to read. We were at the top of the world, 10 miles south of Deadhorse, all alone and at the start of a great adventure. I lay there a while not wanting to sleep, considering what it might be like to reach Ushuaia and the adventures that surely lay in between.

*

Unharmed by our first night on the tundra, we started about our business early. The trailer bags were filled and hot porridge prepared with copious amount of sugar. Dragging the bikes back across the heather and up onto the Dalton, I zeroed the bike computer to record the daily total and got ready to ride. Our first full day was in front of us. Off we went, pointing due south, occasionally a 100 yard section of blacktop making things easier. Our knobbly tyres purred across the tarmac before it reverted back to gravel, rattling our wrists and spines. Sometimes the gravel deepened, sending the bike on a course of its own. At the ten-mile mark we stopped to eat a biscuit and took a slurp of tea from our thermoses. The scenery was awesome, the feeling of space deafening. Perfectly flat in all directions, our view benefited from the Dalton being raised a metre or so above the tundra. All we could see was heather and the odd pond of stagnant water, presumably the result of permafrost melt that spring. Encouragingly there was a distinct absence of bears. Paps began snapping photos but soon gave up due to the mozzies. We kept going, riding in close proximity, tucking in to pick a line through the ruts and loose gravel when the surface deteriorated. It reminded me of walking along sheep tracks back home in the fields of England. Occasionally, a large truck carrying supplies or equipment appeared on the horizon, given away by its huge dust trail. They thundered past, forcing us to hold our breath and pray the bike didn't wander off the edge of the road in the zero visibility. A few seconds later and hopefully without being hit in the chest or leg by a flying stone, the dust would disperse and everything would come back into view.

'I'm getting low on water,' said Martin, above the noise of our tyres.

'I could do with topping up my bottles too,' replied Paps. 'How about we stop here next to the Sag?'

We detached from the pedals and stood the bikes to attention like motorbike riders. I noticed the trailer flags fluttering gently in the breeze and set to work with the water-filter as Martin and Paps ate biscuits in the sunshine and scrutinised the horizon for bears. Here we were cycling bicycles down a gravel road aiming for a town 15,000 miles away. It was madness!

'What are we having for lunch?' I asked, once back on the road.

'It's only 10.30am!' shrieked Paps.

'I can't stop thinking about food!'

'We better use the sausages,' suggested Martin. 'They are starting to go a funny colour.'

'Let's add some noodles!' said Paps.

By the end of the day we were again next to the Sag. The phrase, "winging it" didn't do justice to my feelings of vulnerability. I looked across to my two mates busying themselves with bike adjustments and guy ropes. We were already a team but we were still so wet behind the ears. What wasn't in doubt though, was the level of morale and humour.

'Eating dinner next to the Sag River'

'I'm going for a wash in the river,' I announced.

'OK mate,' replied Martin.

Leaving my towel on the riverbank I stepped out into the middle of the Sag, where the cold water and buzzing mosquitoes made me work quickly. With soap in my eyes and my naked white body scaring away any bear, I turned around to discover Martin catching all of it on video!

Chapter 2

'You guys are stallions!'

'Courage is the art of being the only one who knows you're scared to death.'
Earl Wilson
Born America, 1934

Start Point: North Slope, USA. Mile: 80. 7th August.

We figured on the ride taking a year but that was borne out of guesswork more than anything else and we were definitely in no rush to challenge the World Record set by a young American, Emmanuel Gentinetta, in a frightening time of 261 days. The weight of the trailers was the crucial factor. They were a basket affair pivoting clear of the rear wheel by means of a swing-arm and afforded much easier cornering and superior bike stability over panniers. They also enabled us to "park" the bike and get easy access to a waterproof bag, similar to those used by adventurers on river trips. Strapped to the top of the bag and our rear pannier racks was the mountain of food we had bought in Anchorage. Our rides were touring hybrids built by Ahead Cycles in West Sussex, the frames made of steel and the wheel rims strengthened, making the bikes heavier but tougher. We were also benefiting from suspension seat posts - a goodbye gift from Marke - calibrated to the riders' weight using a combination of plastic polymers. These allowed vertical as well as horizontal travel of the saddle which translated into much less punishment from the road surface. Then there was the transmission, twenty-seven gears, to get over the Rockies and Andes later on in our journey. Yet all this kit meant 8mph was fair for a flat gravel road with knobbly tyres. Anything less signified a worsening surface, headwind or a slight incline.

Midmorning on day three, hills started to appear. We drew closer and closer until the hitherto perfectly flat slope vanished and we were face to face with a short hill that was just long enough to give me butterflies. The trans-Alaskan oil pipeline, a few hundred yards off to the left, followed us up the hill.

'This will tell us a lot,' I said.

Everyone started clicking down the gears until a manageable resistance was reached. The trailer felt heavy, its weight making my thighs burn and heart pump like mad. Out of breath as I crested the top, I waited a few seconds for the other two to join me.

'That was hard work!' I commented, hopeful of an opinion on our first test.

'I'm sweating like crazy,' replied Paps.

'You're not kidding!' said Martin.

We donned our head nets as the mozzies zeroed in. From our vantage point the road continued down the other side into a small valley. It looked like we were about to go into a section of rolling hills similar to those seen in Wiltshire or Yorkshire. The fun and games had begun. With a gravel surface these hills would sap our strength and send eating levels skywards at a time when we were already fretting about our dwindling supply. Paps led the way, enjoying the all too brief downhill. We all then battled against the loose bumpy gravel on the opposing side.

'Paps cuts a lonely figure across the rolling hills of the North Slope'

By the time two more valleys were complete a nasty headwind had appeared and I for one was doing a great impression of a drunken man on a bicycle as I searched left and right across the width of the road to find the best line. We pulled over absolutely exhausted. My arse was on fire. Standing next to the bike, gulping down water, I could feel blood slowly returning. I kept thinking, *'We've got ten more days of this...'* Everyone grabbed what they needed and sat on the turf a few yards from the bikes. It didn't take me long to open up.

'I am fucked. I need to eat more,' I said. 'The gravel is killing me.'

'Me too.'

'Yeah, and me.'

'Can we have 20 minutes? I've got to rest and get my strength back.'

'I'm not going anywhere,' said Paps.

Silence descended as we slurped water and munched through some biscuits. The soft turf was like a thick pile carpet, pleasing to touch and warmed by the sun. I stretched out, turned on to my front and watched the light breeze tugging at a patch of wispy grass a few feet away. The scale of the landscape swept me away again, into my daydream world where for a short while I had trouble understanding what we were doing. Then someone started talking and my dream world evaporated.

'Shall we get going?' asked Martin, in a way that was more of a command.

Sometimes the computer read as little as 3mph and it wasn't long before a big bowl of meat and rice was cooked to improve morale. The conversation was littered with humour and sarcasm as we cracked jokes about our location and how little food was left. The afternoon wore on with the hills unrelenting, another five miles then a break, another, another, each time receiving one biscuit. The last bag was riddled with petrol fumes from one of the fuel bottles I was carrying.

'Petroleum Oreo anyone?' I offered.

Everyone took one without so much as a murmur. Then we heard a magical sound, a sound that gave us hope and stripped away the helplessness of it all.

'Motorbikes!' shouted Paps.

Out of sight for the moment, climbing the hill we were about to descend the sound of two growling, spluttering machines got louder and louder. I could feel the excitement building with every passing second. Suddenly the riders came into view, braking hard to pull over.

'How are you boys doing?' asked one of them once he had removed his helmet and given us a big broad smile. He was a middle-aged American, a mountain of a man who filled his black riding leathers. 'We thought we'd stop to see if you were ok?'

'We're a bit low on food to be honest. Can you spare any?' said Martin, clearly anxious to convey the gravity of the situation.

'Well, we don't have anything on us right now,' he replied. 'We're heading up to Deadhorse and returning tomorrow. Is there a shop up there?'

'There's a cafeteria in one of the hotels which sells stuff and we'll pay you for it,' I confirmed.

'OK, well, we'll be sure to try,' he said.

He, was Dick Trudo from Idaho. Dick and his friend hung around a couple of minutes whilst we explained the situation properly. Then they cranked up their machines and roared off into the distance, scattering gravel across the road as their tyres dug into the surface. Within a few seconds they were out of sight and their engines barely audible.

'I can't believe how little food we have left. Martin and I bought a tonne in Anchorage.'

'I am permanently hungry,' admitted Paps.

'Yeah, me too mate. I can't stop thinking about food.'

Apart from Dick and his buddy, the only people we had come across so far were pipeline workers and truckers, none of whom we had spoken to. Yet, as the afternoon wore on we started spotting folk hunting caribou. Every few miles an RV - or Campervan – was parked to the side of the road. Sometimes it was just a couple of guys decked out from head to toe in camouflage gear enjoying a food break. Other times it was more of a family outing, with wife and children tagging along. It made me wonder if my red hair was in danger of attracting some unwanted attention from a rifle or crossbow.

Maybe we should buy a caribou off a huntsman and strap it to the top of Martin's trailer?

We stopped within a few yards of an ageing RV on one occasion as a deliberate ploy to get food and two minutes later out stepped a couple and their two young kids. Everyone said hello and Andrew and Mary soon dispatched their daughter off to the camper van to fetch some ginger snap cookies for the hungry cyclists! To make matters worse though, by midmorning the next day Martin became dizzy, nauseous and zapped of strength. The mosquito bites had taken their toll. We were forced to let him fall asleep in the sunshine at the side of the road. I fetched the noodles and boiled some water taken from one of the water bottles as hundreds of mozzies swarmed around us.

'I don't mind if we make camp here. It's not like we are going anywhere for a while,' I offered to Paps, adding, 'We could try again later by cycling a few hours tonight?'

'That's fine but the longer we take to get to Coldfoot the more we have to ration,' he replied.

'Let's get him to eat something and see if he feels better later on. How do you feel?'

'Tired, very tired.'

Paps was carrying a comprehensive first aid kit but unfortunately there weren't any pills in it labelled, 'Take one every 8 hours if bitten 100 times by mosquitoes and you need to keep cycling without food.' Just when we were looking for a boost, true to his word, Dick turned up on his way back from Deadhorse.

You legend Dick!

Paps ran over to greet him like an old friend. He hadn't just bought the odd bar of chocolate; he had six rounds of sandwiches with fruit to boot. Whats more he refused to accept any money from us. I don't think Dick truly realised how much trouble we were in at that point even after repeatedly conveying our gratitude to him.

'How do you feel mate? Still rough?' I enquired, a little while later.

'A bit groggy but I don't feel nauseous anymore,' replied Martin.

'Would you like some lunch then? We made noodles and cut up the last sausages.'

'That sounds great. How long have I been asleep?'

'About an hour and you missed the best bit.'

'Why?'

'Dick stopped by and gave us a load of food.'

'Really?'

'Yeah, we have chocolate and sandwiches!'

Dick's food lasted until the next day as we continued to draw closer to the Brooks Range. The mountains were now very impressive, surrounding us in all directions. Martin's strength had returned but the mosquitoes continued to enjoy themselves. His legs and arms were covered in bites. Lines of blood ran down the backs of his calf muscles, denoting where he had picked the scars. During another food break, more bikers pulled over. The two guys looked like spacemen dressed in their futuristic gear, their jet-black sun visors disguising any clue as to their homeland.

'How you boys doin'?' said one of them, taking off his helmet.

The southern states drawl was a dead give away. 'We're OK thanks,' said Paps.

'We have something for you,' announced the biker. 'We met a chap called Dick last night in Coldfoot. He told us about you guys, so we brought along some food in case you were getting hungry.'

'What!' exclaimed Paps.

'When we heard what you were doing, we thought we should help out! My name's Larry and my partner here is called Ronnie.'

We all shook hands and introduced ourselves. Then Larry and Ronnie started delving into their huge pannier boxes and off-loading a whole bunch of goodies. More sandwiches, nuts, freeze-dried chowder and soup along with porridge oats and peanut butter. A feast! Five miles back we had shared a comical moment, passing around an apple, seeing who could take the biggest bite and now we had been supplied again!

'That's famous Texan hospitality there my friend,' confirmed Larry.

'Well, we are very grateful for it!' I assured him.

'We've ridden all the way up from Texas,' said Ronnie. 'But it's not as far as you guys are travelling, right?'

'What's the road like from here to Coldfoot?' enquired Paps, as Martin admired their machines.

'Well, it'll be OK for a while. Then you see where the pipeline follows that valley?' said Ronnie, pointing into the far distance.

'Yeah.'

'Well, once you get to the end of that valley, you turn left and start climbing. It's very impressive.'

'That's the start of the Atigun is it?'

'You've got it.'

Thrilled by our good fortune we watched Ronnie and Larry don their helmets and start up their motors. I sensed an element of jealousy descend as they effortlessly waved goodbye and sped off down the hill, heading north.

'What top blokes!' said Martin, as we set off at a somewhat more sedate pace into the wind.

'I could massacre that pot of peanut butter,' said Paps, trying to gauge our mood.

'Did you see how easy it is on those motorbikes?'

Our good fortune was short-lived because almost immediately we ran into a guy repairing the surface of the Dalton with a huge machine which had turned the surface into a soup. Mud grated between my wheels and brake blocks, coating the chain and my feet, as well as causing Paps to come off and endure a lot of teasing and muddied clothes. We pulled up to discuss what to do as the wind had become very strong, almost to the point of it being a waste of energy.

'Let's get behind that hummock!' shouted Martin, as he pointed to a small outcrop of rock and heather a few yards away.

Everyone took what they needed and wondered over to lie down. Two minutes later the jar of peanut butter was open. 'Cor, that's good stuff!' I said, taking my first spoonful.

'I told you. This stuff is pure energy,' said Martin, as I passed him the jar and spoon.

The wind was funnelling down the wide valley in which we now found ourselves. Fluffy white clouds raced overhead as I stared up at the blue sky. The short sharp hills had gone forever now. The geology had changed. We were in the mountains. The valley floor was golden brown, dotted with heather plants whose tiny pink and crimson flowers perforated our position behind the hummock. Looking across to the far ridge, golden brown gave way to black as the bare rock of the mountainside revealed itself. It was difficult not to marvel at our surroundings. We made some food and got inside our sleeping bags, hoping the wind might relent. Two hours later the conditions had worsened but by the third hour we were convinced it was tolerable so we packed up and headed on. I had to breathe like a freestyle swimmer such was its power.

'This is crazy!' I shouted, stopping less than a mile later.

'Let's get the tents up!' screamed Paps.

The tents flapped around erratically in the wind until we secured all the guy ropes and loaded the inners with lots of gear. Then it was over to Martin's for dinner. The view was spectacular. Thick meadow grass led all the way down to a lake half a mile away, its surface dotted with white horses. Beyond it a backdrop of mountain peaks, their north-facing slopes covered in snow from the previous winter. Angry clouds rushed overhead, blackening the sky and an occasional ray of sunshine broke through to highlight the surface of the lake. Then it started raining.

Late into the evening the wind hammered into us. The inner compartment of my tent billowed back and forth, hitting me in the face as I lay inside my sleeping bag.

'How about we make a cup of tea?' I shouted, after thirty minutes of daydreaming.

'That would be lovely, thanks!' came Martin's reply.

'Bugger off! I'm not making it.'

'I thought you were offering?'

'No, I was merely wondering if anyone fancied a brew. Besides, you have the teabags.'

'I still have some tea in my flask,' said Martin.

'Good, 'cos so have I!'

'Ha-ha!'

'What time is your alarm set for?' shouted Paps.

'1am,' replied Martin. 'If the wind has dropped I'll wake you up and we'll get going.'

"You guys are stallions!"

'Paps and Martin share a joke during a tent dinner on the North Slope'

Martin's 1am inspection revealed horizontal rain but by 6am the conditions were much better. The weather became glorious, hot enough to stride around topless as we cleaned the bikes in a fast flowing river. Then came the small matter of conquering the Atigun Pass, the pass that would take us over the Brooks Range and into more recognisable territory where pine trees and picture postcard Alaskan scenery awaited. Off we set, up the long valley we had been in the previous day. Eventually, as Ronnie had said, the road swung left, hugging the right side of the adjoining valley and began climbing. Ever so slowly we got higher and higher. The wind blew and the road started to resemble a farm track with all the ruts and potholes. We were back to picking a line again. Occasionally, a truck or huntsman came down from the summit, their clouds of dust obscuring our view. We were cycling together today; at times close enough to hear heavy breathing. With regular stops to take on food, water and grab opinions, the road just seemed to keep going and going. The exertion was incredible. All that I could be certain of was that it was hard going and therefore we must be getting closer. Then a particularly droll huntsman past by during yet another food break.

'You boys haven't started yet, wait 'til ya get 2 miles further on, then the fun really begins!' he mocked.

'Looking forward to it!'

There was a good bond growing between us, especially today with the knowledge of the Atigun. This climb had been on our minds for months. We kept slagging off the disparaging huntsman for a while and then got back on the bikes to continue up the farm track. Soon enough the extent of his forewarning became apparent. The view suddenly opened up and we were face to face with a series of switchbacks that twisted up the headwall of the valley. The road then went out of sight. The road went *vertical*.

'Oh my god, look at it go!' I shrieked.

'That guy was right. Look at it!' confirmed Paps.

'I don't think that's the top,' I replied.

'Shut up Wils!'

Conversation fell silent. We were into our own worlds now, concentrating on the task in hand. It was never going to be a single uninterrupted climb, even to where the road passed out of view but there was no desire for chatter. I reached bottom gear immediately and fretted that if the road became even more inclined, I would have to get off and push. That was something we had dreaded, even resolved to avoid at all costs but here I was, on the first true climb, struggling to stay up straight. Luckily, I kept the pedals turning and got to the end of the first switchback.

'Aim for the next corner,' I told myself, quickly looking over my right shoulder to see Martin and Paps following at hundred metre intervals.

God, this is killing me. The guys must be feeling this, right? This is hard, right? They must be feeling bad because I am totally shattered. My chest and legs are screaming at me! How on earth do the trucks get up this thing?

The wind didn't help matters. By now it was rifling down from the upper reaches of the headwall. Combined with the surface and gradient it resulted in my front wheel lifting off the ground as I pulled hard on the handlebars to scrabble forward and the trailer bounced up and down on rocks and potholes. My target changed from being the next corner to a piece of road just 50 metres in front of me, cast in sunshine. Once there and sweating furiously, I chose the next target; a shady bit, this time 100 metres further forward. Off to my right I could see where we had entered the valley. Beyond that was the open emptiness of the North Slope. The view was spectacular but I was in no state to marvel at Mother Nature. All that mattered was the grey dusty gravel just beyond my front wheel.

Get to the shade and take a break…just get to the shady bit and you can stop. You can do that.

Once at the shady bit, I pulled over immediately. Leaning against the bike I swallowed down as much air as I could. Then I reached for the nearest water bottle and watched the boys fighting their own battles below me, steadily drawing closer. They weren't going to like what I saw. From my position, the road continued into another set of switchbacks before again disappearing out of view. Martin came up beside me, noted the fresh set of switchbacks and murmured something I didn't catch as the wind ripped down from above, tugging at our shirts. Then Paps arrived. Martin set off again but I was far happier chewing the fat with Paps a few minutes longer. His colourful appreciation of our circumstances made our plight seem all the more real.

'This is fucking hard work!' he assured me.

'I was cursing after just one switchback and look what we have left!'

Squinting into the sunshine we watched Martin head up the next section, his legs pounding and upper body leaning forward against the wind trying to keep the front wheel on the ground. He seemed to be working so hard, it took him an age to cover just a few hundred metres. Sufficiently motivated I got ready to move but the road was so steep that I couldn't get the wheels turning quickly enough to balance myself on the bike. Instead, I resorted to setting off across the road, perpendicular to the angle as the wind hit me and my tyres slipped on the gravel. Eventually, I got over to the right side of the road just as a truck hurtled past. It made the hill look like a speed bump. Each of us were alone again battling upwards. Much later, another huntsman trundled down from above, his window open.

'You guys are stallions!'

I cracked a smile before being swept up in his dust cloud. His comment played itself over and over again in my mind. This was a big moment. After an age the road started to swing left and flatten out. I could see Martin a few hundred metres ahead of me. He was off the bike, facing me, his arms raised above his head in a triumphant pose. Were we at the top? He had the video camera out, filming my approach. I jumped off the bike, realising we had summitted and hugged him in jubilation, waiting only minutes for Paps to join the celebrations. We had done it. Everyone swore, laughed and joked, eager to relay their own private thoughts and stories of the climb. A sense of euphoria swept us off our feet as we realised a big downhill was ours to enjoy. None of us could quite believe it. We looked south and saw the road follow a wide valley way beneath us and rewarded ourselves with slices of bread covered in mayonnaise and mustard. We were all so overjoyed that a couple of hours past by in a blink of an eye. Nothing could halt our triumphant chatter. Lying in my tent that night, I kept re-running the day in my head, how it had felt to view the switchbacks, then the pain and eventual feeling of accomplishment.

Is that all you've got, Alaska? Bring on Canada, bring on the Rockies!

Chapter 3

'I've been looking for you, for 150 miles.'

'The appetite grows by eating.'
Francois Rabelais
Born France, 1494.

Start Point: Coldfoot Camp, USA. Mile: 240. 12th August.

It won't surprise you to hear that we took full advantage of the buffet meals on offer at Coldfoot. Considering our location the quality was first rate with US$10 buying an All-You-Can-Eat style marathon. This place was made for us. For breakfast the first morning I managed to tuck away two bowls of cereal, a full English fry up, two towering stacks of pancakes covered with maple syrup, a bowl of fresh fruit salad, fresh orange juice and coffee. It provided enough energy to clean the bikes around the back of the diner much to the displeasure of the camp owner who informed us we were hosing down our trusty steeds with drinking water tankered up from the south. Anyway, we spent the rest of the day cleaning gear and relaxing in the sunshine, albeit out of sight of the owner. Occasionally I popped into the diner to 'top-up' on the calorie intake, taking time to study the numerous head and antler of caribou and musk ox that adorned the walls. We had spotted just one musk ox, a beast of an animal with a shaggy coat and physique of a bison that had stood motionless like a bronze statue in the middle of the tundra. There were also photos showing the construction of the Dalton, a 360-mile section of which had been laid in just five months. Other photos showed the special rigs that were constructed to tow the incredibly heavy, prefabricated equipment up to the oil fields and others documenting where rigs had come off and sunk into the permafrost or become enveloped in snow and ice. It was real edge of existence stuff up here.

'Coldfoot Camp'

Hot news in the diner was that extensive forest fires had taken hold to the south creating visibility problems for the truck drivers. Some even said the flames were licking across the highway at certain points so I went outside to update the boys, only to find Paps angling for an invite from a couple from Los Angeles. Every so often another monster truck rolled into camp with its cargo of piping, tanks or engineering equipment. Then two motorcyclists drew up. They were two Argentines, nine months out from Tierra del Fuego.

'So how has the trip been then?' I hope I asked, in Spanish.

'Long. We happy to finish,' one of them said, bluntly in English.

It caused my mind to race.

What are you complaining about? You turn your right wrist and you're suddenly doing 60mph…

For them, the adventure was nearly over. They were just 5 hours from Deadhorse, a distance we had covered in over 40 hours riding and six days in the wilderness.

*

We headed out, unsure if the fires would cause us problems. The trailers were topped up with a mountain of food, allowing us to relax and appreciate the beauty of the Alaskan wilderness. Pines trees lined both sides of the Dalton, the closest ones covered in a fine layer of white dust thrown up by the trucks. It made for eerie surroundings as we cycled hard through the rolling valleys, eventually making it to a sign announcing "Gobblers Knob – Steep Incline".

It doesn't look too bad to me…

The road climbed for about a mile before rounding a corner and being keen to see what all the fuss was about I started off, leaving Martin and Paps chattering at the roadside. By the time I reached the corner my opinion had changed. It was bloody hard going. I rounded the corner and saw the road just keep going, dead straight, climbing far into the distance, hugging the side of the valley.

Martin said there were no big climbs today! In fact, I remember exactly what he said, "Gently rolling hills today, boys."

My arse was killing me because a little rule had become vogue which stated stopping midway up a climb was for losers. So despite my rear end telling me otherwise I was forced to soldier on along the straight for another half an hour. Progress was numbingly slow. To take my mind off the pain I resorted to counting shadows of road markers cast across the road in front of me. The markers were spaced at least 50 metres apart and I kept counting sets of ten before taking a peek on my progress. Ten more shadows and then a quick glance up before bowing my head again. Eight…nine…ten….I wasn't going anywhere. I bounced around on the saddle trying to get blood to my backside, whilst wiping sweat from my face. Mosquitoes buzzed around my ears and my skin burned in the hot sun. Fifteen minutes later I was at the top. Parking the bike, I kicked off my shoes and collapsed with exhaustion on a smart wooden lookout, unable to even sit up straight and drink any water. It had been an overwhelming effort. Some time later the sound of bike tyres drew up next to me.

'What the hell were you doing?' puffed Martin, in a playful tone.

'I don't know, I just couldn't stop.'

'I kept looking up and you were still going. No way could I stop,' he continued, cracking smile.

'I looked back and you two hadn't pulled over so I thought, "they must be fine."'

'Must be fine? Are you kidding? It was killing me!'

'I reckon that was worse than the Atigun, you know.'

Paps arrived and lambasted both of us to the same tune. It was hilarious! We all continued to rest, reiterating how awful the pain and effort had been.

'I can't move, I'm so tired,' said Paps, as both of us lay flat out, staring at the blue sky.

'It's so hot,' I remarked.

'Wils, do you want some M&M's?' asked Paps.

'No thanks. I'm fine.'

'How about a cold coke with ice?'

'Piss off.'

By late afternoon a long rolling landscape provided us the miles to cross over the Arctic Circle. An incredibly tacky photo followed and then we freewheeled down the hill and found a spot to pitch next to Fish Creek.

'Have one of you got the food bag?' I asked, the following morning.

'No. Why?' asked Martin.

'It's not where I left it.'

'Are you sure?' asked Paps.

'I put it in a tree next to the creek but there's no sign of it; no bag, no food or packaging, nothing.'

The boys dropped what they were doing and scouted the surrounding area whilst I went back to the tree, convinced I'd failed to spot it the first time. Convening back at camp still empty handed, Paps voiced his opinion on what might have happened.

'I tell you who might have taken it,' he said glumly.

'Who?' I demanded, as my anger threatened to boil over.

'Well, I heard some people on the road last night. It was really late and I think you two were already asleep. They started shouting "Bear! Bear!" obviously trying to scare us. I had a peek outside but then all went quiet. Maybe they took it?'

'Bastards!'

This was a real kick in the teeth. It was at least a 60-mile ride to the next services at the Yukon River, 60 miles in the heat and hills of Alaska without any food, not even anything for breakfast. It was unthinkable. The thieves had also taken the sun cream that had so far prevented my face and hands from burning in the 30°C heat. We packed up and started tackling the climb we had left the night before. Very little conversation only heightened my anxiety. Each of us kept an eye out for traffic coming in either direction, ideally looking for some vehicle that might be carrying food. One or two trucks past by and then Paps spotted a couple of RVs in convoy approaching from behind. We jumped off the bikes and started waving vigorously. I even considered stepping into the middle of the road and offering a police halt but our gesturing was enough to get their attention. I ran forward towards the first RV whilst the boys took care of the one behind.

'Thank you so much for stopping. I wondered if you had any food we could buy? Ours has been stolen,' I pleaded, nailing the well-rehearsed line perfectly.

'Yes of course! Let's just pull off the road,' said the woman in the passenger seat.

To our good fortune we had flagged down Jim, Joyce, Chuck and Lorraine, wonderful folk out enjoying their retirement with several months touring around Alaska and Canada.

'What about apples? Do you eat apples?' enquired Joyce, from the back of her campervan.

'Yep.'

'And yogurt?' she went on.

'Yep.'

'And you eat ham and cheese, right?'

'Yep.'

'Ah, and I have some tea bags here, will they come in useful?'

'Uh, yeah.'

Their well-stocked fridges and cupboards took a real battering, so much so I felt a little sorry for Jim and Chuck. I could just imagine what was running through their minds...

'Blimey, go easy love; we don't have to give these lads the whole larder. Wait, that's prime ham! I bet they've pulled this gig a few times already...cheeky buggers.'

'The least we can do is give you kids some food,' said Lorraine, as we stood around thanking them. 'I hate the thought of the same thing happening to my son out here.'

Not to be outdone, a pipeline worker out running maintenance checks saw what was happening and came over to give us his packed lunch. It set the tone for what was to come because over the next few days the charity just kept coming. At a café flanking the Yukon River, three guys on holiday from Chicago picked up our tab after hearing about our trip and this came on the back of a young brewery rep fetching us three bottles of beer from his car. The Chicago clan were out enjoying the wilds on a farewell tour since one of them (we didn't know which) was terminally ill. It made our photo together on the steps of the diner all the more poignant.

'How about we use the shower block at the back of the diner?' suggested Martin, once the guys had driven off. 'We can also clean our clothes.'

'Great idea,' confirmed Paps.

I emerged cleanly shaven and hung out my pants and socks across the handlebars of my bike in the sunshine. As I did, Zin pulled up a few yards away in her pickup truck. Zin was a free-spirited, no nonsense type of woman in her forties I guess, that we had met a few days previously. It was a brief meeting back then but she had seemed friendly enough, so I walked over to have a chat. She recognised me straight away, which wasn't hard considering what I was wearing.

'Hi! How are you doing?'

'Good, how are you guys?' she asked, excitedly.

'Great, apart from having our food stolen yesterday!'

I brought Zin up to speed with the theft but then of all the good fortune since. Still appalled, she reached into her purse and took out US$40.

'Zin, please, we are fine,' I retracted, realising my complaint may have seemed like a prompt. 'We've had our food replaced. There's no need to give us anything.'

'No take it, I am totally embarrassed,' she said, stuffing the dollars down my shirt. 'You know who stole the food don't you?' she asked, rhetorically. 'It's military lads off the base.' She was referring to the Air Force Base near Fairbanks. 'They are always up to no good, hunting drunk and shooting out road signs and car windows. I bet that's who took it. Bastards!'

Maybe bears are the least of our worries?

Deeper into Alaska, engaging in conversation about the trip was becoming natural, as were the reactions. An hour after being handed a load of sandwiches, chocolate biscuits, fruit and crisps by two families out trekking another act of generosity came our way. With Martin taking a pee in the woods and Paps and I readying the bikes, a vehicle passing at speed along the highway braked violently on the bridge above the creek. We could hear the driver select reverse gear and then accelerate like a lunatic back up the highway. Eventually the mystery vehicle came down the track to meet us.

'Hi guys! I've been looking for you, for 150 miles!'

It was Anthony, the brewery rep we'd met at the Yukon River. 'Hi Anthony, how are you?' asked Martin, slightly relieved that it wasn't an over zealous policeman.

'Great thanks. I put a big drum of drinking water in the van this morning in case I spotted you and also a bag of trail mix.'

'We really shouldn't be doing this,' I said, a few hours later.

'What?' replied Martin, as Paps giggled in the background.

'Eating around camp,' I explained, whilst leaning in for another handful of trail mix. 'We're in the middle of a forest, with the tents up, totally defenceless against a bear attack and are eating a 3 kilo bag of fruit and nut.'

'Great, isn't it!' replied Martin.

'You wont be saying that if we get a visitor,' I countered, with a smile on my face.

'What the hell, they taste awesome!'

The next day we eventually got off the dreaded gravel. The Dalton was no longer, replaced instead by smooth black tarmac that would take us all the way to Fairbanks. We stopped to change our knobblies for smoother, harder road tyres and the difference was astonishing. With less friction the bike actually freewheeled and gained speed on even the shallowest declines, benefiting from the weight of the trailer. We were like kids, racing each other and using our momentum to pedal like maniacs up the opposing slope. The highway was silent, no birdsong, nothing. The smoke from the forest fires suffocated everything. We tried using masks provided by some kind-hearted pipeline workers but they restricted our breathing even more. All the streams were clogged with soot from the charred landscape making our water filter worthless and forcing us to limit our intake and flag down more travellers. By early evening we made it to a tiny trading post, where, to our joy, the owner was himself a keen cyclist. This entitled us to half price coffee and muffins. We sat there in the comfort of his log cabin-style store, nursing our sore muscles, hitting the repeat button on coffee and muffins for an hour.

'I don't want to get back on the bike,' said Martin.

'Me neither,' replied Paps and I.

'Shall we have another round of muffins then?'

'Damn right.'

The outside toilet was a hole in the ground design, basic back home but more than adequate considering our style of living. As I sat down to do my business courtesy of all the coffee, I noticed a note scribbled on the back of the cubicle door.

'Imagine this at -40°C!'

*

Fairbanks was our first town for 500 miles and with 50,000 residents it felt like London. Suddenly we shared the road with dozens of cars and lorries. Junctions, coffee shops and supermarkets distracted us as we negotiated our way through town to our campsite. It was wonderful to have easy access to the internet, payphones, laundry and food.

Reaching Fairbanks was a big step and a chance to reflect on what we'd achieved. We had overcome problems associated with real inexperience, albeit with the aid of many individuals. Nonetheless, our determination and fortitude had got us here intact and in a healthy state of mind. Sure, we would have far bigger hills and worse weather to negotiate but no longer would we be so isolated and that felt good. Our bodies were adapting well to the weight of the trailers and the long days in the saddle were made manageable by the regular breaks we took at the side of the road. Perhaps the most important aspect was that we were working well as a team. The constant decision-making wasn't causing major problems and therefore, overall, morale was tip-top. The Canadian border, our next target, was only 300 miles away.

'Right, we won't be long mate,' said Martin, as he followed Paps into the Post Office.

'I'll wait here and look after the bikes,' I replied, sitting down on the curb to enjoy the morning sunshine.

People studied me closely as they strolled in and out. A smartly dressed middle-aged woman was one such curious local. 'Where are you travelling to?' she began.

'Down to South America,' I replied, getting up.

'Wow!'

'To be honest we've only just started.'

'Are you raising money for anything?'

'Yeah for children in El Salvador. Money for computers, training teachers, building a pre-school, stuff like that,' I explained.

'That sounds fantastic! OK, well all the best with it, bye.'

'Nice to meet you. Bye.'

Eventually the boys came out and we started riding. Less than half a mile down the road I spotted the same woman hailing us down from her car.

'This is for the projects in El Salvador,' she said in a rush. 'I am really impressed!'

With that she stuffed an envelope into my hand. 'Oh, thank you,' I replied, realising she had passed me a wad of money.

No sooner had I finished my sentence than her back was turned and she was scurrying towards her car. I looked inside the envelope to find US$100 in crisp US$20 notes. I couldn't believe it. Paps came up alongside me, straddling his bike. 'What was all that about?' he asked, as the woman pulled out of the car park.

'I met her five minutes ago. You and Martin were posting your letters,' I explained. 'I only spoke to her for a minute or so.'

'How much is in the envelope?'

'US$100.'

'Blimey.'

'I didn't even get her name.'

She must have gone straight to the bank because the notes were brand new. No searching questions, no fuss, just a straightforward decision.

We blasted out of Fairbanks heading east toward the Yukon Territory of northern Canada. Six days got us to the border as we pedalled hard through the mountains and wide valleys. Pine trees and their deciduous cousins competed for superiority. We shared the road with trucks and 'Cruise America RV's' but on many occasions when the road flattened we cycled three abreast. It allowed us to chat about food, the next food stop and the evening meal. Our second night in Canada, now more than 800 miles from Deadhorse, we reach White

River and meet Bob, a grumpy, kind-hearted owner of an RV site who'd been left by his wife and children to close up for the season. The location was stunning; a beautiful valley covered with pine trees that ran up the sides of the surrounding mountains. When it started lashing down Bob generously offered us a basic cabin for the price of a tent site and even let us prepare dinner in his kitchen. We watched the rain tumble out of the darkening sky whilst eating our meal on his porch but this unfortunately attracted the attention of a passing family looking for a place to stay.

'Look at the trouble you have caused me now! Come on, get inside, get inside!'

We scuttled inside like teenagers on the sharp end of a teacher's scolding. The hot weather had disappeared now, replaced by fresh mornings and a real chance of rain. We could never be sure what we would wake up to and I for one was constantly preoccupied by cloud density, colour and wind conditions. Getting wet on the bike was not pleasant and made things more complicated. Firstly, it meant wearing a jacket and probably waterproof trousers and that meant sweating, a lot. Secondly, spray from the bikes and traffic meant wet socks, shoes and shorts that remained wet through the following day and thirdly, as soon as we stopped to eat, the wind cut through us. Yet, we were still enjoying the rub of the green and just learnt to adjust to what the conditions threw at us. We used breaks in the weather to try drying clothes and our tents by securing them to the trailer or the rear pannier rack using bungee cords. Sometimes it worked well, other times it rained all day. On more than one occasion, we hung up clothes in diners and cafés in the vain hope of drying them out. I am not sure what the other customers made of seeing grubby socks and pants hanging on the backs of the chairs but desperate times called for desperate measures and anyway, the health department never caught up with us. Deeper into the Yukon Territory we headed, crossing braided rivers and hugging the shores of crystal-clear lakes, the surrounding mountaintops dusted in snow. It got us to Cottonwood campsite on the shores of Kluane Lake. The scenery was spectacular and our early finish gave us the opportunity to clean the bikes and do repairs. Then a solo cyclist rolled in, perhaps only the fourth or fifth we had met in 900 miles, Jason was the first to be heading to Ushuaia. He wasn't just cycling directly to Argentina like us, Jason was taking two years to complete his journey, clocking up unimaginable distances with planned side trips. He'd set out from Prudhoe back in June and covered practically every inch of Alaska before tracking into Canada and catching up with us. I couldn't work it out. To me, Jason was a different breed. Obviously he loved cycling, yet, to save up and spend two years on a bike, solo, was just insane. No matter he was carrying a sawn off shotgun in one of his panniers, it was apparent that 8-10 hours a day in the saddle, followed by camping alone in the middle of nowhere didn't phase him at all. I couldn't think of anything worse. I had been slugging my guts out for the past three weeks but at least I had friends around me to tease and be teased by; to strike up conversation with; to rely upon and to chat with around the campfire at night. Jason had none of that. Of course, we were all out here to meet people and to see the world but doing it on a bike, solo, was a terrifying thought never mind adding an extra year to the journey. Comparing notes, it seemed that cycling in a group made it easier to meet people as we had far more stories of chance meetings and hospitality than Jason even though he was a really friendly and likeable chap. An example of this hospitality was the invitation extended to us that evening by Joan and her husband Ray. Canadians from Vancouver Island, like many of their countrymen they were on their way home after several weeks touring around Alaska and western Canada. We headed over to their cosy campervan after dinner, our head torches guiding us through the wet blustery blackness. Within minutes we were chatting and joking over biscuits and mugs of hot chocolate spiked with Ray's brandy. Their kindness and enthusiasm for our trip were remarkable. They reminded me of my mother and stepfather, Ted. I felt like I could relax with them and speak openly, the conversation giving rise to thoughts of the wind and rain outside and the long road ahead. I wanted to leave the bike behind and finish the trip in their campervan as the repetition of everything was already getting to me. The repetition of making and clearing camp, of eating biscuits at the side of the road or of finding a safe place to camp for the night. Somewhere we were all happy with. It wasn't like we were rolling in to a pre-booked hostel or bed & breakfast. When riding we would almost never know where we would end up and in what condition we would have to make camp. As I saw it, the psychological aspect was only going to get more intense as time went on. Our bikes would require ever-increasing levels of maintenance. The same went for all our gear. Therefore even rest days would become repetitious, as we re-stocked on food, did laundry, cleaned kit, serviced the bikes and hunted down bike parts. Only when all the jobs were complete could we relax. How would I cope? There was no support team, no vehicle alongside to escape the headwind or the rain. No air conditioning to cool down from the heat or warm up from the cold. It was just us.

- *We've proved we can do it, I want to go home.*
- *It's the months on the road that defines the challenge.*
- *But I can't face months and months of this. I'm sick of it.*
- *Paps and Martin seem alright. You're just tired.*
- *Maybe.*
- *Come on, you'll be ok.*

*

'Stop being so polite, just help yourself,' said Brian, as Martin leaned in to the fridge to grab another Molsen.
'Would you like another one as well, Brian?'
'Yep, I'm ready!'

Thirteen continuous days in the saddle from Fairbanks had left us exhausted yet a short break in Whitehorse signified the chance to spend some time with a contact of Zin's. Brian Farrell had offered to put us up for a couple of nights, letting us descend on his place, emptying kit bags, cleaning our gear and lounging around eating his food. I found it very difficult to decide whether to position myself next to the smoked salmon dip or Brian's wood burner which heated his whole place, a beautifully designed and constructed log cabin set in deciduous forest a few miles out of town. What I loved so much about Brian was that he seemed to know exactly what we were after. He gave us great food, let us clean our clothes, drink beer, watch TV, gave us the keys to his car to run chores down in town and most importantly of all, made us feel totally relaxed. We talked 'til late about Canada, our ride, his life in the remote Yukon and of course sport and women. The time passed too quickly and I could have stayed a month but as always, we had to keep moving.

Heading out of town a touch forlorn, my malaise was broken by some people waving enthusiastically from the opposite side of the road. Quite unbelievably it was Jim, Joyce, Chuck and Lorraine, our lifesavers from the Dalton highway! We crossed over to join them and I jumped off the bike to receive a big kiss from Joyce!

'Hello! How are you?' she asked, elatedly.

'We're good!' remarked Paps.

'We were coming down the road and saw these three cyclists wearing yellow jerseys and I thought "Oh! It's the boys!" We had to stop and say hello!'

'All I thought was, "Who are this crazy lot?"' I joked.

800 miles on from the Arctic Circle, seeing our saviours again was wonderful confirmation of their charity. In fact, I seem to remember being asked if we could spare some food!

Chapter 4

Room 118

'The little unremembered acts of kindness and love are the best parts of a person's life.'
William Wordsworth
Born England, 1770

Start Point: Whitehorse, Canada. Mile: 1,100. 4th September.

It was just a matter of when and where but it was going to happen eventually. When it did come, we were making our way around Teslin Lake, battling a cold headwind. It was tough going and approaching lunchtime the mileage read a grand twenty. Martin and I stood at the roadside waiting for Paps to appear.

'That's it, I can't keep going like this,' he said, pulling up next to us. 'I'm in too much pain.'

We walked down a track with food and flasks to crouch beneath the road and take shelter. This had happened on a few occasions but he was speaking in a more aggressive and fatalistic tone this time. Paps's knee condition had been diagnosed by specialists and physiotherapists in Australia and London after some of his training rides resulted in pain. The specialists were sure he would continue to experience pain, but what they didn't know was if the condition would worsen out on the road. Paps was suffering from Iliotibial Band Syndrome, one of the major causes of lateral knee pain in runners which is also linked to cycling and hiking. The iliotibial band (IT band), a thickening of tissue which extends from the outside of the pelvis, over the hip and inserts just below the knee, is crucial to stabilising the knee during running. In Pap's case, the symptoms manifested themselves from rubbing and swelling of the IT band during exercise, giving him pain above and below both knees, although the right knee was far more problematic. Regular stretching routines – something Martin had instigated in all of us from day one - could appease the problem but there was also a meniscus tear to Pap's right knee which gave him considerable pain when he applied added force on the hills. Although he didn't experience pain every day, it was clear that cold hilly days were perfect for aggravating the symptoms. Cold hilly days were as common as pine trees in Canada.

We huddled together close enough to pass around some biscuits and discussed what to do next. Then a 4x4 made its way up the track from the lake below, stopping opposite us. The two occupants wound down the window.

'What the fuck are you doing on our land?' yelled the girl in the driver's seat.

For a split second we all froze, half-inclined to return a similarly loaded response, before smiles broke out across their faces and her male passenger apologised on her behalf. 'We are looking for a place to camp, actually,' said Martin.

'You're welcome to use one of our cabins if you like; they're basic but dry,' said the girl. 'We're going into town to get some supplies.'

The lure of a cabin was too much to resist. Gathering up our gear, we freewheeled down the track wondering what we might find. It turned out that we had stumbled across a summer teaching camp run by the Tlingit First Nation people. Abandoned wooden cabins were dotted amongst the trees but I went over to one which had a load of cut wood stacked against it and knocked on the door. All of a sudden six young children spilled out and then an overweight woman in her twenties, who stood filling the doorway. I explained that we'd been invited to stay by Anne and Charlie, and the lady told me to choose any cabin we liked before gathering up the kids and shutting the door. The one we picked wasn't like Brian's back in Whitehorse. It was more like a garden shed your dad attempts over a long weekend, only to sack off and watch the football. About 10ft square, made of wooden sheeting, tarpaulin and a corrugated iron roof, there were two single beds inside and a wood-burning stove in one corner. We unpacked, hung up our wet clothes and I collected firewood from a pile of logs as it started to rain. Before long, Paps had the stove going and Martin had fetched a mattress from an adjacent cabin.

'Paps relaxes with his newspaper in the hut'

Within an hour we were enjoying lunch and then Paps and I spent the rest of the afternoon watching Martin construct makeshift front pannier racks out of duct tape. According to Martin this was designed to balance the bike and remove stress from the rear portion of the frame but Paps and I just thought he was killing time. This was the worst possible situation for Martin. Conditions were eminently rideable but we weren't making any progress and our theory was proven correct when a couple of days later the duct tape was removed and burnt on the campfire after he became annoyed that the kit bags weren't perfectly symmetrical!

Bored from eating trail mix and drinking tea, we went over to thank Anne and Charlie, who were back from Teslin. Anne, who had cussed us up by the highway, wasn't part of the Tlingit community. She was from Toronto but had spent the summer in the Yukon operating as a fire spotter. Like many hundreds of volunteers, her job was to sit in a cabin, scanning the forest canopy for signs of fire and then report any sightings over radio to the authorities. She certainly seemed to fit the bill. I couldn't work out if she was naturally this bonkers or whether the past five months alone in the forest had made her that way! Yet, the generosity of the Tlingit was phenomenal. They were descendants of North American Indians, hunter-gatherers that had moved in from the coast to eek out an existence from the harsh yet bountiful Canadian interior. One or two members continued clearing up and dismantling smoking sheds as Tommy, the designated chef, got the grill going. He threw on a few moose steaks and fried up some potatoes, all for the price of a rack of unused rifle shells I had found at the side of the road. Our burgeoning friendship led to the need for more beer.

'I'm going into town,' said Charlie. 'Do you want to come for a ride?'

'Sure,' I replied.

On the way back, and with an ice cold 12 pack stashed between my feet, the headlights of Charlie's truck picked up a ghostly figure drifting along the edge of the road. A pair of red eyes pierced the windshield before I realised I was momentarily face to face with a black wolf. It elegantly and confidently strode over the ground, totally indifferent to a vehicle travelling past it at speed.

'Scary-looking aren't they?' said Charlie, noticing my awestruck gaze.

'And much bigger than I imagined!'

In the morning Paps and I slept in, enjoying the warmth of the stove whilst Martin went off to hunt moose. They came back empty-handed but he had revelled in the experience. Meeting the Tlingit and learning about their way of life had been a totally unexpected and off-the-wall encounter which had left us rejuvenated. We headed on, our renewed spirits protecting us against the cold wet conditions and Paps's knee problem lying dormant.

*

'Bloody hell! You're crazy!'

Petrol had started leaking out across the camp table from Stu's fuel valve and without realising I lit the burner and put on a pot of water to boil. Within a second the puddle had caught fire. After what seemed like an age, I reacted by throwing a few items clear of the flames, my pitched shriek alerting the boys. The main danger was the fuel bottle exploding and considering it housed half a litre of pressurised fuel the effects were likely to be devastating. Martin lurched forward, picking up Stu and throwing him 20ft across the campsite before stamping on the poor chap. Then I witnessed Paps pick up the pot of water and rush over, smothering Stu and the flames. I apologised for not spotting the danger. Stu was covered in a lot of black soot and had burns to part of his fuel delivery mechanism but it looked superficial. We stood around, not sure whether to laugh or thank our lucky stars that no one was hurt.

Naming inanimate objects started early on and Stu wasn't alone. We had also named the video camera, Keith, and referred to our rear cycle racks as our "Berts", after the singer Bert Bach-a-rach. Naming these objects seemed logical for some reason. For me, it was an easier and more recognisable way of referencing objects, yet, we didn't go on to name other objects like the tents, the trailers or the pots and pans. It was just Stu, Keith and our Berts. The most embarrassing thing was when we spoke about them in front of people, asking if Keith's batteries needed charging or whether Stu could do with a clean. We were well and truly ensconced in our own world.

Eight days later we reached Fort Nelson, a 200-year-old trading post whose main industries these days are oil, gas and forestry. It marked the end of a 1,200-mile easterly track from Fairbanks and our first day's rest since Whitehorse. The journey from the Tlingit had been punishing. It was now the middle of September and the weather was closing in. We had suffered days and days of heavy rain but the scenery had been remarkable and we had seen our first bear. Rounding a bend with the three of us spread across the empty highway I happened to spot it coming down a bank and cross the road to reach a river to our right some 500 yards away. As soon as I saw the threat I shouted "Bear!" and hit the brakes, only to realise that I should have been a bit more tactful. Happily it didn't hear my shriek but just continued across the road and out of sight. We were left in awe. Then my heart started pounding as it dawned we would have to cycle past the animal as it potentially foraged at the side of the road.

'I got a photo,' said Paps, who kept the camera strapped to the handlebars for such occasions.

'What if the bear is by the side of the road?' I asked, worriedly.

'Let's give it a couple of minutes, I think it was heading toward the river,' said Paps.

We waited and then set off at full tilt, cursing the slight incline. I started thinking back to all the horror stories we had heard about bears chasing and pulling cyclists off the road into the forest. What made matters worse was that Martin and Paps had shrewdly worked out that it didn't matter how fast they were going just as long as they weren't bringing up the rear. They were both ahead of me and therefore safe in the knowledge that I would be first on the menu!

'I was shitting myself,' I admitted, once we had all stopped half a mile later to get our breath back.

'You're not kiddin'!' said Martin.

The road took us through an impressive section of the Rockies, following grooves cut by engineers along precipitous rock walls that afforded incredible views into distant valleys. Each ascent was rewarded by a descent alongside fast flowing turquoise rivers gorged with rainfall. Deciduous trees were shedding their leaves, making the road greasy and treacherous, flooding the valleys with colour. Gold, red, yellow and brown permeated a pine green background, as we remained wet for days, escaping into diners and cafés at any opportunity, eager to grab a cup of tea and wonder if it was ever going to stop. Some days we woke to the sound of raindrops and fell asleep to the sound of raindrops. At Liard Hot Springs we jumped into the thermal pools to nurse our sore bodies and I came out like a lobster after spending too much time in the top pool being poached by Mother Nature. Canada was opening my eyes, flooding my mind with endless possibilities.

*

'It's been ten minutes now,' I said, impatiently. 'I want to get riding.'
'Calm down, he'll be here in a minute,' replied Paps.
'We said we'd only call girlfriends when we weren't riding. What the hell is going on?' Another five minutes slipped by and Martin still hadn't emerged from the diner. 'Do you think he is alright? I might go and have a word,' I suggested.
'Leave him mate. Obviously something has happened but he'll be out soon.'
A couple of minutes later Martin appeared. I thought better of venting my annoyance and instead walked over to my bike in readiness to ride. Only then did I notice the tears streaming down his face. My displeasure vanished instantly. 'Are you alright, mate?' I asked, walking over to him.
'Yeah, I'm fine.'
'No you're not, come here,' I said, wrapping Martin up in my arms.
My hug triggered his emotions to overflow even further. It was well known that being separated from Sam for such long periods of time would be one of the hardness elements of the trip for Martin. After six weeks on the road and less than 15% of it completed, that fact was proving accurate.
'Take your time,' I said.
'I'll be OK. Let's get going.'
Irrespective of emotional ties and no matter how much our lifestyle was becoming the norm, learning to accept the routine, the distances and the effort wasn't always the easiest thing, especially as the weather was so damn awful. When hills, wind and rain combined, frustrations bubbled to the surface. It felt like we were being punished for our rapid progress through Alaska and later the same day, it was Martin who let fly whilst we climbed a particularly lengthy hill approaching Muncho Lake.
'All we ever do is fucking cycle!' was his solitary scream.

Only continued riding would get us to warmer, drier climates to the south and Martin was fully aware of the irony. His frustration echoed all our sentiments. We had taken just six days rest in 1,700 miles and spent nearly all of that time doing chores. Three more hard weeks riding separated us from Vancouver and only then did we plan to put away the bikes and go off exploring or spend time with loved ones.

On we went, thankful of all the continued Canadian hospitality and the now habitual roadside breaks when the lead man pulled over and everyone grabbed food and drink and then found an appropriate place to sit. I lived for these. They allowed blood to return to my buttocks but more importantly they gave us a chance to chat, something that was often scarce whilst riding or when no nearby diner offered the chance to sit in the warmth over a coffee. On the road, food breaks were perfect for bouncing around opinions, sightings and having a general moan if the wind was blowing. Conversation covered everything you could imagine and more. We might discuss the effects of eating so many beans or an apparent lack of personal hygiene or the effect of so many hours in the saddle. Other times it would be current affairs, world politics, sport, women or someone might spend a few minutes re-telling a funny story from University days. We were getting to know each other again, only this time we were ten years older and ten years wiser. Now our opinions and characters were well shaped; none of us were married or had children and it showed. We were used to doing things our own way, an untenable situation out on the road, where co-operation and patience would be integral, constant factors. We were already disagreeing over things such as riding style, when to stop, where to camp, what to eat or where to take a day's rest. So far, these disagreements were no more than minor irritations, however, it was likely that as time went on everyone would start fighting their corner a little harder until something happened. It remained to be seen whether this would be at the expense of a member spitting the dummy and riding off into the distance.

*

At Wonowon, a town named for its position 101 miles north of Fort St John and the start of the Alcan, our mood is much better. A day of sunshine and high winds mostly in our favour, results in 74 miles, one of our best totals so far. Wonowon was nothing to write home about. In fact, as we approached all we saw were one or two hotels, restaurants and fuel stations lining the highway. Pulling up, our eyes focused on a scrubby piece of land where a few pines trees afforded some protection from the wind and road, just perfect for our tents and bikes. I went over to speak to a guy pulling hard on a cigarette a few yards away.

'Hello mate, we were thinking of camping over behind those pine trees,' I said, pointing to the spot we fancied. 'Do you think anyone would mind?'

'How long are you staying for?'

'Tonight. We'll be gone by eight o'clock in the morning.'

'You'll be fine there then.'

I reported the good news so we walked the bikes over and set up behind the trees. The tents, still wet from the night before dried immediately in the sunshine and strong wind whilst Martin collected the food and stored it in a derelict building a few hundred metres away. Tonight we were treating ourselves to a meal at the restaurant. These were other occasions we lived for. Quite often it led to the whole evening being spent indoors, writing our diaries and studying the map for the next day's ride. We'd take advantage of one of the best phenomenon's in the western world; refill coffee. Diners also provided a means to sneak strip washes in the toilets or even the odd shower in places catering for truckers so we smuggled along our wash kits, hidden under our waterproof jackets in case a similar opportunity arose. With the burgers ordered, I chanced my arm by walking around to the hotel next door. The guy behind reception was the same chap I had spoken to before.

'Hi there, I was wondering if there's anywhere we can get a shower?' I asked.

'Not really.'

We both knew what I was getting at and by remaining silent he eventually succumbed. 'But I could let you into one of the rooms, I suppose.'

'That would be fantastic! I'll just go and get a towel and tell my friends, OK?'

'Sure.'

'What's you name?'

'Mark.'

Mark had a look about him that said, 'I'm in a dead end job and I know it.' His red blotchy face and slight build reeked of a lifestyle littered with booze and fags but he had a warmth that shone through. 'Many thanks Mark, I'll be right back.'

A couple of minutes later I was following him down the corridor, grinning at the thought of a piping hot shower. 'Thanks for this, we really appreciate it,' I told him.

'I could be fired you know but my boss is a jackass, so who cares.'

'It's really generous of you,' I said, trying not to laugh.

'Don't worry, I can take the heat. Here, use Room 118.'

Half an hour later, we were all clean and enjoying our huge burgers and fries. It was a perfect example of how our mood could change like the wind. Mark's unexpected generosity had made all of us extra sociable, on a day where conditions hadn't even been that hard. It was equivalent to finding a proper campsite that had a covered shelter, somewhere to cook in the dry, to hang up clothes and huddle around a stove. On such occasions our mood would be ten times better. Aiming for a settlement or campground by nightfall therefore became our best strategy. A small dot on the map, which the day before had signified a café and mechanic's garage could today reveal a small supermarket, post office and village life and being around people gave us some feeling of security against the bear risk. One such dot on the map was Hudson's Hope, a charming little town of less than 2,000 people and like Fort Nelson, formerly a trading post. The hours in the saddle had taken their toll so we went in search of a beer at the Sportsman's Inn which we'd spotted on arrival. It was a large, no-nonsense place, where families and couples dined and drank in a relaxed atmosphere that suited our dress code. The first Kokanee didn't even touch the sides but merely fuelled my desire for a day off. I didn't want to get up at 6.00am, scratch around for my clothes and feel the chill of a frosty morning. Nor did I want to pack away all my gear and start cycling. I wanted to lie in my bag and rise for a late breakfast or perhaps stay in bed if it was raining. Conversation turned to Paps's knee and a day's rest was negotiated within minutes and I ordered another round of Kokanees to celebrate!

I was glad we stayed as things turned interesting the next day when we went to the local library to check our emails. We met Rosaleen Ward, a member of staff who had moved to Canada from Wales many moons ago. She let us use her computer and we got talking about the trip. Then Rosaleen suggested she call a friend of hers, Jacquie Kinahan who reported for the local paper, the Northeast News. As we waited for Jacquie to arrive, a call came in from a local resident. Glen wasn't interested in borrowing a book, he was trying to track down the three Brits.

'Yes, they are here checking their emails,' said Rosaleen, a little bemused.

'Great, ask them if they are interested in meeting my daughters,' asked Glen.

At first, I thought it was a joke but the look on Rosaleen's face told us otherwise. Glen seemed eager to farm out his daughters, presumably in the hope that they would be married off and out of his hair. Without meeting Glen's daughters, we didn't know whether to be flattered or insulted!

Chapter 5

'Bye Jeanette!'

'Be still, sad heart, and cease repining; Behind the clouds the sun is shining; Thy fate is the common fate of all, Into each life some rain must fall, Some days must be dark and dreary.'
Henry Wadsworth Longfellow
Born America, 1807

Start Point: Hudson's Hope, Canada. Mile: 1,960. 23rd September.

'Are you sure you know where we are going?' I asked.

'No,' replied Paps. 'I haven't got a clue but these are the directions I was given.'

'I'm sure it's been more than 5kms.'

'Well like I say, according to the directions, this is right,' he reiterated, pointing ahead.

There was nothing more I could suggest, Paps had made the phone call. We cycled on another couple of miles, Paps leading the way. It was pouring with rain by now, dark clouds blackening the afternoon sky. My sunglasses made it seem like night-time so I switched to my normal pair. Within seconds they too were covered in tiny water droplets, half blinding me. As the road started to plummet down the side of a valley Paps accelerated out of reach.

Martin and I followed him down the hill. I watched the computer. One mile, then another as we dropped like a stone. I hung back to avoid the jet of water flying off Martin's trailer wheel. The speed hit 25mph, then 30. I felt the cold sweat on my back as the wind billowed through my jacket. A truck thundered past, Martin reappearing through the spray, hunched forward, hands feathering the brakes. The distance kept mounting; three miles then four miles.

Oh god, I hope Paps has got this right.

We finally bunched up on the valley floor after crossing the Nechako River. 'This is the junction,' said Paps, assuredly.

'I bloody hope so,' I replied, wiping water from my face.

'She said she would meet us here?' asked Martin, a little puzzled.

'That's what she told me,' muttered Paps.

She was Karen Peterson. Karen had agreed to be our host when we past through Prince George, a sizeable town along our route south toward Vancouver. Like Brian before her, she hadn't a clue what to expect. All she knew was that three Brits, now soaked to the skin, were about to descend upon her. Martin went to scout around and eventually spotted Karen, waiting with her 4x4 and horsebox on the bridge overhead.

Well done Paps, I had complete faith in you!

'Hi, you must be Karen! I'm Martin. Have you been waiting long?'

'No, just a few minutes,' she said.

'Hi, I'm Anthony.'

'Hi Anthony.'

'And I'm James.'

'Hi James. Let's put your bikes in the horsebox shall we?' said Karen, opening the trailer door.

My first impression of Karen was that she was shy and introverted. She was slim, her short light brown hair a no-nonsense cut matching her character and her clothes chosen for the love of the outdoors. There was an awkward moment which passed quickly enough and then Martin joined her in the pick up whilst Paps and I rode with the bikes, holding on to the sides when she rounded a bend in the road. I started to relax.

'Well done mate,' I said, water still dripping down my face.

'You weren't the only one worrying about climbing back up that hill.'

'I was praying you had it under control!'

'Me too!'

We had picked up Karen's details from a friend of Brian's, back in Whitehorse. Like our arrival into Whitehorse, getting to Prince George signalled a real treat. Apart from being indoors, having dry clothes, eating nice food and enjoying the comforts of home living, it provided something extra. It was something to be cherished. We were strangers in someone else's home and that showed plenty of trust on Karen's part, especially for a woman who lived alone.

All of a sudden we came to a halt and Karen opened the horsebox to reveal a beautiful house set in a couple of acres of land. Two horses in the paddock wondered over to meet us as the sun broke through. The feeling of wellbeing was palpable. We all looked at each other, smiles etched across our faces. "Make yourselves at home," instructed Karen, so we set to task, hanging out the tents, washing clothes and attending to Stu and Keith before a home cooked stew was put in front of us. I kept thinking how different it was out on the road, cooking in a shelter and then retreating to our tents. Now I was sat at a table in the warmth, drinking wine and chatting to Karen and her friend, Darla.

'Oh my goodness, look everyone!' said Darla, in a hushed voice.

We all turned in astonishment to see a black bear in the back garden. No more than 30ft away, it looked huge. I mean, nothing like the size of a moose or a musk-ox but believe me, I was damn glad there was a sturdy piece of glass between us. What astounded me most was how gracefully it ambled over the ground. Its whole body seemed so supple.

'Stay still everyone,' was the order. 'Don't make any sudden movements and speak quietly.'

'Look at the size of its feet!' I whispered.

Then a second bear came into view, lolloping out of the wood to join its companion. The sheer power was breathtaking. Paps fetched the camera and took a couple of shots but the darkening light failed us. Then without warning they bolted across the paddock and melted back into the trees. The whole episode left me completely spellbound.

'I've been coming to dinner here for the last ten years and haven't seen anything as good as that. You guys turn up and the first night there are two of them out there!' joked Darla.

'Do you charge extra for this, Karen?' asked Paps.

Like Brian, Karen ferried us around, cooked for us, cared for us. I found it hard to get my head around, for we were complete strangers. Twenty-four hours later, Paps, Karen and I found ourselves staying up late, chatting. I took a sip of my coffee as she put another log into the wood burner and started to talk passionately about her love for horses. She was also an avid cross-country skier and explained how she had built her house. The slightly awkward meeting of three wet cyclists less than two days previous was replaced the following morning by a send-off of hugs and heart-felt thanks back at the roadside.

'Karen, it's been truly amazing,' said Martin. 'Thank you so much for everything.'

'It's been a pleasure, I've really enjoyed it,' she replied, her face welling with tears.

I was really sad to be going. I didn't want to ride off into the rain again. I wanted to go back to Karen's, put on a thick pair of socks and sit by the wood burner, drinking tea and eating her homemade cookies. In ten minutes' time I would be soaking wet again, sweating under my rain jacket and staring at a four-mile climb. In nine hours time I would be climbing into my tent, changing out of my wet clothes and then helping with dinner. I couldn't imagine that the rain would still be falling two days later but it was. It was chucking it down.

'Let's get out of this for a while!' shouted Martin.

'There, that shop!' I shouted, pointing back from the highway.

I squelched my way across the gravel car park, parked the bike and traipsed inside. The owner and her husband realised very quickly that we had no intention of buying anything but it didn't seem to matter as whatever charm we had left gained us free access to the coffee machine. Twenty minutes later the huge pool of water collecting around us began to migrate under the counter as I poured the 3rd round. The shop was Tardis-like. Everything known to man was on sale. The bolt cutter section gave way to Spiderman suits and I even noticed some fetching all-in-one thermal pyjamas that for a brief moment I considered buying. Then Martin came over with a 2ft adjustable spanner in his hand.

'How about we add this to the tool set?' he smirked.

Over the following few days the scenery got increasingly more dramatic. We cycled into the heart of the Canadian Rockies, on a westerly track toward the Atlantic Coast. A pair of lynx bolted from a ditch and an hour later we disturbed a young bear scavenging by the roadside. It ran alongside us for a while before coming out on the road no more than 30 yards away. Neither animal nor human knew what the next move was but thankfully the adolescent cub chose to run up a bank and hide behind a tree. There was wildlife abound;

caribou, moose, bison, porcupine even coyote. Red squirrels were very common. They danced around our tents, hoping to pick up a stray biscuit or two but what impressed me most, was the sheer number of eagles and hawks. The landscape was immense; making us sweat as the road went vertical with altitude gains of a thousand metres a day commonplace.

'Martin and I look out over an awe-inspiring Canadian landscape'

Locked away in all this beauty we found the small town of Pemberton in the dark and were forced to pitch in the town park despite various signs explicitly telling us otherwise. We crept through the gates, rolled the bikes over to the far corner next to some trees and put up our tents. Only in the morning, when I got up to take a pee, did we realise the tents were in full view of the local police station.

*

Our Canadian adventure was drawing to a close. We plummeted down from the ski fields of Whistler, past the enormous granite walls flanking Hove Sound and onto a ferry across to Vancouver Island. Everyone relaxed. We sat on deck, basking in the glorious sunshine as floatplanes dotted the sky above us. Only a few more days remained until the big break and besides, we were spending the next couple of nights with Ray and Joan in Nanaimo. Exiting the ferry ramp, we rode across the tarmac to see Ray stood on the back of his 4x4, waving enthusiastically. We felt like prodigal sons.

'This is going to be so good!' I said.

'I know. How long before Ray opens the brandy?' joked Paps.

*

'Ah, what's he done now?' questioned Paps, as I secured my bike to the ferry deck.

I wondered over to him and realised what he was referring to. Martin was stuck at the dockside speaking to a police officer. At first, we assumed it was polite conversation but as the seconds ticked by it became more sinister. Martin appeared to be explaining something by pointing at his trailer and gesturing with his arms. Then the officer disappeared back into the terminal building.

'What's going on mate?' shouted Paps.

Martin looked up and held out his arms as if to say 'Who knows?' so we walked back down the gangplank to see what was going on. 'What's the problem?' I asked, once we reached him.

'He spotted the licence plates on my trailer,' said Martin.

'So what?'

'Well, apparently, he might be arresting me for it,' said Martin, glumly.

'You're fuckin' joking!' said Paps.

'Did you explain that you found them at the side of the road?' I asked.

'Yeah, obviously.'

A few days back, Martin had spotted a vehicle licence plate in the gravel verge and secured it to the side of his trailer. It wasn't the first time this had happened. He had done the same in Alaska and the Yukon Territory and had plans to send them to his young nephew. Unbeknown to the officer, the Yukon plate was currently out of sight inside Martin's trailer bag. Possessing the British Columbia plate was in danger of getting him arrested.

'Have you told him about the other plate?' I asked.

'Not yet,' said Martin, clearly understanding my question.

'What is the officer doing now?' asked Paps.

'He's taken the plate and gone to ring his superiors,' said Martin.

A few seconds later, the officer reappeared. 'Right, lads. We have run the number and I have been told it's off a stolen motorcycle,' said the officer. 'It's very important that you tell me the truth, otherwise you may be arrested. Can one of *you* tell me your route through Canada?' he asked, now looking at Paps and I.

It was obvious the officer wanted us to corroborate Martin's description of our route. 'We came down through the Yukon Territory to Fort Nelson. Then we went through Charlie Lake, Hudson's Hope, Prince George and Williams Lake. After that we crossed to Pemberton. From Pemberton to Whistler and then across to Vancouver Island to here,' said Paps.

'You never told me you came through Whistler!' snapped the officer. 'Why not?'

'I don't know,' replied Martin. 'We have travelled through dozens of towns in Canada. I forgot to mention Whistler, that's all.'

'The motorbike was stolen in Whistler,' said the officer. 'I am at liberty to tell you that you are suspected of stealing that motorbike. Start telling me the truth!'

'I have told you the truth! There is nothing else to say. I found it at the side of the road and thought I would keep it as a memento. I can't remember where we were exactly, but it was a few days ago. Why would I be stupid enough to steal a motorbike and then put the licence plate on the side of my trailer when crossing the border? We are on a yearlong cycle trip, which took two years to plan and we are raising money for a charity. How can you possibly think I actually stole that motorbike? I am not a criminal. I resent what you are implying.'

The officer paused, considering what to do, with the situation on a knife-edge. I was confident that they would realise he wasn't the person they were looking for. That much was obvious. Yet, a criminal record, even if retracted, would probably invalidate Martin's US visa or at least create further problems at the American side of the border. What would happen if Martin was denied access to the US? Would Paps and I have to cycle through America and meet Martin in Mexico? It didn't bear thinking about.

'OK, I am going to tell you what I think,' said the officer, finally. 'I think you've been a very silly boy who has done something extremely stupid. Taking a licence plate out of Canada is a criminal offence. The plate belongs to the State, it is State property,' he continued. 'You have convinced me that you didn't steal the motorbike. Gather up your stuff and get on the ferry please Sir. Please consider yourself a very lucky man.'

Just keep your mouth shut and let's get out of here!

'OK, thank you officer' I said, quickly.

Martin wasn't fool enough to antagonise the policeman with any backchat. He simply got his stuff together and pushed his bike up the gangplank. On deck and out of range though his anger boiled over. 'A silly little boy? He doesn't have a fucking clue who I am!' he started off.

'At least we are onboard, mate,' said Paps, trying to calm him down.

'How dare he speak to me like that, I can't fucking believe it!'

Anyway, things settled down and we left the bikes to go inside the passenger lounge. The hour's journey south from Victoria across the Strait of Juan de Fuca to the American mainland would give us plenty of time to make the sandwiches we'd been craving. The ship was busy with commuters and weekend passengers. One nearby passenger was Mike Klazek. Mike was a 58-year-old Victorian resident, a softly spoken man who taught music at one of its secondary schools. He also played in the local orchestra. He'd brought his bicycle with him today as he was on his way to see a good friend that lived a few miles along the coast. The conversation was simple enough yet once safely through immigration, Mike cycled over to us as Paps went off to get directions. I wasn't expecting what came next.

'You guys are heading east, right?' he began.

'Yeah, we are going to cycle a few miles before it gets dark,' said Martin.

'Where does your friend live, Mike?' I asked.

'She lives in Sequim, towards the east. I'd like to invite you all to have dinner with us,' he said.

'Wow, that's very generous of you,' said Martin.

'I think your trip is just fantastic so I'd like to take you out by way of saying well done. I know Jeanette would love to meet you all.'

'That's very kind of you. How far is it?' I asked.

'About 16 miles, I can usually do it within an hour,' he said. 'I know a bike path that runs along the coast, it's much better than the main highway,'

'Okay Mike, lead the way!'

The coastal scenery disappeared in the darkness and Mike's solitary headlight became our path to an RV site in the centre of town.

'They don't allow campers,' reported Martin, after Mike had already ridden off to Jeanette's place.

'What are we gonna do then?'

An hour of searching got us nowhere, not even a piece of scrubby ground on which to pitch and the hotels were too expensive. I hated these times; finishing a long day and then failing to find somewhere to get warm and comfortable, frustrated the hell out of me. We even considered sleeping rough in Wal-Mart car park but then it started raining. So instead we went to meet Mike and Jeanette at the Thai restaurant and slightly embarrassingly they arrived to see us loitering outside in the cold, unwashed and still wearing all our cycling gear.

'How did you get on at the RV site?' enquired Mike, as the waiters kept bringing out tray after tray of food.

'Actually, we weren't allowed to pitch our tents,' said Paps.

'Oh! Did you find somewhere else?'

'We looked everywhere and the hotels are too expensive but I'm sure we'll find somewhere later,' said Martin, in hope more than anything.

'You are more than welcome to stay with me,' said Jeanette, as we continued to discuss the lack of options.

'You've been more than kind with the meal. We'll find somewhere to camp, we always do.'

'It's no problem. I have plenty of floor space to offer you. You'd be warm and dry. Why don't you come and stay?'

In the end, the offer was too much to refuse and to be fair we couldn't believe our good fortune. Jeanette's place was a huge well-appointed mobile home. She made us feel right at home, handing out clean towels and letting us shower, even treating us to a nightcap before we crashed out in our sleeping bags. My diary entry for the day read...

10th October. 57 miles to Sequim, USA. We woke to pouring rain and set off toward Victoria. After losing Paps, he finds us sheltering under a tree during a tea break. Later, Martin has a narrow escape with the Police at the ferry port. Luckily we are let on board and meet Mike, who invites us to dinner in Sequim with his friend Jeanette and a lady called Gloria. Couldn't find anywhere to pitch. Spent night at Jeanette's place. I love her '70's décor!

Our mood couldn't have been any better when we woke. Jeanette got up early to buy bacon and sausages for breakfast. What a send off!

'Bye boys!' she shouted, as we rode out in the sunshine.

'Bye Jeanette!'

The amount of hospitality we had received through Alaska and Canada was phenomenal. The sight of us out on the road or in campsites intrigued people and triggered a conversation. "How far are you going?" "Where are you headed?" "Where did you start?" Sometimes the conversation led to food, a meal or even an invitation to stay and today was another case in point.

'Hi boys!' said Shirley, excitedly, as we cycled up her driveway.

'Hello!'

'You didn't mention that hill in your directions, Shirley!' said Paps in reference to the 14% grade marking the entrance to their property.

Bob and Shirley were a retired couple we had met only fleetingly a few weeks back. Reaching their place in Silverdale marked no more cycling for twelve days. The three of us shook hands, patted each other on the back and went inside, extremely proud of ourselves. Bob and Shirley had built their house many moons ago, on a piece of land overlooking the Kitsap Peninsula. The open plan design and large windows made the most of views that extended west across to the Olympic Mountains and into Washington State. This was a stunning region, made even more beautiful right now with the deciduous trees in full autumn glory. Like those before them, Bob and Shirley took care of us for a while, took us out of the wind and rain, away from cooking on the stove, away from the bikes. As I have said, these were special moments. Everyone knew that it wasn't going to last forever, even our long break would come to an end at some point. The dreaded headwind or the next hill was always just around the corner, yet a night or two with friendly faces made all the difference. These stops gave us the impetus and enthusiasm to carry on. Our hosts' energy and passion for what we were doing provided a boost to morale, a reassessment of our goals. We would stop feeling downtrodden and start to see the achievement and progress we were making. 'It's only ten more days to Karen's place' or 'Once we get to California it's only 1,000 miles and we are in Mexico!' we would say. Statements like these showed how far we had come. Considering ten days or 1,000 miles on a bike as 'only' values was routine now, it was how we thought. No way that would have happened before the trip, when a thirty-mile ride was an accomplishment. Thinking in blocks of distance or time helped to manage its enormity. When you are cold and wet all day in Canada, there is little solace in thinking about Mexico. What you want to know is when you can get off the bike, a target to push on to. Even for Paps, managing the mental battle was still the biggest challenge.

Fresh from a good night's sleep, Shirley dropped us off at Bremerton to catch the ferry over to Seattle. From there we spent three hours on a bus listening to music, chatting and eating piles of junk food. We were on holiday. Arriving into Vancouver a nervous excitement ran through me as I said goodbye to the lads and headed off across town.

'Hi, my name is James Wilson. I believe my family is staying with you? The name is Barber,' I said, once at the hotel desk.

'They are out at the moment, Sir,' said the receptionist.

'Can I go up and get changed? I am sharing a room with my sister, Lucy Wilson.'

'Sure, I will get you a key card.'

Letting myself in, I threw my bag onto one of the beds and noticed a bottle of whiskey next to the TV. A note was lying next to it. "Hi James, we thought you might appreciate this! See you later, love Lucy."

"That's my family," I thought.

Chapter 6

"You never listen to a thing I say!"

'It is not necessary to understand things in order to argue about them.'
Pierre Beaumarchais
Born France, 1732

Start Point: Silverdale, USA. Mile: 2,935. 24th October.

It was obvious that Mum, Ted, and Lucy had come out to pamper me. When I announced I was going to attempt cycling across two continents, a year before heading to Alaska, the whole family looked a bit bewildered, perhaps even a tad exasperated.

'You're going to do what?' had asked my elder sister, Helen.
'It's a personal challenge and we are raising money for charity.'
'How long have you known about this?' she continued, gathering herself.
'For a year but I didn't want to say anything until it became more than talk.'
With nearly 3,000 miles in the bag they were starting to appreciate the scale of what we had asked of ourselves. This translated into VIP treatment as swish hotels and restaurant dining replaced my mildew-infested tent and cooking on Stu. I could hardly contain myself. A couple of nights in Vancouver were followed by three more nights in equally salubrious digs back in Victoria, whereupon Ted and I snuck off for a day's fishing on the western side of Vancouver Island. All too quickly our time together came to an end and they returned to England, leaving me with a few days to kill before meeting up with the lads and continuing the ride. There was no better option than taking Ray and Joan up on their offer of some accommodation.
'It works best on massage setting you know,' said Ray, as I jumped into the hot tub.
'I think it's doing the trick already, Ray!'
'Are you ready for another beer?'
Time alone made me ponder the forthcoming leg through America and reflect on the awe-inspiring beauty of Canada. The scale of the country and its humble citizens had made a big impression on me. Although I longed for the sunshine of California our Canadian experience had been nothing short of exceptional. The temperate environment, golden colours of autumn and intelligence of the country's people resonated strongly with me. Penning a letter each to Zin, Brian and Karen to update them on our progress, it was time to dig deep, concentrate on the task ahead and get cycling again.

*

'What goodies did you get then?' I asked, as the lads stepped out of the supermarket laden with shopping bags.

'Oh boy, we have got so much food!' Paps replied, excitedly.

'Great! What can we have now? I am starving,' I said.

'We went a little overboard in the pastry section,' continued Martin. 'Give me a minute and I'll dish out the cakes. We've got four each!'

'What do you want me to take?'

'Take the rice, if you like.'

'Give me the porridge and sugar as well,' I said, getting up from the curb and unhooking the food sack from my Bert.

Ripping packaging open and filling Ziploc bags always caught the eye of the public and today it was the people of Shelton that saw us sprawled out across the pavement, feverishly restocking the larder. As usual, we took an equal share of water, fruit, biscuits and cakes. Other items were apportioned by habit. I took the rice and porridge, Paps the meat, noodles and some vegetables. That left Martin with the remaining veg, as well as the pasta and bread. He also seemed to have a never-ending supply of custard powder, which he made when in the mood or still hungry after dinner. This wasn't all we carried though. We also had mayonnaise, sugar, tea bags, powdered milk, jam, tinned meat, tinned tuna, sardines, cheese and seasonings and due to my newfound addiction, I also insisted on keeping a healthy supply of peanut butter. All this made the trailers feel appreciably heavier but the weight didn't last long. Within a couple of days the food mountain just melted away and it was time to pull off the highway again and find a shop. No amount of food seemed sufficient on a hilly day and sometimes two lunches appeared wholly normal yet excess body fat continued to fall off. By now, my ribs shone through as skin stretched tightly across my chest.

Back on the curbside we chose to keep the cakes in reserve and opt for making a quick sandwich. With our backs against the supermarket wall we basked in the midday sunshine, watching Shelton's public come and go. As we did, a clapped-out black hatchback rolled into the car park, pulling up a few metres away. Out stepped two lads and two girls, all of them dressed in black. I tried to avoid eye contact as the lads had tattoos across the arms and calf muscles and one of them, a six-foot man mountain looked irate enough to hit his own granny. They walked past us, towards the supermarket entrance and straight into an unfriendly looking skinhead who had been cussing his girlfriend a few minutes before. It was as obvious as me requesting a second sandwich that they were going to clash.

'What the fuck are you looking at?' said the six-foot Goth.

'Why? What's your fucking problem?'

'Why were you staring at me, man?'

'You were staring at me, you jerk!'

With this, the tattooed Goth pulled off his t-shirt, puffed out his chest in an apparent show of strength and got ready to fight. It was so entertaining that I actually stopped eating. Then the girlfriends got involved and the whole event turned into a slanging match. Lots of shouting, cussing and ego stroking but no one seemed prepared to throw the first punch. Within seconds two police cars screamed into the car park to be greeted by the supermarket manager.

'Oh! I thought it was really going to kick off' said Martin, disappointedly.

'Yeah, I know. Just when it was getting interesting, the cops turn up,' I said, returning to my sandwich.

Luckily, the afternoon's ride was delayed a little while longer by meeting Rick who wondered over with his young son. 'Where you headed, guys?' he asked.

'Down into Mexico,' said Martin.

'Really? I'm a cyclist myself, the name's Rick,' he said shaking hands with us.

'Are you a member of a club around here then?' asked Martin.

'Yeah, I do weekend rides, just road cycling really. I've got some spare jerseys in my car that you can have. I'll be back in a minute.'

Waiting for Rick to return, I found it hard to put the knowledge of the four cream cakes in my bag to the back of my mind. 'They might be a bit big for you but you are welcome to them nonetheless!' he said, mocking his portly frame.

It was a kind gesture but Rick was no touring cyclist. Don't get me wrong, receiving gifts was great but trailer weight ruled in our world. The jerseys were now just further items of surplus kit that since Prudhoe we had been jettisoning in an effort to become a leaner, sleeker, more efficient outfit. Stuff was either given away, burnt on the campfire or sent home, making for some hilarious banter as we marvelled at the ridiculousness of some apparently "essential kit". Neither the battery charger with a British plug nor the hunting catapult made it into the top three. Number 3, was my washing bowl. Although collapsible and clearly a camping item, it never saw the light of day. We washed plates, pots and cutlery in streams and lakes or under a tap. If we weren't near a water source, a cupful from a water bottle was poured into the dirty pan and a little detergent added. We made do. At Number 2 was the solar shower! Quite why such an item was required in Canada still remains a mystery. Never once used or even considered, its only purpose was to annoy Martin each time he spotted it at the bottom of his trailer bag. Yet, for me, the Number 1 spot and king of the absurd was Martin's skipping rope. Later confessing to being "somewhat over prepared" Martin had always been a fitness freak but wouldn't you think 15,000 miles cycling would keep him in shape?

*

Location: Bullards Beach, USA. Mile: 3,210.
(Continued from Prologue)

With Paps still motionless and considering his next move, Martin looked at me as if to say, "Come on, tell him to stay!" The problem was, I didn't share his spirit. I knew Martin was digging deep, trying to pull the team together but I was so angry that I just wanted Paps to walk off. I couldn't physically say, 'Yeah mate, please put your tent up,' even though I knew I should.

On reflection our first major crisis had been a long time coming. Three months on the road had taken its toll and everyone's patience was being tested by the appalling Oregon weather. It wasn't that I didn't feel bad for Paps, on the contrary, the pain and discomfort were such that he had sensibly suggested stopping at Christmas to go home and be with his girlfriend, Naomi. After all, if the knees were so painful, why carry on and make the situation worse and chance crippling yourself? The thought of him having to give up horrified me but quite frankly his attitude had drained me.

What made the situation more complicated was that Martin and I began to suspect that the knee problem popped up when it suited him, a product of studying Paps's behaviour over the past three months. The knee was almost a fourth person by now and it seemed to need resting when it rained a lot or when it was windy and unpleasant. On other days, even when it was hilly and cold but crucially, sunny, the condition never materialised. I tried not to think the worst but inconsistencies made doing so very hard. It also felt like we weren't operating as a team that shared all the tasks and rallied around. As far as I was concerned, we had been doing our level best to make his world as tolerable as possible. This was most evident at camp where Paps was so used to having dinner made for him that it was a case of him getting his tent up and waiting to be served. Perhaps it was our fault for not nipping it in the bud? Sometimes, we joked about it to stir interest and Paps did help with dinners and made nearly all the campfires but never once did he cook alone. It sounds childish to bicker but you have to understand, why should Paps get special treatment? We were all dealing with the rain, the wind and the hills. We all felt tired and dirty at the end of a day and had to clean our bikes and do laundry on rest days. Yet somehow, because Paps was coping with a knee problem it entitled him to call the shots. His attitude and the superiority in the way he spoke angered the hell out of me. During his moods, which lasted anything up to two days, we resigned ourselves to coping with aggressive body language and cycling with a stranger. Conversation became entirely two dimensional, as Paps remained silent and unapproachable. Responding with one word answers or discourteous grunts and definitive statements like, 'I need a day off.' Paps was as frustrated with Martin and I and our lack of understanding as he was with his knee and this struggle had finally resulted in a full-blown argument in the rain and wind of Oregon. The dam had failed.

'I don't want to leave,' said Paps, with his back to us.

'Yeah and we don't want you to leave either,' said Martin.

'It just feels like I have been on my own since the restart.'

Paps turned his bike around and wheeled it back into camp. Putting his tent back up, I served the porridge and we all got out of the rain and wind. The crisis had come and gone. I sat on top of my sleeping bag, eating my bowl of porridge, pondering what had just happened. I was damn glad Paps hadn't gone and felt guilty that I hadn't been strong enough to tell him so. Paps recalls…

From my perspective it had been a tough week and my spirits took a huge battering. Being 3-5 miles behind on some sections reminded me of my predicament. I simply couldn't fix what I didn't understand and knew we had to keep cycling to get out of the bad weather. It all came to a head two days before Bullard's Beach when we were cycling along a difficult coastal road and my knee gave way completely. I was alone as usual and I had to stop due to the pain, almost crying from the sheer frustration. What was galling was that I had to walk up a hill for the first time, something that both my friends missed completely. I remember getting into camp and not being happy, no surprise there, and greeted by general statements of concern but nothing more. Due to the frequency of my bad days at this point, the boys hadn't clicked that my position was now worse. Nevertheless, I was annoyed because after relaying my 'stopping on a hill', we got up the next morning and set out as if everything was normal and we should do another 50. Unbelievable.

That day into Bullard's Beach my knee somehow held together although for the last 10 miles I was cycling at perhaps 20%, trying to ease the pressure on climbs or indeed cycling on one leg when things got really bad. I remember Martin staying with me for some of those final miles but I asked him to go on and catch Wils, as I felt so useless. I didn't want him hanging around me even though he was trying to help. It seemed that trip mileage was more important than my health and that's what kicked off the argument. I recall asking if we could rest that day or at least have the morning off but it was decided that we really needed to get the hell out of Oregon. Nine times out of ten that is fair enough but I was in bad shape. I remember Martin saying something that morning that got me going - something about us hating half days and I lost it. I told him that he had started to think like a computer not a friend and was more interested in distance and routines than in me. I guess I would have liked one of the boys to have suggested we have a day off but that suggestion never came. I didn't go because deep down I knew it would be a huge mistake and just like every time thereafter when I really wanted a ticket home, something, perhaps a willingness at all costs not to give in, made me stay.

The restart from Silverdale had begun well. We had progressed quickly through the state of Washington, traversing westward to meet the Pacific coast at the mouth of the Columbia River. The huge, 4.1 mile long Astoria-Megler Bridge which spans the river, took us into Oregon. After a brief laundry stop, where we sat around half-naked in towels waiting for our clothes to dry, we continued down the coast. Everyone held their breath in anticipation of the storms that famously roll in off the Pacific during this time of year and by the time we had reached Beverley Beach, the stunning coastline was giving us a real pasting. It was miserable. Us, our bikes, our kit, everything became wet and dirty. If that wasn't enough, the cycling was made harder by the strong winds that buffeted us on roads covered with leaves, twigs and fallen branches. Traffic whizzed past in near-zero visibility, inches from our left shoulders, the rolling coastline making us sweat under our waterproofs and curse when we got a puncture. Food breaks were taken anywhere an opportunity presented itself such as under the eves of a locked toilet block within a state recreation ground.

'It's the water between my socks and shoes that is making that squelching sound but my feet are dry,' I said, happy that my waterproof socks were working.

'Mine aren't,' came Paps's reply. 'They are soaking.'

'My pants are wet though.'

'My arms are wet. How are my arms wet? I have got my jacket on.'

'It's sweat, not water.'

'Great!'

'Damn it's cold,' I said.

'Do you want some tea, Wils?' asked Martin, hidden from view in an adjacent alcove.

'I've got some, thanks mate.'

We all peered out across the clearing, watching the rain. Above us angry clouds continued to build as the next weather system rolled in off the ocean. Thunderous waves clapped against the rocky shore below us and seagulls danced on the wind. I started to shiver.

'Do you mind if we get going?' I asked. 'I am getting cold again.'

'No problem, I am chilly now too.'

'And me.'

It turned out that the bad weather in Canada was only an aperitif. Oregon was the real deal. Yet, it was hard to ignore the beauty of our surroundings. The crashing surf and wind in our ears gave the jagged coastline a haunting feel. We followed the road along forested cliff tops before plunging down to sea level, where huge rock stacks stood tall in the sand like beachfront sentries awaiting an invasion. Lighthouses marked each headland. We'd make use of state campgrounds to try to get warm before setting off again into the maelstrom.

'What are we having?' I enquired.

'I thought we could do the sausages with mashed potato?' said Martin, searching through his food.

'That sounds good. I hope no one comes in whilst we are cooking, it's a bit cheeky.'

'We don't have many options I'm afraid.'

'Better than doing it in the rain,' said Paps. 'Damn, I have forgotten the pots, I'll be back in a minute.'

'My tent is leaking,' I said to Martin, as the shower block door closed behind Paps. 'Where one of the guy rope patches joins to the inner.'

'You should have pitched under the trees like me, rather than out on the grass.'

'I am leaving some clothes in here overnight,' I said, changing the subject.

'Yeah, I think it's too cold for them to dry completely though.'

The sausages and mash tasted fantastic and lifted our spirits, so much so that we started to laugh about our surroundings. Here we were, three men eating

"You never listen to a thing I say!"

dinner on a bench in the men's shower block of a state campground on the Oregon coast. Wet socks, wet tops and wet gloves hung from cubicle doors, dripping water all over the floor. Every so often one of us was forced to get up to reengage the light switch which had a ten-minute timer. It was 6pm; pitch black outside and still raining. What a day it had been...

'My food bag has disappeared and Paps, your Tupperware boxes are scattered everywhere!' I had said after stepping out of my tent. 'I think you guys should take a look.'

'It'll be the blasted raccoons,' shouted Paps from inside his.

'Hang on mate, I am getting up now,' said Martin.

I collected up Paps's boxes and food wrappers and then started hunting down my food bag in the wet undergrowth beyond the edge of the campsite. Martin scouted an enormous 6ft high log pile in the opposite direction. Fifteen minutes later, there was still no sign of it.

'What was in it?' asked Martin.

'Porridge, sugar, tea bags, the water filter, some Veg, I'm not totally sure. Maybe some rice? I am going to check over there,' I said, pointing to a clump of trees I hadn't searched.

'OK, I'll look by the creek.'

A few more minutes went by and I was giving up hope. *Surely the racoons couldn't lift such a heavy weight, could they?*

'I've found it!' shouted Martin.

I ran over to find him crouched next to the creek. 'I can't see it.'

'There, floating in the creek against the bank, next to that dead branch.'

'How are we going to get it?'

'You might be going for a swim young man!'

'Fat chance, let's find a stick.'

What Martin found was more like a branch as we set about trying to hook the bag. Although the creek was only ten foot wide, the opposing bank was vertical so it meant reaching out at least eight feet from the other side.

'Are you sure you've got me?' I asked nervously.

'Yeah, go on, I've got you!' said Martin, holding onto the back of my trousers as I leaned out across the creek with the stick in both hands.

'OK...a bit more....bit more,' I instructed.

'I can't go any further or we'll both be in!' he said, clearly enjoying the comedy of it all.

'I've got it!'

'I bet the racoons weren't happy when it slid down the bank!'

'They've made a mess though,' said Martin as water poured out like a sprinkler head. 'But we have the water filter.'

'Thanks mate. Let's get out of here and I'll buy everyone breakfast.'

*

The day after Bullards Beach, we were again braving the wind and rain as the next squall rolled in. Everyone was in better spirits for some reason and rounding one particular headland we decided the wind had become so outrageous that we should get Keith out and film it. Neither Keith nor I caught a single thing they said as their words were whipped away back up to Canada. As far as I was concerned, it couldn't get any worse but at least we had come prepared, for late in the day, as I descended into another small bay and followed the road inland, I rode past a tent at the side of the road with three bicycles lying next to it. I pulled up and walked back along the road through the pouring rain to investigate.

'Hello. Is anyone there?' I offered, as I approached.

The tent door opened to reveal three very dejected, wet cyclists, one of whom had her arm in a makeshift sling. 'I thought you might need some help, are you all OK?' I asked.

'We're alright. She took a fall on the corner back there,' said one of the lads.

'Do you want me to get some help? We are trying to reach Gold Beach tonight, maybe someone can pick you up?'

'It's OK. We are just gonna rest here for a while. I don't think her injury is that bad.'

'We met a few days ago back at Reedsport, right?' I said, recognising one of them.

'Ah, yeah, that's right! How are you doin'?'

'Well, apart from the weather we are fine thanks. It looks like there might be a campsite over the road if you decide not to carry on. Have you got enough food?'

'Yes thanks.'

'OK, all the best then.'

'Bye.'

We had met the Aussies back in Reedsport, "sinkin' a few tinnies" as one of them had put it, in the room next to us.

'So how far are ya goin'?' one of them had asked me.

'We are heading down to Argentina,' I said. 'But we are just trying to get to Mexico for Christmas at the moment. How about you?'

'Well, we only started in Washington. It just depends but perhaps we can get to Mexico. There's no plan.'

'You enjoying the weather?' I asked, with a heavy amount of sarcasm.

'We didn't realise it was going to be like this actually. We don't have any waterproofs.'

Everyone knows that Australians are famously laid back but honestly, cycling through Washington and Oregon during November without rain gear? It was suicide. Huddled together in that tent, I think they were beginning to realise a few jackets might have been a good investment. We left them to it and pressed on, soaked to the skin and freezing cold until we spotted a steel container which provided us some momentary shelter. The flasks were empty and we all began to shiver straight away.

'I am frozen,' I said.

'I saw a sign back there, indicating an RV site around here,' said Martin.

'Left or right?' I asked.

'I reckon we head right.'

'Let's go!'

We headed off, along an access road that ran parallel to the main highway and soon came across it. No sooner had we registered and got the tents up, the clouds cleared and everything was glistening in sunshine. Gerhard, who for some reason became known to us as Hans, owned and ran the site and according to him, his 'All-You-Can-Eat' suppers were stuff of legend.

'I am going to make a mockery of this. Hans won't know what's hit him,' said Martin, as we headed off to the dining area.

To be fair, Hans's supper was superb, especially the braised sauerkraut and meatballs. Yet the highlight of the evening wasn't his cooking but rather his singing as he took centre stage with microphone in hand. We all looked at each other in disbelief. What happened next was like a scene from the 'Wedding Singer', as Hans ran through his repertoire of well-rehearsed melodies, accompanied by Jane on the electric keyboard. Pure comedy.

'Hans sets to work'

*

After no more than two miles the next morning the wind picked up and the rain was lashing in. We fought against being blown into the middle of the road.

'This is silly, I nearly came off back there,' said Paps, as we bunched up on the 2ft wide hard shoulder.

'Let's try and get to Gold Beach. How far is it, mate?' I asked, looking at Martin.

'No more than 3 miles, probably around that headland.'

On entering the small town of Gold Beach and after Martin had been blown into a ditch, we took refuge in the first available diner. Rain clattered against the window and customers eyed the three drowned rats.

'What can I get you guys?' asked the waitress.

'Three coffees please, oh and a portion of French fries,' said Martin.

'No problem.'

'Have you heard the weather forecast by any chance?' asked Paps.

'Yeah, a storm is coming in apparently.'

'This isn't it?'

'No. It's not meant to hit until late afternoon. This is just the edge.'

'That settles it then. Looks like we're staying,' said Martin, looking at Paps and I. 'How far have we come from Han's place, Wils?'

'Ten miles.'

'That's the longest, hardest ten miles of my life!'

Chapter 7

"It's the boonies down there!"

'There are no foreign lands. It is the traveller only who is foreign.'
Robert Louis Stevenson
Born Scotland, 1850

Start Point: Gold Beach, USA. Mile: 3,320. 6th November.

Paps was a few hundred yards up front, leading the way into another bay as several lines of traffic thundered past on their way out of San Francisco. We had the benefit of a three-foot wide hard shoulder but I was navigating with the aid of the passing headlights. When we bunched up at the next set of traffic lights I started up straight away.

'I've had enough of this, I want to get off this highway,' I said.

'There's nowhere to camp,' said Paps.

'We haven't found anywhere in the last five miles. Now it's dark and bloody dangerous. Let's just doss down somewhere.'

'How about we go on the beach?' offered Martin.

'Or we could look behind that supermarket?' I countered, pointing off to the left.

The back of the supermarket presented no option, chiefly because a Security Guard wasn't in the mood to let us sleep on the tarmac so the only alternative was the beach. This wasn't the first time we had run into problems. As expected, camping rough in the lower 48 was not like Canada or Alaska. In America, nearly all the land flanking our route was private, much of it with prominent 'Keep Out' or 'Trespassers will be prosecuted' signs stamped against the fencing. State-owned land, like forestry plots or parks were similarly well patrolled and nearly all the beaches we came across were off limits to camping. This left very few options apart from designated camp areas or RV parks, all of which charged for their services. Today was just another case of us running out of time as we searched frantically to find somewhere to sleep. We rolled the bikes back across the highway in the darkness and into a small car park that fronted the beach. Fortunately once on the sand, a little hollow afforded us some protection as we laid the bikes down and rolled out our mattresses. Safely inside my sleeping bag my body started to fall limp with the benefit of a little music to drown out the urban clatter. The stars sparkled brightly in the night sky, moonlight reflecting off the incoming waves and I drifted into a deep slumber.

By 6am the car park next to the beach was busy with surfers arriving to catch a wave or two before heading off to the office. They strutted around half-naked in black wetsuits, applying a little sun cream to their faces whilst we ate breakfast and got ready to ride. The bad weather was behind us now. We all sensed the approaching heat of southern California and even the odd food break had us basking topless if the sun was out. Our route out of Oregon had taken us through a beautiful section of Redwood forest where we woke one morning to wild elk grazing around our tents before we hiked through the forest to a deserted white sand beach.

'Martin basks in glorious sunshine on a deserted beach'

On sunny days we shared the road with groups of bikers out for a blast on the tight twisting Highway 1 that hugged the spectacular coastline. The landscape was changing. Parched grassland and scrub dotted with Eucalyptus trees now dominated our surroundings. The day before we had cycled over the Golden Gate Bridge in glorious sunshine. Standing on such a famous structure in the same clothes and accompanied by the same two friends I had started the trip with made for a poignant moment. Had we just cycled here from the Arctic Ocean? For a moment I dismissed it out of sheer disbelief. It felt like I had seen someone else do it on the Discovery Channel. Persisting on all those hills, through all those wet days and stopping all those times to eat a biscuit at the side of the road had somehow got us here. I paused, soaking up the unexplainable. No matter that the day ended in disarray at our improvised beach camp, we were now well heeled touring cyclists.

"It's the boonies down there!"

'Paps and Martin on the Golden Gate Bridge'

*

Three days after the beach camp we were back in San Francisco, this time without the bikes. We had left them at a campsite to the south, to return and spend the weekend with a friend from University. Pete now lived in Atlanta with his wife and young son and had come a long way from his modest upbringing in London. He was Vice President of Underwriting in a large insurance firm which meant regular business meetings around the States and Europe. No surprise then, that one of them happened to coincide with our arrival in San Francisco! It also meant we got to stay at the Hilton.

Seeing Pete was strange. Even though we found it hard to imagine each other's lives, I did feel a pang of guilt for not cementing a career, like he had done. I was messing about on a bike whilst he was supporting his family, building capital for the future. I had to keep reminding myself that it was precisely this that I was trying to break away from, at least for a while; that I was trying to explore things from a different perspective. The boys chatted away, leaving me in my own world again, like I was back on the bike or back staring at the gravel verge during a food break.

Soon enough we were toasting beer after beer in a brilliant little pub a few blocks away chock-a-block full of young trendy locals. The carpet was soaking wet from spilt beer and the air so smoky that for an all too brief moment we were back in Bangor. Gone was the bike, my wet clothes and the Oregon weather.

*

I jumped off the bike, unhooked the trailer, flipped the bike upside-down, detached the rear wheel and then went about finding my head torch. Only the last remnants of light remained on the horizon. The wind was howling in off the ocean, twice knocking the bike over and making it awkward for a quick repair. Alone in the darkness, I started cussing over and over.

Stupid bloody tyre, I'll have to buy a new one. Damn, I can't see anything, is the glue dry or not? Four miles short of the campground and it decides to puncture. If this inner tube punctures again this bike will be in the bloody ocean.

Martin came jogging back to see what had happened. We set off again and eventually rolled into a campsite in the pitch-black. It was full for the Thanksgiving Holiday but we found a place, showered and made dinner. Then I got talking to a couple washing their dishes outside one of the campsite's shower blocks. They let me sample some of their leftover lobster and then invited me to join them and their friends at their campsite no more than a stone's throw from the tents. Martin and I strolled over not knowing quite what to expect.

'Hi there!' I said, walking up to find half a dozen people huddled around a roaring campfire.

'Hi boys, come and meet all our friends. Everyone, this is James and…'

'Martin.'

'This is James and Martin; they are cycling from Alaska to Argentina. Is your other friend not joining us?'

'No, he's asleep. It's tiring work this cycling game!'

'Ah! Come and take a seat. Would you like some pie and ice cream?'

Martin and I went into autopilot. Out flowed a few stories about the Atigun, our stolen food and the Oregon weather. More than anything we revelled in being amongst such friendly people, to have the chance to hear about their lives and experiences. The annoyance caused by my tyre vanished as quickly as the pudding.

'So how far do you cycle per day?' asked a lady, clasping a mug of cocoa to our right.

'Anywhere between forty and eighty miles but it depends on a lot of things. Today we did eighty-three, despite a detour due to road repairs and a nasty squall that soaked us for an hour coming out of Lompoc.'

'Well you probably won't see rain again for a while. It gets pretty dry from here on south.'

She was right. It was the 25th November and we wouldn't see rain again for another 106 days.

*

'We need to make a decision or we won't be crossing the border tonight,' said Paps.

'I know Paps but I can't risk going into Mexico without a new middle ring. I'll get some directions and you two can stay here and we'll get moving when I get back,' I said, trying to thumb a lift.

'Ah, here we go, there is someone coming now,' I said, spying an approaching red 4x4. 'It looks like he is stopping!'

We had just spent the last two hours being directed and redirected around San Diego, negotiating junctions and lots of traffic. The two bike shops we had found in that time had been unable to help and everyone was now slightly hot under the collar. Today's objective was getting across the border *not* wasting time in San Diego.

'I was wondering if you knew a bike shop around here where I can get a replacement part?' I asked, leaning in to the off side window.

'Yeah sure, I'm a cyclist myself. What do you need?' said the driver.

'A new chain ring.'

'I know a great shop a few miles away. I don't mind taking you if you like?'

'Really? That would be brilliant.'

'I'll open the trunk and make some room in the back.'

As my saviour jumped out I gave Paps the thumbs up. We were back in business. 'My name is James,' I said, offering my hand.

'Greg Jones.'

Greg was tall, dark and athletic. 'Pleased to meet you Greg,' I replied. 'We're trying to get to Tijuana tonight but I'm not sure if we're going to make it now.'

'You should do, the border is only 20 miles from here.'

Paps and I loaded my bike into the back of Greg's jeep, carefully trying not to ruin his sparkling racing bike and then Greg and I set off across town. Fifteen minutes later a mechanic was already working on my ride. Things were so much easier with a local!

'So what was wrong with the ring?' enquired Greg, as we watched the mechanic.

'We had some work done in preparation for crossing into Mexico and now the new chain keeps slipping because the teeth on the middle ring have worn down so much.'

'They didn't spot it when you had your overhaul?'

'The guy turned out to be a bit of a cowboy. We're finding there's still stuff to sort out.'

'It's the luck of the draw, I guess. Shall we grab a coffee whilst we wait for them to finish?'

We found a place overlooking the beach a couple of blocks away. Like many people before him, Greg empathised greatly with what we were doing. He was ten years older than us, had the job, the family and the comfortable lifestyle, yet he admitted to being truly envious of our ride and the good it was doing for the children in Central America. What people failed to grasp, Greg included, wasn't so much the physicality or obstacles such as the wind or rain but rather the mental stress. A three-week ride encompassing the length of Britain is a big distance but it's manageable. Just dig in for a while and you'll be set free having achieved something that most people would be in awe of. That didn't apply in our case. We had cycled Britain four times over and hadn't completed a third of the trip. That alone told us of the distance that still lay ahead. Indeed, Mexico was where the real fun and games would begin and where the stress levels would be cranked up another couple of notches. Eight hours a day in the saddle, twelve days without a break or four hundred miles in a week carrying our own gear. These were the things that got the public's juices flowing. Yet, for us it was the way in which those miles were done that made the trip so massive. When we explained that the real factors were finding food, maintaining kit and sleeping rough whilst trying to make progress, our audience's eyes just glazed over. They didn't get it.

Us: We tell people it's the constant decision making, the constant conferencing over when and where to buy food, when and where to sleep the night, never knowing what lies ahead. That what tires us most is doing all the miles and then having to clean the bike, clean our kit, write reports and plan ahead, when all you want to do is open the front door, grab something from the fridge, and go to the pub with your mates.

Audience: Bollocks. You're having the time of your life.

Maybe we were having the time of our lives yet the challenge was massive. Emails from family and friends back home also told us people's perception was wildly different from reality.

Email to England: Life on the road continues to have its ups and downs but we are managing to get on well enough and we are all looking forward to getting to Mexico and sampling something different. I may be out of touch for a while as we are about to cross the border and head down the Baja. Trust all is well with you. Speak soon…

Email from England: Wish I could join you guys for some time away from the stress of everyday life. It must be so great to see so much and have no worries for a year. Did you manage to visit Universal Studios or perhaps Sunset Boulevard on your way through LA? At least be sure to get across to the Grand Canyon, I hear it's worth a visit. Keep me up to date. All the best…

Greg and I pulled up to find the boys relaxing on the grass exactly where we had left them.

'All sorted?' asked Martin.

'As good as new,' I smiled.

'Ah, brilliant!'

'Any ideas how we should get to the border from here, Greg?' asked Paps.

'Well you'll be okay for a few miles but then the Interstate takes over and so you'll need to ask someone. I've never been across on a bike.'

'Not a problem, we are used to getting lost!'

'You need to be careful you know, it's the boonies down there. Do any of you speak Spanish?'

'James does and Martin and I know the basics.'

'Watch out, the police are corrupt as hell.'

We bid farewell to Greg and began the tricky task of getting to the border. The scale of our map made it virtually useless and we couldn't follow the motorways so we were forced to negotiate the labyrinth of main roads and one way streets. Eventually we resorted to asking locals and navigating by the advanced tool of "reckoning."

'I'm sure we should be heading more toward those hills.'

'You're probably right but that guy said, "Keep going until you reach an overpass."

An hour later and we spotted the city of Tijuana on the horizon, thanks to the view afforded by a hill we had climbed. With the light fading we got lucky with one or two reckonings and some accurate directions from a car mechanic and then a young lad out on his skateboard. On the shoulder of the Interstate for the last half mile, we past through the border station complex alongside hundreds of motorists. Suddenly, we found ourselves on a 4-lane highway with no shoulder and in very murky conditions.

'Let's not mess about, it's lethal out here.' I said, excitedly. 'Follow the sign for el Centro!'

Firmly in the Spanish speaking world, cars raced past as we tried to get off the highway and head for the city centre, no more than a mile away. We cycled a few blocks in amongst the traffic with buses cutting across us to pick up passengers from the curbside. We were close; the hostel was only a block away. Pushing our bikes through the chaos and up onto the curb, the whole of Tijuana seemed to be monitoring the three apprehensive gringos. The city was teeming with life. This was it; the trip had been turned upside down in the space of ten minutes. Welcome to Mexico. Welcome to the start of our Latin American adventure.

Chapter 8

Punctures, Diarrhoea and Paralysis

'If you don't like something change it; if you can't change it, change the way you think about it.'
Mary Engelbreit
Born America, 1952

Start Point: Tijuana, Mexico. Mile: 4,460. 3rd December.

Ten months before flying to Prudhoe I left my job and flew to South America to learn some Spanish. The first three months I lived with a Bolivian family in La Paz. I took classes during the day and spent most of my time with the family in the evenings. Twice a week we played "Volly" - a form of volleyball where players use any part of their body and the walls of an enclosed court to return the ball over the net, a fantastic game, played with real speed and competitiveness that left me gasping for breath in the high altitude conditions. After a while I stepped up my language practice by putting a notice in the Linguistics Department of the University. It led to meeting Justo Martín Tancara Limachi or Martín, for short. We'd speak in Spanish for an hour and then English for an hour, helping each other with vocabulary and grammar. It worked well and we became great friends. Martín used to come to the house every morning and we'd sit in the kitchen drinking black tea and eating bread and jam whilst chatting and laughing at each other's accents and poor pronunciation. Things took on a whole new dimension though when I relocated to Argentina. Within days I had met Carolina, a tall, slender, dark-haired bombshell. I was captivated. She ended up coming to England a couple of months after I returned and helped with some of the fundraising events before we fled to Alaska. Neither of us knew what would happen but speaking to her from Fairbanks I knew I wanted our relationship to last. We stayed in touch, me phoning from campsites or writing letters from my tent. I was so envious of Martin and Paps during the Vancouver break when they were with Sam and Naomi, sharing experiences and reaffirming their relationships. But now the wait was finally over. It was just three weeks until she flew in to Mexico City and we planned to head straight to the beach for the Christmas period.

*

Having now got to Mexico, our immediate goal was a port town located 900 kilometres away down the eastern coast of the Baja peninsula. From Santa Rosalía a ferry would connect us with the Mexican mainland to the east for a further 800 kilometre blast to Mazatlán, where we intended to leave the bikes for Christmas.

Apart from one or two hair-raising encounters with large trucks on the Baja's terrifyingly narrow highway, we flourished in our new surroundings. Gone was the heavy traffic and urban sprawl of southern California, now it was full-blown desert, where we traversed huge tracts of cacti ridden country. Abandoned cars, packs of dogs, litter and colourful, poorly built houses accounted for each small village or *pueblito* we past through. Getting things done was harder and more time consuming but speaking to the locals was fun and new. The boys were adjusting too, getting by with phrases and grammar they had picked up since tuition began on the Dalton. The waterproofs were banished to the bottom of the trailer bag and we cycled topless through mile after mile of bone-dry rock fields and bare escarpments, fuelling the hard miles with many yummy pastries bought at roadside panaderías.

The best place we found for our first night in the desert was an area on the inside of a right hand bend covered in dead grass and littered with thorns. What concerned me about it were the huge number of fist sized burrows in the sandy soil. Suddenly, I was reminded that we were now in the land of snakes, scorpions and spiders. As it turned out, the fear of being bitten wasn't what kept us awake half the night.

'Rrrrghhhhh...clac...clac...clac...rrrrghhhh...clac...clac...clac!'

As we were about to find out, Mexicans liked to make a lot of noise. Truck drivers kept thundering past our campsite, slamming the engine revs through the roof to negotiate the bend. It was like trying to sleep next to a pneumatic drill.

On we pushed, thankful of tailwinds and a mountainous central spine that never really materialised. Star-filled nights were cool but not cold, making a pleasant change from the heat of the day and we were also enjoying a change in diet, for breakfast now consisted of jam-filled French rolls and fruit; a much quicker alternative to boiling water on Steve, the new stove we'd been given by a shop in San Diego.

Guerrero Negro ('Black Warrior') wasn't an appealing place by any means, in fact it was the bleakest place we'd seen in four months, a forgotten windswept backwater. I walked into town in search of a phone, along a wide dusty boulevard where blocks of shops were separated by the occasional plot of rough ground filled with packs of stray dogs. Most of the side streets were unpaved, causing large clouds of dust to blow up into my face every time a gust of wind struck. The town was at least benefiting these days from a flow of tourists eager to spot the grey whales that come to a nearby lagoon between the months of January and March to give birth. For us though, Guerrero Negro was no more than a refuelling stop and a bed for the night.

'Is there a phone shop around here, please?' I asked, after walking for fifteen minutes without luck.

A little surprisingly the guy holding a 25kg sack of oranges understood my Spanish. 'At the end of the street there is a shop opposite a petrol station.'

I carried on another ten minutes, my legs weary from the long day in the saddle and eventually I found it. It wasn't a call centre but rather a general store offering a call service. 'I'd like to make a call to Argentina please,' I said, to the lad stood behind the counter.

'No problem,' came his reply. 'What's the number?'

'Here it is,' I said, passing him a piece of paper. 'How much is it?'

'US$1.40 a minute.'

I looked at him ruefully as if to say, 'Blimey, that's pricey!' and he smiled back with a knowing 'Yeah, I know!' There were no cubicles in which to take the call, only a portable telephone resting on a heap of newspapers in front of him. All manner of people flowed in and out of the store so I had to wait a few minutes whilst he served two or three of them. Then he eventually dialled.

'I don't think it's the right number,' he told me. 'There is no service.'

'I'm sure it's the right number. Can you try again?'

In truth, it was the first time I'd used the number in Mexico so we were both unsure. Anyway, he kept dialling without success and then much to my surprise he phoned up his uncle to check the code.

'I am trying to call my girlfriend!' I said, by want of an explanation.

He smiled immediately, 'Don't worry, we'll make it work!'

He seemed to be enjoying every minute of the challenge having all but given up serving the long line of customers waiting to my left. Each time he dialled, we both crossed our fingers.

'There's still no service so I'm going to call the phone company,' he said. Five more minutes went by as he chatted to the phone company and operated the till with his other hand. I stood around slightly embarrassed by it all. 'They say there are too many ones in the number,' he reported. 'So, I am going to try with one less.'

'OK, whatever you think,' I replied, shrugging my shoulders.

We both stood there, listening to the dialling tone, while the queue grew ever longer, now backing up past the rice and pasta section. 'Yes!' he exclaimed as the call went through. We both broke out in smiles and clasped hands before he passed me the phone.

'Muchísimas gracias!' I said to him, as Carolina's voice came on the line.

*

Short of options we'd been forced to kip next to a road junction with a roadside café. The two chaps who'd been kind enough to let us camp on their piece of rough ground were running the grill so we ordered a few tacos and sat at a table listening to the engines braking outside.

'Rrrrghhhh….clac…clac…clac…rrrrghhhh…clac…clac…clac!'

'Ear plugs tonight then!' I shouted, as I swatted away flies patiently awaiting our order.

Riding the Biscuit Highway

'Paps and I sit in stony silence at a truck stop on the way to Mazatlán'

The previous night was spent crossing the Sea of Cortez on the ferry from Santa Rosalía. Laying out our sleeping bags on deck allowed us to marvel at thousands of stars as we pitched back and forth to the motion of the waves and then watched the sun rise *above* the ocean. Yet the run into Mazatlán proved to be anything but simple. The mood of the group steadily deteriorated as illness struck me and then moved on to Paps who was forced to nip to the ditch or behind a bush as many as 20 times a day. He had continued to ride but now his knee was playing up. Martin, on the other hand, was struggling with a trapped nerve in his back, giving him severe pain through his right shoulder. His right arm was virtually useless, forcing him to cycle one handed and my patience was being stretched by a run of bad luck with the bike.

'Arrghh! No, not again! Fucking hell!' I screamed, at my third puncture in the space of five miles. Everyone pulled into a lay-by to hear me blaspheme and wonder if I was going to launch my bike into the scrub. I was at melt down. 'This fucking tyre!'

'Go and stand over there!' shouted Martin, whilst levering me away from the bike. 'Go on. I've got this.'

'No,' I said stubbornly.

'No, go on! Go and stand over there and calm down!'

I did as I was instructed. The day was in freefall. On we went, Paps silent and Martin half paralyzed, through the heat and the hills, hunting down the 86 miles that would see us into Mazatlán. Tempers were being stretched to the limit.

'Here he comes now,' I said to Martin. 'He hasn't seen us. Paps! Paps!'

I ran across the lay-by toward the road, shouting and waving as I went only to see Paps cycle past, seemingly unable to hear my screams over the noise of his music player which went on when he didn't want to speak to anyone.

'Paps Paps!' I screamed at the top of my lungs.

Don't fucking ignore me! I know you can hear me, I'm right here!

I returned to Martin, convinced Paps was playing mind games. Now a hundred yards away we both looked on to see him suddenly stop and look around. Martin shook his head in disbelief.

We arrived in the dark, all of us knackered. I managed to arrange a basic hotel to store our bikes at no extra cost but no one seemed to care. With the two-week break now in force, I put it to the back of my mind and tried to relax.

'Put them in Room 2 please,' said the girl at reception, pointing across the hall. 'I'll just get the key for you.'

With key in hand I went over, opened the door and wheeled in my bike. Only then did I notice some bikes and trailers leaning against the wall. 'Are there other foreigners staying here?'

'Yes, three Americans,' replied the receptionist.

'Which room are they in?'

'Room 105.'

I headed back along the narrow, brightly lit corridor and knocked on Room 105. A tall, dark-haired twenty something answered. 'Hello, are you guys the cyclists?' I asked.

'Yeah?' came the telltale American accent.

'The receptionist told me about you. We are cycling too.'

'Ah! How are you doing?'

This chance meeting shed light on a longstanding puzzle. Back up in Alaska and through most of Canada we were continually scratching our heads over how people seemed to know who we were and exactly what we were up to.

Joe Public:	Hey, you guys are brothers right?
Us:	No.
Joe Public:	Oh, but you're cycling to Argentina?
Us:	Yeah, that's right.
Joe Public:	And you started in Prudhoe Bay?
Us:	Yeah, how do you know that?
Joe Public:	We read about you in the paper. How's it going?

Brothers Mike and John Logsdon started out just nine days before us. It had taken 5,760 miles - a distance equal to flying from London to Delhi – to catch them, even though they had cycled thirty-five days less than us by getting to Mazatlán. Thirty-five days! They had spent two weeks in Fairbanks to allow John to recover from knee surgery, a week in Vancouver (where they woke one morning to find the house in which they were staying full of models doing a photo shoot), two weeks in their home town of San Francisco and two weeks with family and girlfriends in Los Cabos, a beach resort at the southern tip of the Baja. Rock hard road tyres and assistance from their father who carried their trailers the length of the Baja had kept them ahead of us. Had we been messing about? Had we not pedalled hard enough? Were their tyres really that much more efficient?

The brothers were doing the trip as a lasting tribute to their mother who had died of a brain tumour ten years previous. The ride was also providing financial support to the National Brain Tumour Foundation. Upon passing through Los Angeles they met Nate Ajello, a fellow American who wanted to join them because his mother had also died of a tumour. The brothers accepted and Nate flew down to Los Cabos three weeks later having quit his job, let his flat and bought a bike and trailer. So like us, they were now a three-man team. Swapping stories over a beer in the central plaza was incredibly refreshing. Here was instant access to people who understood what despair, anger and gratification a few thousand miles in the saddle felt like.

The Americans were spending Christmas in Mazatlán and then continuing along the coast, whereas we all took an 18-hour bus journey to Mexico City. After a couple of days in the capital the boys headed to the Pacific coast to spend time with Sam and Naomi and I went to the airport to pick up Carolina. This was the day we'd both been looking forward to for months.

'What time is the taxi picking us up?' asked Carolina, two days later.

'Five thirty,' I said.

We weren't going to the beach. We were heading to England.

Chapter 9

Pink Flamingos

'Love is whatever you can still betray...Betrayal can only happen if you love.'
John Le Carré
Born England, 1931

Start Point: Mazatlán, Mexico. Mile: 5,760. 9th January.

'Hello mate!' I said, as the door flew open.

'Hello!' replied Paps, enthusiastically. 'How you doin'? Come and see the state of Martin.'

Paps made way and then followed me along the short entranceway into the middle of the room, where I saw a very forlorn-looking Martin peering out from beneath his bed sheet, his head propped up by a single pillow.

'Hello mate, how are you?' he said, in an effort to be perky.

'Better than you by the looks of it,' I replied, grinning at him. 'How did the marriage proposal go?'

'I was a little nervous but it went OK.'

'Congratulations!' I replied, shaking hands with him. I perched myself on the windowsill to benefit from what little breeze was on offer. 'What the hell is going on lads?'

We were all back in Mazatlán, post Christmas break and I'd been expecting to ride out tomorrow. 'The Christmas break has been a bit of a disaster!' quipped Paps. 'Vomiting and diarrhoea for days, then to top it off, Martin went to see a doctor about his shoulder and the doc made it worse.'

'You must be joking,' I said, my opinion of all things Mexico dropping yet another notch.

'I was starting to get some movement back,' began Martin, shuffling up a fraction as if to ready himself. 'But thought it best to get it checked out as I was still in pain. The doctor we found yanked at it, prodded me and now I can hardly move it again.'

'Some doctor then. How long have you been like that?'

'Four days. I'm in agony to be honest.'

'We need to get it looked at.'

'Wait 'til you hear what else has happened!' said Paps, prompting Martin to divulge more gossip.

'When I left Mexico City I thought it was a direct service to Zihuatanejo but it wasn't. It took me all the way to Acapulco!' said Martin, sending Paps into a giggling fit. 'It meant a further nine hours along the coast in a second bus.'

'No!' I screamed, my laughter causing me to fall off the windowsill.

'But that's not all,' said Martin, reluctantly. 'I also sent my passport home with Sam.'

I broke down again. 'Anything to get off the trip, right?'

'It was in her suitcase and I totally forgot about it.'

'What happened to you then?' asked Paps, as the conversation turned in my direction.

'I had food poisoning too, the day after Carolina arrived. Twenty minutes before boarding I was sat on the loo, vomiting into a bucket. We got on the plane but one of the cabin crew noticed me and they wouldn't let me fly,' I continued. 'So we had to get one with Lufthansa the next day. But that's not everything either,' I said. 'When we came back to Mexico City the Customs Official stamped 30 days into my passport,'

'Ahah!' shrieked Paps.

'So, I now have 25 days to cycle 1,700 miles to the Guatemalan border!' I said, with a smirk on my face.

'Yeah, well at least you *have* a passport!' retorted Paps.

Down the hall our American counterparts were not so inclined to see the funny side of things. In the two weeks we'd been away travelling on buses, sitting in planes and vomiting over half of Mexico they had gone nowhere. They were still trapped in their hotel room awaiting bicycle parts from California. According to Nate, they were going stir crazy.

For me, the trip to England had left me in a mess. I was angry and the thought of the next few thousand miles felt unsurpassable. As I write this, resentment continues to course through me over my sister's wedding – for which Carolina and I returned to England.

Ever since Helen and her long time partner, Dan, had set the date of their wedding, she had reiterated how important it was that I be present. We'd always been close, even seeing eye to eye on the majority of things through the notorious teenage years, which is why, when I went to Alaska, I was fully intent on being in England for her special day. Rightly or wrongly though, all that changed when I got on the bike. The challenge we had set ourselves was far larger than any of us ever imagined. Mountains of continual self-doubt, periods of depression and a strong desire to chuck the bike into a ditch and go home came at a price. The strength and will power needed to forge ahead into many more months on the road couldn't be put at risk by returning to England. After five months of slogging my guts out the trip was bigger than nearly anything. Not the health of a family member but certainly bigger than Helen's wedding. Going back to England with only 35% complete, seeing the family and entering a wedding marquee where I had to listen to "50 miles a day doesn't seem too bad to me" might break the belief. The special feeling of completing the ride from start to finish would also be lost, like running 13 miles on a Monday and Thursday, only to claim you have run a marathon. With the integrity gone, I was fearful that my will power would be lost with it. Would I ever make it to Ushuaia? We'd been living a day-to-day existence and we all knew how fickle and unforgiving the line between success and failure was. But Helen and my family just couldn't see it. Each time I checked my emails or made a call home, I was engulfed in wave after wave of pressure to return and my cries for understanding and lenience went ignored.

So why did Carolina and I go? Why did I forego all that I have spoken about above? Put simply there are few things more important to me than my family's opinion of what I am doing and I finally realised I was in a no win situation. From the content and veiled threats it became apparent that a non-appearance risked writing off the project altogether; living in Bolivia, fundraising for the children, riding down the Americas, all of it discarded to a family file entitled, "The Selfish Brother". A good portion of me didn't care but a bigger portion did. Every time someone mentioned the words, Bicycle, Wedding, New Year, etc the file would be brought out and the finger pointed in my direction. Most importantly, I couldn't let my hot and cold relationship with the family's figurehead collapse completely. I knew my character; I would react by ostracising myself. I had to let go, I had to swallow my pride and by doing so destroy the purity of the trip.

Why doesn't Mum understand? Why doesn't she support me? Can't she see that I've earnt the right to stay out here and finish the trip?

It is not my intention to convince you that my wishes trump that of my family. Quite frankly, it doesn't matter. Yet, in telling the story of our cycle ride – albeit from my perspective – returning to England is critical for so many reasons. Now I was hurt. Now I was angry, bitter and resentful. It had a detrimental effect on my attitude, making me more selfish and undoubtedly played a part in my actions and future struggles with Paps. On countless occasions, when I had needed a bit of resolve or inspiration my thoughts had turned to Mum and Ted. "Keep going, keep fighting, they are going to be so proud of you." I thought this challenge was something they fully embraced and saw for all its worth, a stunt which would ultimately demonstrate the determination and self-belief that they had installed in me. How wrong I had been. Perhaps I should have taken notice of Ted's comment before the trip that "It's just too ambitious James, too far, you should rethink," and it meant cycling on, still 10,000 miles from Ushuaia, knowing that my family thought my presence at Helen's wedding was worth jeopardising the completion of a 15,000 mile unsupported challenge which had taken two years to plan and helped raise tens of thousands of pounds for charity.

Reaching the steps of the family house at 12.30am the morning of the wedding, Helen broke down in my arms, hardly able to stand. I had entered a different world.

*

Our convalescence in Mazatlán had crept into its fourth day. During that time we'd got Martin some decent medical attention and a truckload of drugs inside him. He was permanently wasted, sometimes unable to process what we were saying or even lift his head off the pillow as the muscle relaxants kicked into overdrive. The doctor reckoned they could help release the trapped nerve in Martin's spine but recommended no cycling for at least 3-4 days so I seized the opportunity to get my visa extended. Paps and I killed more time by surfing the net, eating pizza and drinking wine. When we eventually got going, now well into January, riding came as a bit of a shock to all of us. Martin was still punch drunk and none of us were in the mood for cycling. The end of the first day couldn't have come soon enough.

'I'm going to see if we can stay here,' I said, spotting a group of brick houses set back from the road in the fading light.

I parked the bike, clipped my helmet to the handlebars and strolled up the dirt track, one or two chickens scampering from underneath my feet. There was plenty of rough ground on which to camp but I was in search of permission first and so marched up to the nearest house. The whole area seemed deserted. I cautiously opened a gate which led to the front porch.

'Hola?' I shouted, forewarning anyone of my presence. 'Hola?'

'Si?' came the voice and then the body of a middle-aged lady.

Striding out of the front door she came in her red and white dress and white apron. The sight of a gringo standing in her garden didn't seem to bother her in the slightest. 'Hello, I was wondering if we could camp in the field tonight?' I asked, hoping she understood my Spanish. 'There are three of us. We have food and water.'

'My son's house is empty,' she said, unreservedly. 'He is away at the moment so you can sleep in there if you want?'

'Are you sure?' I replied.

'Follow me and I'll show you!' she said, waving me over.

I followed the lady further up the track all the while expressing our gratitude, and across to a single storey brick building set amongst some scrawny trees where a partly collapsed barbed wire fence marked the property's boundary. The lady opened the metal door, which screeched against the bare concrete floor and led me through a darkened kitchen to a surprisingly pleasant lounge where curiously a 5ft high toy flamingo stood in one corner. The single bedroom had two beds with an adjoining bathroom. It was an unexpected palace.

The boys aren't gonna believe this!

Usually, when I had something good to report I tried disguising my excitement until the very last moment but on this occasion I was so overwhelmed I broke into smiles well before making it back to the roadside.

'It's good,' I heard Paps say to Martin, as I approached with a big grin on my face.

'We have been given a house for the night,' I said, coming to the point.

'What?'

'Follow me!"

That night we cooked under the watchful eye of the flamingo and enjoyed the light afforded by a single bare bulb until the generator was switched off at nine-thirty. The only thing that concerned me was Martin's discovery of a plate-sized spider lurking in the bathroom. I kid you not, this thing was colossal. Even though Paps jammed the bathroom door shut with a piece of wood I was left wondering if the not so itsy bitsy spider was going to emerge through the 2 inch gap at the bottom, especially as it was my turn to sleep on the floor. What if it had any brothers and sisters? And if so, where were they and how bloody big were the parents?

*

South of Mazatlán the heat became a serious drain on our strength. As the days went by, and having picked up Martin's passport in Tepíc, it became appreciably hotter and all manner of insects started to appear as the humidity also climbed. We were forced to stop riding by midday and escape the 40°C heat, using the time to cook. The hilly route along the coast made us work like never before. We'd slurp down ever-increasing amounts of water with layers of salt coating our bodies by sundown.

'The Mexican heat takes its toll on Paps and I'

'It's pretty grim, I think we should move on,' I reported, after scouting a piece of waste ground set back from the highway.

Everyone agreed so we carried on a few hundred yards before spotting a beach at the end of a dirt side road. 'I had no idea we were so close to the coast,' I said.

'Let's go and check it out,' replied Paps.

We dismounted and started pushing the bikes along the sandy track. Almost straight away a foreigner stopped to chat in his 4x4.

'Hello there,' said the driver in English.

'Hello. Do you know if we can camp on the beach?' asked Martin.

'I wouldn't recommend it, besides why don't you stay at the RV site?' he said. 'It's only a few hundred metres down the main highway and I think they allow campers.'

To some extent or other we always researched the route and Paps or Martin always had a half-decent map available but the amount of times we got caught short scrambling for accommodation options was staggering. Had we not bumped into this vacationing Canadian, we'd have missed out on being treated like celebrities. It turned out that the RV site was run by a Canadian lady called Mary and was chocker block full of North Americans, the vast majority of whom were retirees from Canada. In fact, it was just like camping in Canada but 20°C warmer and with a beachfront view! Within an hour of arriving we had been invited to the weekly buffet dinner and were having our glasses topped up with margaritas. Then Mary addressed everyone.

'Can I have everyone's attention please,' she began. 'I want to make a quick announcement. Tonight we are honoured to be hosting Martin, Anthony and James, 3 Englishmen cycling the length of the Americas.' Some 100 people turned to focus their gaze on us, forcing me to take a break from chomping down my fifth taco. 'If you haven't yet had a chance to speak to them, please do so. They are raising money for children in El Salvador and are accepting donations!'

By the end of the night we had pocketed $600 pesos and decided to stay a day, play ping-pong, swim in the sea and of course, eat. Best of all, a chiropractor on holiday with his wife and their two daughters, offered to straighten us out on his table.

'Considering you've just ridden 6,000 miles you're in remarkably good shape,' said Steve, as he worked on my shoulders and neck. He seemed to know exactly what our diet consisted of and what ailments we were suffering from.

Meeting Steve was a stroke of luck for all of us, none more so than Martin who now had no trouble body surfing in the Pacific every lunchtime as we continued our way along the sun-scorched coast. It was one such lunchtime that we happened upon the coastal village of Maruata, a truly breathtaking place. Turquoise waters broke onto to a pristine white sand beach several hundred metres long where one or two locals stretched out on hammocks, selling cold drinks, mangos and watermelons under a load of thatched awnings. We forgot about riding and spent the rest of the day body surfing and lying in the sun. We drank beer in the evening sunshine, cooked a meal and the three of us conversed in Spanish for the first time. No bike maintenance, no washing of clothes, just pure down time. It was how we imagined the trip should feel.

*

'Christ it's hot!' remarked Paps, over the din of the Cicadas.

'Let's have another beer then?' I suggested.

'I think he's locked the shop.'

'I'll ask him to open it again, come on, it's too hot to go to bed.'

We were another 61 miles further down the never-ending Mexican coastline and it was our tenth night in the space of twelve days camping within earshot of the waves. The pitch site we had found ourselves was - like Maruata - one of the nicest places we had camped. The following morning as I was getting dressed inside my tent, the sound of the breaking surf was usurped by four simple words.

'My bag has gone,' said Paps.

Suddenly I remembered my half-filled trailer bag that I'd left strapped to my trailer with a single bungee cord. Scrambling for my clothes and torch I emerged from my tent to see it untouched. Paps's bag was the one missing, the only one to have been stored *inside* his vestibule. To rub salt into the wound, he was also the only one to consistently harp on about some form of security around camp. The theft sobered me up. As I swept the beach for any remnants of his belongings I kept chastising myself. My apathy should have cost me, not Paps. Martin scouted the road but to no avail. A big bunch of dollars, some bankcards, clothes, bike parts and spare disks for Keith were history.

'We need to get to the nearest town and file a police report,' said Martin, stating the obvious.

I kept thinking how remarkably calm Paps was about the whole thing. Within half an hour we were in Caleta de Campos a couple of kilometres away. Even though none of us expected the Mexican police to find any trace of the bag, the theft was going to cost us time and plenty of inconvenience. For the next two days we waited around for the police to turn up and actually went in search of them in a taxi. Then we accompanied the Sergeant and his officers back to the beach to explain what had happened, spoke to the newsagent who doubled as the town's Mayor and also the only person authorised to sign and date the police report, and waited for the police station to open again on the Monday morning. At one stage the Sergeant told me that we'd have to pick up the report from Lazaro, a town 1.5 hours away by bus but fortunately I convinced him that we didn't have the money to travel. It was an unbelievable effort.

Mexico had already provided us with more than our fair share of bad luck. Trapped nerves, diarrhoea, passport and visas problems and now a robbery and there was still more than a thousand miles to the Guatemalan border. We set out from Caleta de Campos a tad forlorn and in search of happier times. Could Mexico claw back our affection or were we destined to come to blows as we watched it suck the fun out of cycle touring?

Chapter 10

Mud huts and Casinos

'Poverty is like punishment for a crime you didn't commit.'
Eli Khamarov
Born England 1948

Start Point: Caleta de Campos, Mexico. Mile: 6,450. 30th January.

'This wave looks good!' I shouted, as another set of six rolled in from Hawaii. 'Go! Go! Go!'

The Pacific's immense breakwater tossed us about like puppets on a string. It was exhilarating stuff. The water massaged my sore muscles and washed away the grime and salt from my skin. Before long we coughed and spluttered our way back up the beach, to find Paps waiting with the evening's sandwiches. The sun hung low in the cloudless sky, flooding the horizon with yellows, oranges and reds. We were alone, hidden from the highway several hundred metres down a farm track. The next night it was very different indeed.

'Here we go boys!' I said, triumphantly. 'I bought some Modelos in case we got thirsty!'

'Good man!' came Paps's reply, as he watched me dump several cans of beer on the table in front of him.

Tonight we were enjoying the comfort of a cavernous but bare house that had never been lived in. Desperate to find more than some poxy rumble-strewn field – something of an annoyingly familiar occurrence in Mexico - I had been bold enough to stop on a whim and stride down an impressive driveway to speak to a guy who at the time I presumed was the owner. Only later did I discover that he was merely renting the five acres or so surrounding the property and that the house was in fact not a house at all but rather an unfinished Casino financed by a local governor who had run out of money. Left to ruin in the intervening 20 years, the whitewashed walls had faded somewhat with the tiled floor barely visible beneath droppings of the tenants' wildfowl that roamed everywhere. A small pack of dogs lounging in the shade of a few palm trees out on the veranda reassured me this was rural Mexico.

Anyway, the tenant – a friendly leather skinned middle-aged man with a generous amount of stubble and a slight stoop – invited us in without much fuss and led us and our yellow bags up a huge staircase to a large room where a small metal framed table and a chair stood in one corner. Thanking him profusely he popped out to a balcony that ran right around the building and returned a couple of minutes later with another chair and his overweight wife. Then we hung around slightly awkwardly; all four of us watching her sweep the rat droppings that littered the bare concrete floor. Once done though, we were able to settle in and get set up for the night, even enjoying a cold-water strip wash in the outhouse at the far side of a jet-black swimming pool.

Finding the beers turned out to be a bit of an adventure. It all started when we realised there was no milk to make a flask of tea. I was packed off to the nearest village with the farmer's teenage son and even had my bus fare paid for. Within minutes the young lad was slamming the minibus door and we were on our way. Very quickly I was instructed to pass forward the few coins to the driver who merely held out his hand and deposited them into a small wooden box that sat beside him by the gear stick. Then I settled down to receive the nervous gaze of every passenger around me. This was nothing new of course. In fact, I smiled slightly as I remembered a remark Martin had once made when irritated by the constant gawping and piss taking.

'To these people we are just a freak show, dressed in funny clothes, living at the side of the road or passing through like a circus act,' he had said. 'What they don't realise is that we have a family, worries, responsibilities, that we are here of our own choice.'

He had a point. Surely we were to be congratulated in getting off our arses and making a difference to some children in El Salvador, rather than continue along our stereotypically western lives where we chased professional careers, sat in traffic jams, had too many creature comforts and material possessions and the luxury of an employer paying for time spent on a far-flung beach? Why didn't any of them spot the difference and come over to have a half-decent conversation? To seize the opportunity to talk to a Gringo, in their language, on their turf? The answer of course, is very obvious. Why on earth should they? To them we might have been living cheaply and roughing it a bit but in the grand scheme of things we still stood for Gringo materialism, even imperialism. One glance told them all they needed to know and we were pigeonholed in a blink of an eye. They and us were born on opposite sides of the fence and a bit of dirt on our faces and the odd rib shining through wasn't going to change a thing. Interestingly, the reaction we received depended a great deal on the circumstances at the time. Whenever we were eating at a café or mingling with the locals in a street market their natural shyness and conservatism kept any exuberance under wraps. Like the bus journey I was currently on, we became objects of intense scrutiny but no more. Yet, when we were eating by the roadside or pedalling along and a truck load of workers came howling past, hemmed in like a load of POWs, we became the biggest bit of piss-take going. Yelps, cries, whistles, indiscernible Spanish, pointing, finger gestures, the lot. It made generosity shown by the casino farmer all the more poignant.

'Out of reach of the hecklers, Martin and Paps make lunch in the shade of a barn, as I doze on the concrete'

Within a couple of minutes my teenage chaperone and I had arrived in El Papayo and I was busily searching the dark recesses of a storeroom at the back of a small shop as the owner shouted directions at me from her stool. In the end I came out with the milk plus a few packets of biscuits, one of which I gave to the young lad. More crucially I had the beer. Back at the bus stop things got interesting. Before long and after I had run out of things to say to the silent teenager, a large man approached me. He stood out from the locals because his skin was much darker and his clothes bought abroad or from a major Mexican city.

'Hi, how you doing!' he asked enthusiastically, trying to gain my confidence.

Addressing me in English took me by surprise, 'Good thanks,' I replied in my best Spanish.

'What are you doing here?'

'Travelling, with a couple of friends. We are staying at the old Casino up the road.'

The conversation went on a few minutes, creating a bit of interest for a few onlookers. Indeed, by the time my new acquaintance cut to the chase three or four of them were within earshot, no doubt struggling to make sense of our bilingual conversation.

'Would you like a woman?' he asked, still persisting in pretty decent English.

'I'm sorry?'

'I have a woman for you. She's beautiful,' he continued, predictably. 'Big tits!'

'Really?'

'Huge!' he confirmed, stretching out his hands to exaggerate the size of the woman's breasts. 'I know you will like her. She is over there, look,' he said, pointing to a woman loitering on the far side of the road wearing a short skirt and indeed virtually bursting out of the tight top she had on. 'So you like her?'

'How much?'

'US$50.'

'An hour?'

'Yes or US$300 for the night. If your friends want a girl I can arrange it too.'

'You're joking,' I said, now speaking in English. 'That's way too much.'

'OK, US$200.'

'I have a girlfriend.'

'But you must be lonely, right?'

Weeks on the road did create a *firm* desire for love and affection from more than just a load of mosquitoes or your right hand (energy levels permitting of course) but I had no intention of parting with any cash.

'Were you tempted?' joked Paps, as I passed him another warm Modelo back at the Casino.

'For about a second but then I saw her face,' I replied. 'I got her number though if you fancy giving her a call?'

'Piss off!'

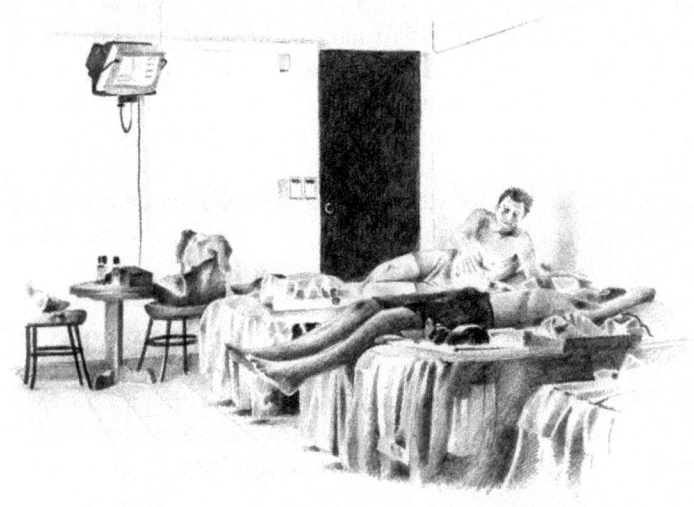

'Paps and I enjoy TV and junk food in Acapulco'

Mud huts and Casinos

Clockwise from top left: Dick Trudho arrives with supplies on the North Slope, Alaska; Paps wraps up for another downhill in Canada; Martin enjoys a stretch after a hard day in the saddle; The legend that is Brian Farrell, Whitehorse, Canada; Martin leads us into The Rockies; Martin and Paps on Canon Beach, Oregon; Being re-supplied by Lorraine, Chuck, Jim and Joyce, south of the Arctic Circle, Alaska.

Clockwise from top; Breakfast on the Baja, Mexico; A Salvadoran child hides behind a British flag; A 5ft pink flamingo watches over me as I set to work on dinner, Mexico; The heat of Mexico; Paps and I talk to the school-children of Chalatenango; Posing for the paparazzi, Chalatenango.

Mud huts and Casinos

Clockwise from top; Martin and I cool off in the Pacific at the end of the day, Mexico; "The Machine" at lunch in Guatemala; Paps returns to his bike after washing in Lake Nicaragua; Martin grimacing as his bottom suffers from yet more punishment; Me looking very forlorn having doubled back from the minefield, northern Peru; Paps at sunset in the desert

Clockwise from top; A sign in Peru tells us to "Smile…you're in Pacasmayo"; Paps and I hog the road, southern Peru; Martin collapses during a food break; Holding out the flags as we leave Coquímbo, Chile; The never-ending straight roads of La Pampa, Argentina; Paps makes sandwiches in Argentina; Madness firmly in control as Paps and Martin pose in their underwear in the Atacama Desert, Chile; The victorious salute, Ushuaia, Tierra del Fuego.

Mexico and its oppressive heat was making us work hard. Finding food also slowed us down, often requiring two of us to drop the bikes and walk along a dusty track, following directions to a random house where we'd wait on the porch for the owner to bring us a plucked chicken, some mince or a piece of beef. Tent life was also hard work. When the biting ants or insects had a night off, we'd ditch the tents and sleep in the comfort of the open air but being forced inside was intolerable. No matter what the suggestion - "You sweat less if you sit up" or "I find it's better if you lie on your back" - there was no escaping hours of mopping your brow and wiping pools of sweat from your mattress. Going for a pee gave the mozzies plenty of time to go hide in the corners of the tent. They'd bide their time until I had declared it safe and then pounce on my sweaty body. Like Canada, it was only possible to avoid the tent if we found a café but pitching near a café or petrol station meant engine braking lorries and humans living nearby with noisy dogs or cockerels. Yet petrol stations or Pemex's to us - that being the state owned brand that dominated Mexico - often had a fresh piece of grass on which to camp and occasionally even an air-conditioned café. They also provided a degree of security that was missing with the rough camps because Pemex's were patrolled by policemen armed to the teeth with shotguns and machine guns. On one occasion when asking to pitch on a beautifully manicured piece of grass at the back of a Pemex, the two plain-clothed policemen agreed to let us use it as long as we bought them a cold coke each from the café. This never-ending pursuit and deliberation over campsites became a daily game. Say no to a possible pitch site in pursuit of a better piece of grass and you risked being forced to pitch in elephant grass swarming with insects and god knows what other creepy crawlies. When out of reach of a coffee, beer or coke though, there was nothing to do but retreat to our tents. I'd stare at the inside, read magazines, newspapers, study Spanish, write my diary or listen to music. We'd even play games like trying to guess our location on a particular date but this only went so far. I'd study the way the tent bellowed in the wind, the ghostly shadows created by my head torch and listen to the noises made by the creepy crawlies scuttling beneath my ground sheet. On the bike I found it hard to concentrate on anything but in the tent my mind wondered everywhere, back to my school days, to my first girlfriend...

What would life be like if we were still together?

I certainly wouldn't be on this crazy trip. More likely I'd be a father, have a mortgage and already spent 10 years paying into a pension fund. Either way, I didn't regret how my life had panned out, not now that the trip had materialised. My twenties had been a joyous time, full of self-discovery and adventures. I had worked hard, gone back to University, travelled a bit and then conjured up this huge challenge to see the other side, to test myself. The fact that we were doing the trip told me all I needed to know about my priorities and desires but lying in a tent in Mexico with so many months left to cycle did make me consider what I wanted after the trip. Like many friends, I too wanted a family, children, a stable environment for them to grow up in and if I wanted that then my priorities had to change. This trip was a final sojourn, a perfect ending to all that had gone before and the perfect opportunity to open a new chapter. We all knew it.

*

'I wish Paps wouldn't cycle off at the end of the day,' I complained breathlessly, as Martin came up alongside me. 'He must be a kilometre in front.'

'Let's ask these people how far the next town is,' suggested Martin, as we reached a line of people waiting for a bus in the middle of nowhere.

'According to one of them, we are ten kilometres away, much too far,' I reported a couple of minutes later. 'Has Paps stopped?'

'Yeah, I can see him waiting at the side of the road,' Martin said, trying to get his attention in the fading light.

'One of them suggests we speak to the landowner that's up there,' I continued, pointing up the dirt track to a couple of men stood talking next to a 4x4. 'They reckon he has a field.'

'Sounds good to me. Paps is coming back.'

The landowner did indeed have somewhere for us to stay. This was a huge stroke of luck considering the impenetrable forest we had passed for the last hour. Paps couldn't have cared less though. He was fuming. 'What are we doing? We can fucking make it if we put our foot down!'

'It's too late,' I offered. 'We need to get off this road, it's a death trap.'

'We'll make it easily! Come on!'

Today, Paps was on the losing end of our democracy rule, a bitter pill to swallow and it led to a complete breakdown of relations that night. As we set off up the dusty track I was praying that the field wasn't the ant-ridden version or the type where we had to stamp down 6ft high grass otherwise Paps was sure to go nuclear. As if by magic we arrived at a clearing in the forest where one of his tenant farmers was working on a tiny half-built mud hut. A brief conversation ensued, whereby I presume the poor chap was told to look after us for the night. Sheepishly we pushed the bikes off the track and up onto the cleared piece of land and shook hands with our host. Then the landowner disappeared.

'We have tents,' I said, trying not to intrude too much.

'No, sleep inside, sleep inside!' he insisted. 'There is space on the floor.'

Eager not to seem aloof or unappreciative, Martin and I set about laying out our mattresses and bags on the sand whilst Paps put his tent up outside. The hut was tiny, half-filled with a bed and lit by an oil lamp in one corner. It was very murky by now but the farmer went on digging a pit in the ground, occasionally adding a bucket of water to form the mud needed for the final wall. Martin and I cracked on with dinner in a silent stand off with Paps.

'How about making a couple of sandwiches for him and his daughter?' I suggested, as I opened the sardine tin and Martin lined the rolls with mayonnaise.

'It's the least we can do.'

We were ravenous, low on food and nearly out of water, hence Paps's intent on reaching Pochulta but we were still a lot better off than our hosts. We put head torches on to see what we were doing yet the farmer had no such luxury and kept working, his young daughter ignoring his commands in favour of studying us from behind a small tree. I was exhausted, mixed with feelings of resignation and intrigue as a constant hum of cicadas rang out from the forest. I gave Paps his ration of two sandwiches and then offered the next round to the farmer who passed them straight to his daughter with instructions to carry them up the hill. When we asked if there was a local source of water, the farmer stopped what he was doing and told us that there was drinking water at his house up the track.

'We are going to get some water,' I said, unsure if Paps would respond. 'Do you want any of your bottles refilling?'

'Yes please, the two on my bike are empty.'

Martin and I marched up the dirt track, following the farmer by torchlight. Soon we were at a small brick house that he and his wife were renting whilst he finished the mud hut. The youngest children, one barely three and the other half that age, hid behind the legs of their mother, unsure of what to make of us whilst we transferred some water into our bottles from a large 5-gallon drum. Eventually the conversation started flowing and I removed my head torch to speak softly to the mother. None of them had met a foreigner before, only ever seeing the odd westerner cycling along the highway. She thanked us for the sandwiches and we thanked them for the water. It was a great little moment. For me, it became the most random campsite of the trip.

The slightly romantic, almost pacifying experience created by the mud hut camp was destroyed the next morning. We had learnt to cope with the cavernous noise and blast of wake created by trucks whizzing past but I still couldn't come to terms with riding over dead dogs embedded into the tarmac. It was a scene we had been familiar with for over a thousand miles. The country teemed with them, abandoned by their owners, left to breed and roam around picking at lumps of rubbish at the roadside. Every 500 yards there was another one, a reminder of the real Mexico. We learnt to hold our breath and even close our eyes to block out the smell and grotesque nature of their bodies. Some of the carcasses had clearly been killed years ago, now semi-permanent fixtures, their bodies having decomposed to leave a partially covered skeleton driven into the tarmac. Other, more recent fatalities lay along the hard shoulder, bloated out of all proportion, as if filled with helium and about to float away. Thankfully we never saw a dog being hit but I did see a carcass with the white line painted over the top of it. Mexico didn't stop there. We'd ride into a town or village or even just past one guy waiting for a bus and suddenly we'd be hit by a barrage of "Pisst!" We'd look left, "Pisst!" We'd look right, "Pisst, pisst!" Suddenly there are so many pissts on the go that we'd nowhere to turn. Not a single Mexican would say anything, not even after getting our attention, nor would anyone raise a hand or break into smile.

'What the fuck do they want?' said Martin once, with his temper in tatters. 'You've got my attention, come on, what do you want?'

Fed up with it all, I actually stopped the bike on one occasion and confronted the pisster but he declined to answer any of my questions and merely walked off. What was he expecting? A trick or two? Maybe I should have juggled a few balls or spun a few plates? Or tried to translate the murmuring and grunting sounds he was making? Surely it would have been far easier, never mind politer, to just say 'Hola!' or 'Como están?' (How are you?), and many Mexicans did opt for a more recognisable form of greeting. I mean, it wasn't even beyond the realms of possibility to be grunted at or pisst at by a Mexican lying in his hammock at the roadside. Yet, no matter how infuriating this was, we still preferred it to the cries of "Gringo!" that had accompanied us ever since Tijuana. Its enunciation fell into broadly two different forms. The first was given by young children out playing along the roadside or perhaps penned inside their school playground. This form of, "Gringo! Gringo! Gringo!" was the affectionate form, a definite means of saying hello and telling your friends that you had spotted a fair skinned foreigner. We were also greeted affectionately with this tag by some of the adult population, who waved and smiled at us but the second form – the derogatory form - used most notably by adolescent males or their fathers was the one that sickened me and often left me wanting to turn the bike around and complete the remaining 9,000 miles in Canada. These shouts of "Grrrringoooo!" just reeked of bad blood because they were never accompanied by a wave, nod or smile. I didn't take it to be racially driven but I can't ever remember hearing myself or anyone else in England, leaning on their garden fence and shouting "Latin American! Latin American!" and then pointing and jeering like they were some freak show. These solitary, haunting cries got the attention of everyone within earshot whereupon group pointing and jeering ensued and that's why we took exception to it. The message of, "Wow, I've seen a gringo!" came through loud and clear, like we were some sort of trophy prize a birdwatcher would treasure after spotting a rare species. This trend was set for another five months.

*

Even though it was barely light, the first climb of the day already had me sweating. I spotted the road twist and turn its way up the contours of the valley, the boys tucked in behind me and our pace slowed to its usual five or six mph. Then, without warning, my derailleur made an awful sound, the chain clogged and the pedals locked, causing me to come to a complete stop. There was just enough time to decleat and stop myself from falling over with the bike.

'That looks bad,' I said to myself, studying the damage.

'The derailleur is completely destroyed and the frame is bent,' remarked Paps.

Like Canada had done with the licence plate debacle and America with my search for a new chain ring, Mexico was also doing it's best to delay us from leaving a little while longer.

Chapter 11

'Smelly, dirty and full of death'

'Usually when people are sad they don't do anything. They just cry over their condition. But when they get angry they bring about a change.'
Malcolm X
Born America, 1925

Start Point: Salina Cruz, México. Mile: 7,050. 12th February.

Martin and I headed towards the only remaining shop in town. In truth, I was putting a brave face on things, having already accepted my fate. Nonetheless I explained what we were after and Martin and I waited nervously as the owner started sifting through a number of boxes at the bottom of the counter. His shop was tiny yet filled with mountains of gear. My eyes wondered past him to half-built bikes and stacks of boxes filling every inch of space. Worryingly, I saw nothing that gave me any confidence.

'One like this?' he said finally, holding up a brand new authentic Deore 9-speed derailleur.

It was one of those moments, so rare and therefore so incredibly special. Only three hours ago I was staring at my bike, fearing the worst. Since then we had managed to get a lift to the nearest village with a farmer and then a further lift with a chap, who quite strangely stopped to pick up a tyre from a ditch. Finally, we had arrived into Salina Cruz. Watching the mechanic and his son beat the hell out my bike frame with lump hammers made me wince but soon enough everything was running like new and they had me doing a lap of the block to check their workmanship. The mechanic even passed me back US$45 after I mistakenly gave him ten times the amount he was charging. Most importantly, he had kept us on target for the Guatemalan border in five more days.

*

Keith's diary, Tapachula, Mexico. 18th February.
'Right, the camera is rolling, we are live boys!' remarks Paps, from inside a grubby street side restaurant.

'We are just about to leave Mexico,' comments Martin, whilst looking at Keith.

'Here you go boys, take your three head of cow tacos,' I say, as the chef - covered in sweat and grill fat - wonders over with our order.

'I need this map held up, I want you to show us where we are,' said Paps, looking at Martin.

Martin opens up our map of Mexico allowing Paps to follow our route from Tijuana all the way to Tapachula. In doing so he accidentally knocks one of his tacos into Keith's storage bag.

'It's gone all over your lap!' states Martin.

'Yeah it's too late now…so there it is, Mexico!' says Paps, with Keith pointed at the map.

'Smelly, dirty and full of death,' comments Martin.

'And now you can look at how I have spilt my entire plate load of food into my bag and all over me for the second time in two days,' says Paps.

'…and it's not like we eat that well to be fair.'

'Final thoughts on Mexico and crossing?' asks Paps, with the camera now in my face.

'Thank god we are leaving. 2,700 miles of dead dogs, cattle and rubbish with the odd nice beach…that's it.'

Paps pans across to get Martin's reaction, the camera rolling whilst he finishes his taco. 'Wils has summarised it all.'

All of us were desperate to leave Mexico and had been ever since the middle of January. It had taken us five weeks to cover the 1,700 miles from Mazatlán to the Guatemalan border, a good effort considering sickness, Paps's stolen bag and temperatures reaching 45°C. Mexico might claim to be a sun-seekers paradise, steeped in Mayan history and with plenty of culture but we had seen precious little of it. In our eleven-week traverse from Tijuana, Mexico had shown us its true colours. I can honestly say that apart from the resorts of Puerta Vallarta, Zihuatanejo and Acapulco, where foreign tourists inject a huge sum of money into the local economy, we saw probably half a dozen beautiful beaches in the whole of Mexico. The rest were ruined by half-built buildings with sewage running down the sand or strewn with rubbish. As for the highway, well where do I start? "Smelly, dirty and full of death," as Martin said, seemed to sum it up perfectly. The pattern of cycling 500 yards and seeing a squashed dog on the tarmac never ended. Sometimes we could smell the death without spotting the carcass. Occasionally it would be a dead horse or cow, the animals' feet sticking up out of the long grass like some sick Monty Python sketch, its body left rotting with 20 black vultures feeding on it. It didn't stop there. Refuelling stops were marked by the deafening engine-braking phenomenon and fly-infested restaurants. At one point the Mexican way of life was perfectly highlighted by an oh-so Mexican trait and by an oh-so delightful Mexican waitress. Devoid of any interest or courtesy whatsoever, she came over to our table, picked up the 9 empty coke bottles we had recently drained and promptly threw them straight out of the window and down an embankment. The bottles went the same way as many thousands before them, along with cans, plastic bags and rotting meat and vegetable waste. We just looked at each other, lost for words. Just imagine the smell, flies and disease such a practice creates in 40°C heat. On we'd go, dripping in sweat only to stop and drink yet another batch of gaseosas - fizzy drinks – whilst we watch a pack of dogs cross the road in front of us, one of them intimately entangled with a bitch while five others waited their turn. Mexicans didn't blink. This was Mexico. I had a conversation one day with a friendly, inquisitive young lad as I waited for Paps and Martin to buy some food from a supermarket in Zihuatanejo. He asked me what I thought of Mexico's people, its beautiful beaches, the wonderful food and gorgeous climate. I don't think he was expecting the answer I gave him. Normally we always put a positive slant on things, no matter what our experience, and we even *liked* the Baja but by the time we reached Zihuatanejo, Mexico was rubbing us up the wrong way. Our relationship with it had deteriorated and although there were still fun, faith-inspiring moments, Mexico had become largely indefensible. 'But it's a poor country, lads,' I hear you say. 'This is what poverty looks like. This is the short straw that you so luckily never drew.' We all understood this. We all appreciated that we were going to see some serious deprivation and a paucity of opportunity but it was their attitude we didn't like. We knew this because as soon as we went over the border into Guatemala it was like being on a different planet, never mind in a different country. Guatemala was far poorer but far cleaner, cared for, you could almost smell the self-respect of its people. Verges were cut, fences stood up straight, piles of bricks and wood were stacked neatly and there were no dead dogs in the road. Goodbye "woe is me" Mexico, hello pride-drenched Guatemala. We soaked it up like a sponge.

*

'Hello there!' I said, as the farmer and his wife made their way toward us. 'I hope you don't mind us camping here?'

We were already stood in the middle of their banana plantation that flanked the highway, risking the odd encounter with a snake or spider as we kicked away some of the larger twigs and dead leaves covering the ground. 'No, it's fine,' said the farmer. 'Why don't you make camp over here? There are less rocks.'

Very quickly we were alone again and able to get the tents up as the light faded. It had been a long hot day in the saddle, a day where smoking volcanoes flanked our entire route on one side and the ocean on the other. My new fad was sucking in deep lungfuls of sweet sugary air each time a truck sped by with its load of freshly cut sugar cane. It was magical. Guatemala was fresh and exciting.

Neither Martin nor I were in the mood to sweat it out in the tents so we went in search of our customary early evening coffee and left Paps to it. A few hundred yards up from our campsite was a kiosk selling hot and cold drinks and a selection of sandwiches so coffee in hand we positioned ourselves outside and chilled out a while as cars and sugar cane trucks whizzed past in the darkness.

'That was tough going today,' I said.

'Yeah but in a few weeks we'll be in Panama City.'

'I wish this drunk would move on,' I said, changing the subject. 'He's been asking us the same question for the last five minutes.'

'What?

"Can you buy me another beer?" Ignore him and maybe he'll get the message.'

'Are you the people staying in the field?' interrupted a young lad, who I'd spotted hanging around for a moment or two.

'Yes,' I replied.

'We want to make you some coffee and my friends want to meet you,' he said, eagerly. 'When are you going back?'

'After these drinks.'

'I will meet you at the entrance, by the road,' he confirmed by way of leaving.

'OK, see you soon!'

I filled Martin in on what was happening before we began walking back a few minutes later. The young lad had grown impatient and come to meet us half way. 'Vengan, vengan!' he insisted. 'We have coffee for you!'

'What's your name young man?'

'Luis.'

We arrived at the entrance to the banana plantation to find at least ten locals hanging around in the blackness. Faces of young and old alike squinted as we scanned the crowd with our torches. It was overwhelming. I could hear people whispering but no one came forward to speak to us, even after Martin and I had said hello.

'Are these all your friends, Luis?' I asked, hoping to start some sort of conversation.

'Yes, they are from the village,' he replied. 'This is my mum and my sister.'

'Hello, how are you?' I asked, as we shook hands with a pair of bewildered women.

'Where are you from?' asked Luis, taking a question whispered into his ear by a lad to his left.

'We are from England,' I replied.

'And where are you cycling to?'

'To Argentina,' I replied. My answer didn't register so I kept talking. 'We have been cycling for six months. We are helping children in El Salvador.'

'Not Guatemala?' asked Luis.

'No, just one place in El Salvador.'

'What's the matter with your friend, why is he inside his tent?'

'I think he is trying to sleep.'

Then my brain was swamped as all the once-timid children followed Luis's lead and grew in confidence. They started bombarding Martin and I with a myriad of questions. What are your names?...How old are you?...Are you married?...Do you have girlfriends?...Say something in English! The sugar-rich coffee arrived. Most of the girls had become infatuated with Martin by this stage, his tanned skin, flowing locks and muscular build lighting up their faces with every move he made. When he didn't understand what they were asking, I translated and when I didn't understand we laughed and apologised for our poor Spanish. Our white feet then became a bit of a party piece before we headed off through the field to show them our bikes and tents. One or two knelt next to Paps's asking him questions through the fabric but he wouldn't come out and join in. There was no pretence, no angling for money or gifts. Meeting us was unusual, a big deal for these kids. We'd be yesterday's news in the morning but right now we were hot property.

Guatemala signalled the start of a five-week, six-country traverse with a series of planned stops to get off the bikes and ease down on the punishing schedule. The optimism that a fresh country brought was contagious. The first break was up in the highlands spending a couple of days in the colonial city of Antigua. Surrounded by black volcanoes and benefiting from a pleasant temperate environment, it made the perfect get away from the heat and humidity of the coast. We walked its cobbled streets, taking in the pastel coloured buildings and numerous plazas, later climbing Volcán Pacaya, an active volcano with a number of red-hot lava funnels. The cool mountain air washed away the stress and frustration of Mexico and plenty of western tourists gave us the chance to speak to someone in our own language. Morale improved, yet, underlying gripes and group politics were about to make another startling appearance. Martin recalls...

Ever since Canada, Wils and I had enjoyed the chance to sit and chat about something other than the route or bikes. We would walk into town or to a service station just to stretch our backs, have a coffee or beer and see normality for a while before the isolation of the tents. We always asked Paps to come but he rarely did. Usually, he said he was too tired or didn't feel like it so we would get him whatever he ordered. The magnitude of this point didn't sink in until Antigua.

After a few beers on his own the second afternoon, it was plain to all that Paps had something on his mind. I was not aware that Wils had already spoken to him and knew the problem. I detected his unhappiness and drew it from him.

'What's up mate?' I said. 'Come on give it all to me.'

That comment was like opening the floodgates. 'I am an outsider in this group,' said Paps. 'I'm pleased that you two are so damn pally but I feel pushed aside and quite honestly everything you talk about bores me silly. You talk about shit like motorbikes and Land Rovers and it's fantastical. You are not going to buy any of that shit. You just talk crap all day and it doesn't interest me. You go out in the evening and talk about the same thing. It's just rubbish. I'm not interested in a single thing you say.'

Once the initial onslaught subsided I asked Paps if he had any more to tell me. He felt that we ignored him and disregarded any ideas or plans that he put forward. I apologised. What Paps didn't realise though was how often Wils and I would discuss what a shame it was that he was not with us and how good it would be if all three of us were to sit and natter for a while.

I spent the next few days going over the conversation in my mind, revisiting his issues and assessing the validity of each point. With some issues I could see his point of view but there was no intent or malice in my actions and I felt sorry that it had made him feel this way. The other points, however, angered me. We were clearly different people, interested in different things. I didn't tell him he bores me or he talks shit just because I am not interested in the subjects that he is. I knew my relationship with Paps had broken down at this point. It had changed irrevocably, at least for the trip. Suddenly I felt disposable in his eyes.

The Paps/Martin incident was far bigger than the argument at Bullard's Beach in Oregon. For my part, I accepted that all three of us might see things differently, have a different way of spending our time, money and energy but what I failed to accept was the way Paps had verbally attacked Martin. The previous night, Paps and I had gone out for a few beers and used the chance to vent off a bit of steam at each other. I commented how his moods left me depressed and angry long after he had emerged from the darkness. We also chatted about Martin and how he did some things differently and Paps revealed how a number of them annoyed him. Crucially the conversation always had a positive slant and by the end of the night, I assumed that although nothing was fixed, Paps and I had got a lot of things off our chests and that some degree of harmony had been reached. After all, this process had been going on for months. What was different about the Antigua blow-out was that Paps had spent the afternoon relaxing in a sports bar, taking advantage of the cheap beer. His tongue was loose and he was ready to let rip. News of what had happened was really hard to take in and get my head around. It may all sound fairly ordinary, just a bicker or quarrel to be expected but to those that were part of the intimate world that we were living in, where support, friendship and strength from your riding partners count for everything, it *did* mean everything, to all of us.

I started thinking along a different track after Antigua. I started to consider riding solo or riding with Martin if he was willing to break away from Paps. This was a huge mental step, one that I hadn't entertained before because I realised that things weren't ever going to change. The cycle of a few good days followed by a few bad days was only going to repeat itself and the chances were, it would get worse as time went by. Did I want the rest of this year – my year - to run like that or was I going to be man enough to change it? Paps's moods weren't some sort of secret, they engulfed everyone and gnawed away at me from the inside. I had even started to predict them, to spot them before they flourished. Even so, I didn't seem able to stop them and neither did Martin or Paps. Like the night at Reedsport, when Martin made a slap up dinner and I did the laundry and bought beer, no amount of goodwill could bury a mood and sow a seed of optimism in Paps's head. The mood disappeared only when he wanted it to, only when he was ready to talk and be sociable. That's why I knew it was set to continue. The heat and insects were set for another four months and the mind-blowing routine for another five or six. Heading back to the coast, a stony silence took hold and a deep despondency ran through me. I kept thinking, "The sooner I am brave enough to act on my own convictions, the sooner I have a shot at being in control of *my* trip". I imagine Martin and Paps were both lamenting what had happened to some degree or other because it was written all over their faces. How the hell had we got to this point?

"Smelly, dirty and full of death"

'Martin's bike gets an unexpected wash from a Central American river'

The next day we rejoined the main highway and met two Canadians, Barry and son, Nat, who had ridden down from Vancouver and were making their way as far as Panama City. We rode along together the whole afternoon in two's and three's chatting about life on the road, them with their panniers and us with our trailers.

'Where are you thinking of staying tonight?' Nat had asked Martin, as we rode along bunched together.

'Normally we ask permission and just pitch in a field.'

'Really?' came Nat's reply. 'We stay with the locals on their property.'

He wasn't joking. Nat and Barry had a well-trodden routine of pressing themselves upon the locals and we were about to witness it firsthand. As the light faded, and with the three of us unsure whether to buzz off and find somewhere of our own to camp, Nat pulled his bike over and asked an elderly gentleman leaning on the fence of his property if he minded five gringos descending on his place for the night. The poor old chap seemed understandably bewildered by it all but waved us in nonetheless. Within minutes Nat and Barry were unloading their kit and erecting their tent on the front patio. I looked at Paps and Paps looked at Martin. How could they be so obtuse? What gave them the impression that these people wanted to fetch buckets of water and even dish up some food for a bunch of Westerners?

"We do this all the time," said Barry, proudly, taking off his socks and leaning back in a chair.

Well done Barry, how imperialistic of you. Wanker. I thought your ilk died out two hundred years ago with the slave trade.

'Really?' said Martin, without a scrap of interest in his voice.

'Yeah, it's great,' continued Barry. 'We get to speak to the locals, learn about their way of life and more often than not we get a shower and somewhere to sleep. Normally the water is cold but you take what you can get.'

I don't give a shit if you get to speak to lots of locals, how can you be that arrogant? Sleeping in a field or in someone's garden is something but setting up camp on the front patio, relaxing in their deckchair and asking the grandmother to bring a bucket of water to soak your aching feet, is just starting to take the piss. I thought people who travelled this way would be immune to such self-importance but clearly not. More than anything, it showed how much of a clique the three of us had become. Like Nat and Barry, we had our own system, one that worked and one that we understood.

'I don't like this at all,' I whispered to Paps, as we made our dinner under torchlight.

'Me neither, mate. Don't worry; we'll be out of here by the morning.'

We made are excuses and disappeared through the El Salvadorian border formalities. Then the appalling silence descended once more between the three of us. Barry and Nat were the least of our worries, we had our own battles to fight and they needed sorting out.

'I want to stop and sort this out,' Martin said, as we all cycled together across the road in silence. 'I know that all of us have got stuff to say and I don't want it going on any longer. Let's pull over at the next restaurant and have a coke. Paps, is that OK with you?'

'Yeah, sure.'

'Wils?'

'That's fine,' I said, my heart thumping with adrenaline.

I knew what was coming and so did Paps. I kept rehearsing what I intended to say but each time I got my words entangled and lost the thread. A couple of kilometres later we came into the small town of Casa, a bustling little place that serviced the highway's commuters. We stopped opposite a suitable spot, parked the bikes within view and went and sat down. The restaurant was packed with customers, most of them tackling chicken tortillas and beans or fried fish and rice. The conversation dilly-dallied for a while as we waited for our cokes but then we got down to business. Martin and Paps discussed what had happened. There was a general meeting of minds and Paps made it clear that he regretted the ferocity of his words. I was half-inclined to just gloss over my issues, like I had done a few times before but this time something made me come out and say my peace.

'Right, well I'm not sure what to say, really,' I said, truthfully. 'What I can't understand is how a friend I have known for 12 years can give me the cold shoulder for two days and then as soon as we meet two complete strangers he is the bubbliest, most happy-go-lucky person I have seen in my life,' I said, in reference to Paps chatting with Nat and Barry. 'You were talkative, sociable, you were asking questions, laughing. I couldn't believe what I was seeing. I don't understand it. Your mood vanished. I appreciate that things are strained between us but seeing you like that was very hurtful. I want you to see it from my perspective. I feel like I really try with you, that I try to help with the knee issue and the differences in opinion but I'm getting very little back. Two complete strangers got more from you in twenty minutes than I got in the last two days. What's the point in riding with you? This trip is about support and companionship. If I'm not getting *anything* back then it makes sense to do without the moods and go it alone. I have thought about what tools, spare parts I need to buy. I have considered everything,' I continued, noting a change of expression on Paps's face. 'Yes, it's bloody tough and it's what we set ourselves but I can't handle your moods.'

'I had no idea you were thinking of riding solo,' said Paps.

'Neither did I. Believe me, I don't want to.'

'Neither do I,' replied Paps. 'This is something that we started and should finish together. I haven't come out here to cycle alone. If you two decide to go off then I'll just go home. I don't like cycling, so doing it alone makes no sense at all.'

The dam had been plugged, again. Would it hold firm or would the weight of seven months on the road and the knowledge of five more be too much? Could the three of us do as we had said, and stick together through thick and thin, no matter what came to pass? Truthfully, none of us knew.

Chapter 12

The Children of Chalatenango

'Joy lies in the fight, in the attempt, in the suffering involved, not in the victory itself.'
Mahatma Gandhi
Born India, 1869

Start Point: La Libertad, El Salvador. Mile: 7,745. 25th February.

'Look at this place!' said Martin. 'We have a room each, there's a pool and apparently we get a buffet breakfast thrown in! Whey hey!'

We had finally reached the capital of El Salvador, San Salvador. Things got off to a slow start because of our early arrival but it at least gave us time to lounge around the hotel Plan had checked us into. We pillaged the buffet breakfast, lazed by the pool and ventured out only to eat a pizza but this was followed up the next day with our scheduled visit to the project area. Here was where we'd witness the fruit of all our hard work.

The rallying point was Plan's offices down town. Patty and Raul, two operatives charged with looking after us told us to don Plan T-shirts and jump into a minibus along with a half a dozen young members of the Salvadoran Cycling Association with whom we would share the road later in the day. Today was going to be far bigger than any of us had imagined. Apart from the minibus and two or three Plan 4x4's, there was also a film crew, press vehicles, an ambulance (in case of an accident whilst we cycled between the schools) and at least four police motorcycle riders. All of a sudden we had gone from eating at the side of the road in grotty cycling gear to being VIPs with our very own motorcade.

El Salvador, meaning "The Saviour", is the smallest country in Central America, a place wreaked by political unrest and natural disasters throughout its recent history. During the late seventies and through the eighties a 12-year civil war ended with more than 70,000 dead and the country in severe financial straits. Flash flooding, earthquakes and forest fires are common, so too the risk of epidemics such as dengue fever or rotavirus which affect mainly children. Combined with an increasing level of violence among the young, (attributed to the dearth of opportunities and high unemployment rate) these factors encourage many to migrate to neighbouring countries. Many of those that do stay rely heavily on government handouts, so much so that a culture of non-working had taken hold which was serving to put the national economy under even more strain. Plan had been working under these conditions since 1976, yet it had succeeded in sponsoring over 40,000 children throughout 392 communities, working on the principles of survival, development, protection and participation. It concentrated its efforts on alleviating infant mortality, improving the coverage and quality of education, reducing violence against women and children, reducing environmental, economic and social vulnerability and participating in the country's wider development process. All of this was done in coordination with the Ministry of Health, and other government and non-government organisations via training and teaching in promotion of rights, implementation of water and sanitation systems, food security and nutrition, natural disaster prevention and reconstruction and above all, children's education.

Back on the bus, we reached the first school – *Escuela de Colima* - an hour's drive from the capital, now firmly in a dusty, sun-scorched rural environment. Stepping out into the heat our newfound fame was about to spiral skyward. Plan's camera crew got ready and one or two dignitaries showed up including Han Dijsselbloem, Plan's Country Director. All manner of people focused their gaze on us, some of them teachers, others field staff, community representatives and parents. Then quite suddenly on Han's instructions we were told to step forward into the school grounds where a couple of hundred children began clapping and cheering at us like we were Hollywood celebrities attending a film premiére. The wave of applause and look of delight on the children's faces were so overwhelming that I had to consciously instruct my feet to keep moving. We continued into the playground and were directed to a long cloth-covered table with chairs that had been set out on an improvised stage. The three of us took our assigned seats, along with the student representative (a girl of around 10), Han, the Salvadorian Minister of Education and the Headmistress. This was major celebrity time. Several hundred sets of eyes were now focused on our every move.

- Perhaps we have misjudged the feeling of sentiment? I mean, it's only us.
- You've made a big impact, you idiot.
- If they only knew how much of a mess we are in as a team.
- Yeah, well look where it's got you! More importantly look at the significance to these people!
- It's unbelievable.
- Enjoy it, you've earnt it.

I tuned back into proceedings as the Headmistress was introducing and thanking "Los cyclistas" and then began focusing on the upgrades made by Plan. I only understood half of what she was saying but just along from me, Paps and Martin were getting a running translation from Raul who was perched behind them. When I was invited to the microphone nerves got the better of me and I asked Han to translate what I was saying. Paps also said a few words and then we made way for the Minister of Education, who had not visited this part of the country for 12 years. Somewhere in the middle of all this hedonism we were presented wooden parrots and T-shirts and then various sets of children came forward to act out their well-rehearsed songs, poems and dance routines. I'd be lying if I said I felt totally comfortable watching three 15-year-old girls dance in front of us but hey, this was their way of thanking and respecting all that we had achieved.

'Can you believe all this?' I said to Paps, as we took a tour around the school.

'I'm blown way.'

Inside the newly built pre-school we were joined by some older students for a question and answer session in front of the cameras. What do you eat? How often do you buy food? Where do you sleep? How do you wash? Why did you choose El Salvador? Then we were ushered along a short ride to the next school. Off we set, 3 Brits and 6 Salvadorans, blazing a trail along the rural highway. Following us was the motorcade. Every so often one of the 4x4s came by so that the camera crew could film us and take photos. At *Escuela de Aguaje* we were again greeted by hundreds of pupils, this time waving British and Salvadoran flags. It was a similar routine, Paps saying a few words and the pupils demonstrating their new found computer skills. We spoke to the staff and then a couple of students demonstrated what they'd learnt about crop cultivation in the school garden. Very quickly we were on the bikes to the third and final school of the day, *Escuela de Tejutla*. By now there was so much going on and so much Spanish to translate I was exhausted but then came a reprieve with a short display between three lads dressed in colourful pyjama-like attire in a courtship dance with three equally well turned out girls. The slight glitch with the music only served to make the experience more authentic and afterwards some of the younger kids rushed in to ask us lots of questions even though the bell had gone for afternoon classes. Paps and I were swamped and then I made the fatal error of signing an autograph.

'Front row seats for the dance'

What followed was pretty embarrassing to be honest, as student after student queued up to receive a dubious bit of Spanish written into their notebooks by a sweaty six-foot ginger man. I just couldn't turn any of them away. Most taxing of all was thinking of some half decent, coherent messages as just signing my name felt highly inadequate.

'What's your name young man?' I asked, of an impeccably dressed youngster in his blue and grey uniform.

'Eduardo!'

'OK…Eduardo, how old are you?'

'Seven.'

'What's your favourite class?'

'English!'

'Really?'

'Yes and football!'

We both laughed like drains, where upon I scribbled down the following.

"Dear Eduardo…education is just as important as football so study hard! James Wilson."

Eduardo gave the note the quick once over and then scampered off to class and I went back to complying with the next autograph hunter's demands, only getting to lunch after most people had finished the main course! It had been twenty years since I was at primary school but I was stunned by how much fun the kids seemed to be having. The English teacher, although too shy to talk to us in English, was extremely proud of his position and eager to know whether the welcome sign was grammatically correct and free of errors. It was. The whole day had been a revelation. These people were falling over themselves to make a difference. All they were looking for was a modicum of funding, a push and a prod in the right direction if you like. They didn't want unsustainable handouts, they were after life skills and through Plan they were getting them.

*

The long-awaited site visits had come and gone in the blink of an eye. In the morning we would leave San Salvador and resume our relationship with the saddle and white line. The thought of many more thousands of miles weighed heavily on my mind and I lay on my bed, staring at the ceiling, ignoring the mountain of gear strewn around my room which needed packing. A package of fresh bike parts had arrived from the UK, meaning Paps could finally replace his makeshift trailer bag for the authentic version.

…*Paps…Paps…Paps…*

I continued to stare at the ceiling, consumed with despondency, thinking only of Paps and the road ahead. I couldn't put the two together. I lambasted myself for my negativity and unshakable gloominess but the thoughts wouldn't go away. Martin and I had resolved to end it tonight. Martin recounts…

On reflection, now that the trip is over, I realise that recent conditions had been incredibly intense and we all felt uptight and exhausted. A few days beforehand I had pulled us to a halt to beat the problem out over a coke. That discussion, the one where Wils admitted he was fully prepared to 'go it alone', had put the cat amongst the pigeons. It was a serious admission and one which established that both he and I were extremely dissatisfied with the way we were being treated.

We knew that the riding had been tough and Paps' knee was giving him trouble. Our complaint was the way issues were handled. Instead of talking about concerns or worries, Wils and I felt shut out for days, and confronted by a wall of silence. This made hard conditions harder still, not knowing if you were going to get any acknowledgement at all that day let alone a conversation or even help around camp. Our riding requirements had also been on different pages from the beginning. Wils and I were keen to ride hard on a riding day to cover the miles in as few days as possible, allowing us time off the bikes to enjoy our surroundings. Paps on the other hand, preferred to stop earlier in the day. Cumulatively this resulted in being a long way off target at the end of the week; a fact that I personally found hard to deal with especially when we realised it meant less off the bike experiences.

By the time we had finished seeing the projects, Wils and I had decided the best course of action was to go it alone. Neither of us liked the idea and even admitted that it felt like splitting up with a long term girlfriend whom we loved but could no longer live with. I kicked myself for not having stamped it out back up in Canada or being more tolerant now. Am I being unfair? Is Paps really in that much pain? Have I blown this out of proportion and am I just being a cry-baby? These questions had rolled around in my mind for months. When I realised Wils was of the same opinion I felt relieved but somehow, I still had to deal with it one way or another. The time had come, the decision had been made and tonight was the night.

The three of us went over the road, opposite the hotel to get a bite to eat. Wils and I glanced at each other, unsure of how we even broach the subject. A discussion ensued but when it came down to announcing our departure, Wils and I quite simply chickened out. We couldn't say to our friend;

'Sorry pal, you are a right royal pain in the arse and I'm off.'

So the next day we rode on, hoping that somehow the crease would iron itself out. I felt worse knowing I'd not been strong enough to sort it in the beginning and was too weak to sort it out now. The only solace was that after two stern discussions, Paps was fully aware of how serious the situation was. I kept thinking, "You never know, conditions may improve..."

Before the supposed break up and after I had stopped staring at the ceiling, I had spent an hour and a half on the phone to Carolina, trying to make sense of it all, not quite believing what Martin and I were about to do. I asked her repeatedly to give me her honest, unbiased opinion because I couldn't work out what was real and what was stress-related. Looking back, it was a pointless exercise. If neither Martin nor I knew what to do, how could anyone else? How had we got to this point? How, in the middle of Central America did it seem plausible to ride off, leaving my closest friend at the side of the road seven months after leaving Prudhoe? Clearly I knew that I'd have a better time away from Paps' moods but when the time came, when I had Martin's support, I still didn't have the balls to say, "I'm off." On reflection, anyone with a more single-minded or ruthless inclination would have ridden off weeks ago so I wasn't about to do it now. At the end of the day he was my friend. It was as simple as that.

*

San Miguel was just 50kms from the Honduran border and most importantly a refuelling stop. The heat was oppressive, sucking the life out of any conversation. In its absence I took to studying my coke bottle and noted the date imprinted on the side.

'Mine's a 1995,' I said, blankly.

'Mine is a 1995 too but it's got a green tinge,' said Martin.

'Mine is a 2002,' said Paps.

That was the end of the matter until an hour later when we stopped again to get out of the sun and take on more liquids.

'Mine is a 2002,' said Paps, studying his bottle of coke.

I picked up my bottle and announced, 'And mine's a 1995!'

All eyes focused on Martin's coke bottle, again the only one to have a green tinge. 'It's a 1995!'

The place we found to camp that night next to the highway was to all intents and purposes a building site. Fragments of brick, glass and metal were scattered between burnt tyres, burnt ground and used needles. It forced us to spread out over quite an area to find a somewhere to sleep. What gnarled though was that 50 yards away was a lush piece of grass at the back of a petrol station that the pump attendant refused to let us use in case he got a bollocking from his boss. Laying out our mattresses atop our flattened tents we ate spam baguettes in the fading light. Then everyone settled down to get some sleep. An hour later I was still staring at the stars and slapping my skin in an effort to kill all the midges and bugs that were landing on me. It was so hot that beads of sweat starting snaking their way over my shoulders and down my back, the heavy coating of insect repellent making things worse. Then three large birds started squawking in a tree thirty yards away, their silhouettes marked out by a couple of street lights. Soon enough my patience was broken. I found my head torch, put my sandals on so as not to be cut by a piece of glass or an infected needle and then went about finding some half bricks. I could hear one or two giggles through the blackness as my artillery started zeroing in on the unwanted guests. After about half a dozen throws that whizzed past without success, I sacrificed pace for accuracy and immediately hit the branch on which they were perched.

That'll teach you to disturb my luxurious campsite! Now, piss off!

Five minutes later, they were back on their favourite branch and I had my sandals back on looking for more stones and half bricks. This was our last night in El Salvador and it proved to be just an appetiser for what was to come next, for twenty-two hours after battling the squawking birds we were in Honduras, with another 70 miles in the bag and firmly in the mood for a shower and bed for the night. Unfortunately, San Lorenzo had only one ATM in town and it swallowed Martin's bankcard. That left us with very little local currency, no food or water and no hotels accepting credit cards. Out of town we rode, looking for somewhere to pitch alongside an estuary where a few restaurants lit up the road and people walked back and forth in the early evening.

'How about we ask one of these restaurants to shout us an evening meal?' suggested Martin. 'We could pay them in the morning when the bank opens and I get my card back?'

Courtesy of a restaurateur, an hour later we were enjoying a two-course meal with cold beer, having washed in the estuary and then again when he offered us some clean water from a water tank. We even found a piece of concrete next to the restaurant on which to lay our mattresses and retired to our beds happy men. At 1am though, things changed.

I thought we were well hidden but an extremely drunk Honduran on his way home or perhaps to another watering hole had spotted us and come over to say hello. All three of us were now wide-awake and hoping he would do what no drunk had ever done in the past; realise that he was surplus to requirements and move on. Quite the opposite in fact. After a few seconds of unintelligible Spanish he very quickly pulled up his grotty, beer stained T-shirt and pulled out a silver pistol from his trousers.

Fair play, I wasn't expecting that…what now maestro?

Still gibbering on about something or other the drunk started waving his hands around and gesticulating with the gun which every few seconds was being pointed in our direction. Then out came a bit of English.

'I protect you!...OK?...I protect you!' he declared. 'You OK with me…It very dangerous around here!'

Yeah, you're not kidding…

'Thank you,' I said, in Spanish. 'But we are fine, we just want to go to sleep.'

Not having come face to face with a drunk carrying a loaded pistol before, none of us knew what to say or do. Then he started off again in Spanish, still wielding the gun. I don't think any of us, including the drunk, knew what was going to happen next. He seemed to be friendly enough but was so hammered and so unpredictable that there was still plenty of time for him to pull the trigger and one of us to be on the way to hospital or worse. Fortunately, he suddenly decided that we weren't worth protecting, or shooting, because he abruptly muttered something and then staggered off down the street and out of sight. I only had time to look at the boys and whisper, 'Jesus Christ!' before we heard the gun go off a few yards away.

"Crack!...Crack!"

We remained motionless, saying nothing for a long while. Then one or two locals appeared, along with the restaurateur who enquired as to our wellbeing before running through the restaurant to pick up the phone. Within minutes the police had got a statement from the restaurateur and sped off in their patrol cars in pursuit. We just turned over and went back to sleep.

We knew something like this was constantly in the offing. Cycling and sleeping rough put us in close proximity of heavy traffic, drunken motorists and those people eager to take advantage of our naivety and basic security measures. In fact, the only form of defence we had against being mugged was our numbers but that was no match for a gun or knife. Not to be outdone though, the night at the Wild West Inn was followed up by a night in a farmyard, just inside the Nicaraguan border. This "cock up" was all my doing. The pressure was on to find somewhere safe to kip, away from needle-infested campsites and gunslingers and having just eaten a grotty meal at an even grottier restaurant in the shockingly poor town of Somotillo, my idea of where to sleep became a split second one. Cycling along the potholed highway scanning for a suitable pitch site, a man standing in the doorway to his house gave me a friendly wave. Without thinking I hit the brakes, shouted ahead to the boys and then went off to speak to my new friend.

'Hola!' I said, taking off my helmet and sunglasses as I approached him. 'Como está usted?'

'Hola!' came the man's reply. 'Bien, gracias.'

The whole family spilled out of the house to see what the foreigner wanted. I explained and without flinching, the man waved me in and through his property – a two room mud hut housing six people – to the backyard, where baked mud was again a strong theme.

'You are welcome to sleep here,' he said, pointing to several square metres of bare soil.

We both stood there for a moment, studying it. I was thinking quickly.

- *It's a bit cheeky, I feel like Barry and Nat.*
- *It's just a piece of hardened mud and there's not a deckchair or foot soak in sight.*
- *Ok, let's get the boys.*

Everything seemed to be running smoothly but then nightfall descended and the farmyard came alive. I should have known better. Ever since arriving on the Mexican mainland we had been dealing with similar experiences. Life congregated along the highway even in rural areas and an empty field or derelict building didn't guarantee you any respite from a cacophony of noise. Tonight was to be the crowning glory of snorts, barks, clucks and gobbles. We couldn't see them but the pigs, dogs, chickens and turkeys had formed an orchestra and were playing for all their worth in full surround sound. It was deafening, a farmyard version of the Last Night of the Proms. What is more, we had front row seats and couldn't leave until first light. I had messed up badly.

*

Like Honduras, Nicaragua was extremely poor. It seemed that if you had a pair of shoes and a change of clothing then you were fortunate because the number of naked or partly dressed children we saw playing in the dirt at the side of the road was staggering. Nicaragua was greener than Honduras and seemed to have more going for it, certainly along our route. We past by Volcán San Cristóbal, through the colonial city of León and then out along a 31km stretch of cobbled road built by order of a former president who wanted an appropriate level of opulence to precede a palace he had nearby. Then a 19km climb took us to altitude and above the cloud base where we experienced our first cool night in months sheltering from a vicious wind behind the wall of a communications tower. We rode along the southern shore of Lake Nicaragua, where beautiful red-roofed farmsteads dotted the rolling ranch land and farmers sat on horseback tilting their berets at us as we passed. Nicaragua had something different and it was a magical few days.

*

'Do I take it that neither of you are cycling Colombia?' I asked, a few days later.

'I don't think it's worth the risk,' replied Paps.

'Me neither,' agreed Martin. 'The thing that got me was Mike's comment in Mazatlán about risking his parents' retirement money to pay the ransom if something goes wrong. I don't want my mum paying for me to be released when there was no real need to go there in the first place.'

'I understand,' I replied. 'I just wanted to make sure.'

'Are you still thinking of going then?' asked Martin, with a hint of incredulity in his voice.

'I think so.'

Having had the boys' definitive answer on the Colombia question, I found the confidence to open a real snakes' nest.

'I'm not sure if riding through Colombia alone will be enough,' I continued. 'I can't get rid of feelings from Guatemala and El Salvador and I want to cycle on my own for a while.'

'I thought we'd covered this but obviously not,' said Paps, exasperated at the continued talk of separation.

'Me going to Colombia allows everyone to do exactly what they want for a while,' I remarked. 'You guys want to see parts of Ecuador and Peru that I don't, so it doesn't make sense to wait three weeks for me to cycle it and then stop for a week in Lima to see Machu Picchu. If we cycle on our own for a while we can meet up again somewhere in Peru or the top of Chile. We will be refreshed and have experienced different things.'

'I don't want to cycle on my own from Quito to Arica,' said Paps. 'It's 2,000 miles.'

'I didn't anticipate having to cycle Colombia on my own either,' I countered. 'We were all going to do it a few weeks ago but I respect your reasons for not going. After all that's happened I see this as the only way of staying together until the end rather than separating for good now.'

'I'm not happy about it but I have no choice so I'll go along with it,' said Paps, still trying to contain his frustration. 'I'll cycle to Lima but after that I want it all buried. I don't want this being brought up again.'

Paps was right, the subject did need burying but he probably didn't realise quite how much I was trying to save the chances of us finishing together. There hadn't been an argument in over two weeks but I couldn't quash the voices in my head over what had happened in Antigua, Casa and San Salvador. In fact, I had nothing to complain about at all. In response to our threat to ride off if there were any more "infractions", Paps was now on his best behaviour and hadn't put a foot wrong. This change in attitude made me go in search of faults that just weren't there. I analysed every comment, every look, every bit of body language that might give me cause to ride off. I couldn't go on like this for another six months and neither could Paps. Life on the road was tough enough without denying him the right to complain about the conditions or give his opinion on campsites, food or where to stop for rest days. A break had to be initiated, one that gave us a fresh dimension and drew to a close all that had happened over the previous few months. I needed some closure and felt better immediately, like a huge weight had been lifted from me. The difference in my outlook was remarkable. Riding through South America now seemed quite straightforward when an hour ago it had made me sick to my stomach.

Two other notable events happened within the next ten minutes; a six-foot snake slithered between Paps and I as we rode out of town and it started to rain. The 106-day drought from Lompoc, California, was over.

*

'This gravel road is killing me,' I said, my face dripping with water after washing in the cafe toilet.

'Only another 20 kilometres of it left!' remarked Paps, sarcastically.

The waitress came over with our ice-cold cokes. Within a matter of seconds a look of disbelief appeared across Paps's face. 'What's the matter?' I asked him.

"I've just checked your bottle and it's a 1995, mine is a 2002!'

'Oh no, not again!'

'Look! Martin's has a green tinge to it. If it's a 1995, I'm gonna go wild!'

Martin sat forward and checked the date on his bottle of coke. 'It's a 1995!'

Chapter 13

"This might sting a little."

> *'I can resist everything but temptation.'*
> Oscar Wilde
> Born Ireland, 1854

Start Point: Uvita, Costa Rica. Mile: 8,450. 14th March.

No one appeared from around the bend so I walked the bike across the road to the small supermarket I had spotted. A short while later I was still pondering what was going on.

Still no sign of them…must be a puncture.

I determined the bike was visible to any passer-by and went inside, occasionally taking the time to stick my head out of the door in case the boys emerged. At the fourth time of checking I caught sight of Martin howling past like a madman.

He's got no trailer!

I raced out of the supermarket yelling his name but he couldn't hear me and within a couple of seconds he was gone. A nauseating horror descended upon me.

Something's happened…it must be Paps, there must be a problem…shit! Shall I follow him? No, it'll take too long…shit…umm…stop a motorist. Yeah, that's a good idea, stop a motorist.

I raced across the road and waited nervously, my thoughts kicking into overdrive.

Martin was flying. This is serious…Where the hell is Paps? Maybe he's been hit?

I finally intercepted a couple rejoining the highway and they sped off in pursuit of Martin with instructions to turn him around. The road fell silent again as I waited next to my bike, hoping he would appear.

Maybe Martin didn't understand what they told him? Maybe they didn't stop him? Maybe they haven't seen him?

An agonising fifteen minutes went by before Martin reappeared, screaming up the road at full throttle.

'Fucking hell, mate!' he shouted, once within earshot. 'You need to stop! You can't go riding off like that, Paps has come off.'

'Is he OK?'

'No, he's not OK, I think he's broken his arm. I left him trying to get a lift back to Uvita. Come on, let's go!'

Martin's adrenaline was overflowing. Back up the road we went, pedalling frantically as the jungle came alive with the rising sun. After a couple of miles we arrived at the crash site, sweating furiously. Paps was nowhere to be seen, only his mangled bike and a couple of trailers marked the spot. I dismounted and saw large blood stains at the edge of the road and blood spots scattered across the highway.

'Jesus, look at the blood!' I stated. 'How bad is he?'

'I don't know,' said Martin, panting from the exertion. 'He was conscious. I checked him over and then came after you. Let's get a lift to Uvita. Someone must have taken him to the hospital.'

'I'll wait with the bikes and trailers,' I said. 'You go and find him.'

Paps recalls...

Wils was out front, perhaps 500m ahead of me with Martin an equal distance behind and because of the gentle topography and winding road all of us were in our own worlds. Not yet hot enough to sweat, a clear breathless morning with hardly a noise emanating from the jungle on both sides; it was as good as it gets for cycling. It makes what followed all the harder to explain.

Cresting a small rise, I saw Wils disappear from view around the next bend. The little downhill section allowed me to stretch a few muscles as I began to freewheel. I started on my legs, nothing more than tightening and relaxing muscles and then moved onto my wrists and back. It was a routine I had been doing for months. Yet, on this fateful day, I decided my back needed further work, so I began another technique which involved keeping my hands steady on the handle bar whilst sliding back off my seat and lowering my backside down behind the saddle, all the while pulling at the shoulders and upper parts of my back. It's an unusual position much like downhill mountain bikers perform to lower their centre of gravity. Things went rapidly wrong from this point onwards.

As soon as I moved off the saddle the front wheel went into a spasm, flicking violently from side to side. 'Oh shit!' I thought, realising I had done something stupid, 'I am going to pay for this!' Before I could bring myself back up, the bike flipped onto its left side and I went down with it. I don't remember being dragged along the road still clipped into my pedals. My memory only clicked in once I'd come to a stop. My mouth was clenched and my body tensed. I had my arms out to my left side, my left shoulder on the road with my legs wrapped around the frame of the bike. Untangling myself, I got up quickly hoping no one had seen me go down!

I knew immediately the damage was significant. In shock and with adrenaline pulsing through me, I didn't react to the pain straight away. Instead, I looked down to see blood pouring out from both ankles, knees, shins and elbows. There were also two "holes" on my left arm, next to a swelling that had already appeared on my elbow. Pulling it in close to my chest, I staggered across the road throbbing in pain, thinking I'd broken my left arm. My back and shoulders were screaming at me. I'd gone down on the tarmac at 30kmph without a shirt on but thankful the gloves I was wearing saved my hands from the same fate. I continued to walk back and forth across the empty road, aware of the odd bird call and waiting for someone, anyone, to appear. Wils was totally oblivious to what had happened but I knew Martin wouldn't be far behind.

- Where am I going to get treatment? I need the pain to stop! Am I off the trip?

- You idiot! You were asking for that! You can't tell them what happened. Think of something else, think of an excuse.

"This might sting a little."

With all the problems we were having as a group by that stage I didn't need someone to tell me so. Goodness knows what was going through Martin's mind as he crested the hill and saw me stood cradling my arm in the middle of the road.

'Jesus Christ, mate!' he said, screeching to a halt alongside me. 'Let me see your arm, can you move it?'

'No.'

'What about the rest of you?'

'My back hurts the most.'

'You've lost a lot of skin from the road. We need to get you to Uvita.'

'Wils has no idea what's happened,' I said. 'You need to go after him.'

'Are you gonna be OK if I leave you?' asked Martin. 'Forget the bikes, just try to get a lift and we'll come and find you, OK?'

'Yeah, OK.'

As soon as Martin had dropped his trailer and disappeared round the next corner I managed to flag down a local tour guide showing a German couple around for the day.

Like Paps said, the day had begun just like any other. One of us led off, today that happened to be me and I'd gone barely 10kms before stopping to fill up on food. This was extremely fortunate because had the supermarket not existed, I would have kept riding at least another 10kms before pulling over to stretch and that would have put me 12-15kms from the crash site and out of reach. Martin was fully aware of this, hence his immediate decision to drop his trailer in an effort to catch me. Lucky too that the motorist had indeed spotted Martin and pulled him over, otherwise he would have been half way to Panama.

Back at the crash site I managed to thumb a lift for Martin courtesy of a kind gent in a transit van. Then I stood in readiness to thumb a lift for me and all our gear. The time passed slowly and only encouraged me to sit on the edge of the drainage ditch in the morning sunshine, staring at the tarmac. I tried not to look at the blood and mangled bike. Thoughts raced through my mind about his crash. They made me feel lonely. I thought about my family, picturing them in England. Then suddenly my mind flashed through images of the road, places we'd stayed, every bend and town from that lonely place to Prudhoe Bay, the memory of lying flat out with Paps at the top of Gobblers Knob, him offering me a cold coke that didn't exist. It made me smile but then feel very sad. The scale of this journey was too big. We were out here proving we could do this challenge, our team in tatters, my relationship with Paps in tatters. Deep down I was at breaking point. I wanted to pour out all my emotion. I wanted someone to take me away from it all.

A few vehicles passed by over the next 20 minutes and then a 4x4 from the opposite direction. It pulled over and out jumped Martin and then Paps.

'Hey!' I said, in surprise. 'How are you?'

'Pretty banged up!'

'This chap offered to take us to hospital in Ciudad Cortes,' said Martin. 'The one in Uvita is shut.'

'OK. How far is it?' I asked.

'About 15km. Let's get the bikes and trailers on.'

'So what happened?' I asked, once we were on our way.

'I lost concentration,' said Paps. 'I was just daydreaming, staring at the jungle and before I knew it my front tyre had clipped the edge of the tarmac and I was down. I couldn't believe it.'

'How is the arm?'

'I can move it. It's my back that hurts the most.'

'That's because you threw yourself off the bike at 30kmph!' joked Martin.

By the time we had checked in and waited an hour to be seen, Paps's good spirits had disappeared.

'Wait here, I'm going to see if there's a doctor in this bloody place,' I said, in frustration.

I marched through to a treatment area, ignoring a couple of stewards and succeeded in getting a doctor to examine Paps.

'The bone is heavily bruised but not broken,' reported the doctor, an hour later.

I translated for Paps as the doctor continued speaking. 'We are going to clean all his cuts and then dress them.'

'Is there anything you can give him for the pain?' I asked.

'I will prescribe some medication which you can pick up from the pharmacy. Wait here and you'll be seen by one of the nurses.'

This was great news. In celebration, I went to fetch the camera from Martin, eager to record at least some of the post crash trauma. The dinner plate-sized piece of flesh on Paps's back was red raw, glowing like molten lava. Grooves in it indicated the direction of his fall with large pieces of grit lodged in the tissue. A small team of nurses ordered Paps onto a gurney and began tending each wound on the front of his body by firstly removing the larger pieces and then swabbing out with alcohol. Each time they dabbed, a sharp "Argghh!" and occasional swear word exited Paps's mouth. I kept shooting frame after frame, for prosperity. Then one of the nurses turned his attention to Paps's back. Face down on the gurney, everyone in the room knew this was going to hurt.

'The nurse says this might sting a little, so brace yourself,' I said, camera at the ready.

'Argghh! Wils, get them to give me something for the pain!'

"This might sting a little."

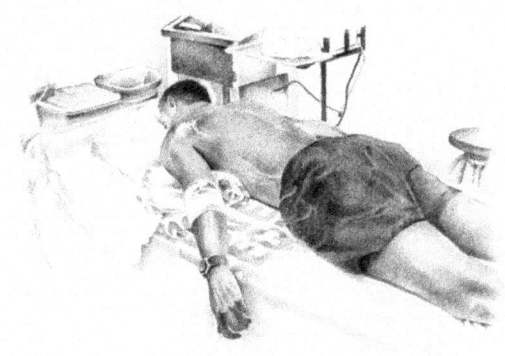

'Paps can't face the pain'

The injuries Paps sustained changed things for everyone. Although he had taken a fall in the mud of Alaska and I had come off at low speed in Canada, both because of the wind, the chance of someone doing some proper damage was probably inevitable at some point. On tight, twisting downhills he would just disappear even though Martin and I were going as quick as we dared. We'd all had a narrow escape because of traffic, the road surface or even the weather and we were all susceptible to the odd fast corner or reckless manoeuvre. On the perfectly smooth and quiet highways of Canada, Paps and I would compete for the highest top speed, something we eventually shared at 42mph. I mean, Paps and I had even overtaken an RV on one section of downhill in America and we all used to drink, eat and even pass items around whilst on the bikes. Therefore when the crash happened we were thankful that Paps and bike sustained only relatively superficial damage. By the end of the day Sick-note had been discharged and we'd found a nice place to rest up out of the oppressive heat. The injuries meant he couldn't walk around outside without bandages and a t-shirt and they only led to the sticky puss ripping when a fresh bandage was put on or when he needed a shower. Martin and I left him resting and went to get something to eat. Straight away we discussed what to do.

'He needs to be at altitude and heal in a temperate environment,' said Martin. 'You are the only one doing Colombia so you might as well cycle to Panama City, it's only 600kms away. I'll take him to Panama City by bus and then he can fly to Quito early and rest up.'

'I'll look after him,' I responded. 'You cycle to Panama City.'

'Look, it's a five day ride to Panama City so missing that is the least of my worries. What's five days riding out of one year? Nothing. You'll have the chance to cycle the lot and we'll see you in Panama before you go to Colombia.'

That's pretty much how it was settled, and we'd use Plan's offices there as the rallying point. Considering what had happened only three weeks ago in Antigua, this was a huge act of selflessness on Martin's part. His generosity and my willingness to accept it, when perhaps I shouldn't have, meant he faced getting two bikes, two trailers, himself and Paps from our location on the coast up to San José and then across to Panama City. It was a journey involving at least three bus journeys and an overnight stay in the Costa Rican capital. Paps kept his feelings on the news under wraps...

At the time I would have preferred it if James had agreed that the group should stay together. It was the first major accident. His decision to leave two days later smacked a little of one-eyed ambition or selfishness. What does it say when one team-mate stays and the other goes? As for Martin, well I wouldn't have got through all the travelling and rest I needed, without him. He was at his best even though it must have been a chore, baby-sitting me, carrying all my kit and helping me get dressed. We were having big problems as a team at that time but it was reassuring to know that when the proverbial shit hit the fan that friends will be friends and Martin was just that.

What follows is very hard to admit but deep down, Paps was right. My anger over his attitude was now controlling everything. Beyond me sorting out the hospital treatment and accommodation he didn't deserve my care. He deserved only the consequences of his behaviour and I wasn't about to sacrifice Martin's generosity in favour of providing a false statement of unity. I was too angry. I had become embittered by my family, by Paps, by the notion of putting others before me. Now it was my turn. It is an awful thing to front up to but honestly, I was numb. I wanted to be alone. I wanted out, away from the group politics, from having to do everything because of my Spanish and the crash was the perfect way to bale.

*

I said goodbye, nervous and desperate not to fail and realised immediately that solo cycling was shit-scary. My near obsession with the bike computer reached new heights. I couldn't keep me eyes off it. From day one it had been my means of gauging progress against the clock. I'd spend hours calculating and then recalculating expected distances, building a picture in my head of when I could relax and enjoy the scenery, stop and have a chat or when we needed to hit overdrive because we'd been messing about too long finding a piece of beef for lunch. Once or twice this addiction had got the better of me...

'Let's stop and have a biscuit and a cup of tea at 30 miles,' Martin or Paps would say.

'OK, I'll tell you when,' I would reply.

Because my computer had become the official distance marker, the boys relied on me to tell them when we had reached a given point. Now, if we happened upon a lay-by and a beautiful view of the Canadian Rockies at 29.8 miles, I still couldn't bring myself to pull over. I had to see at least 30.0 miles on the computer. So, instead of stopping, I'd tell them there was "three-quarters of a mile to go" or more, even though it probably meant we took our break in the bottom of the next valley, surrounded by pine trees. It summed up the mental aspect of the trip to a tee, at least for me and it led to Martin checking my computer during breaks after suspecting that I was telling fibs!

Back in Costa Rica, and with Panama City 370 miles away, I wanted to see what was possible if I cut the stops to a minimum and cycled hard, really hard. I had the advantage of less weight in the trailer as non-essential items were on their way to San José with the boys and I could choose when to rest and when to buy food. I also had no-one to talk to or wait for whilst someone else fixed a puncture. Martin had been harping on about this type of riding ever since northern Canada, his philosophy being 'let's get the riding done and then enjoy time off the bike' and although we had changed our riding style a few times since then, we had never consistently ridden hard just to knock off miles off.

With 94 miles showing on the computer I dragged my bike off the road and knocked on the door of a large bungalow that had an open expanse of grass offering plenty of space for a night's rest. An elderly gentleman answered the door, dressed impeccably in grey trousers, navy sports jacket and a trilby style hat. He invited me to set up where I liked and then closed the door. A huge amount of satisfaction coarsed through me. I laid out my mat and bag, made sandwiches, had a wash under his garden tap and studied the map intensely.

I might reach Panama City by the 19th at this rate. I wish I could tell the boys. How are they, I wonder? Are they in San José?

Night-time descended but I was in no mood to sleep. I was buzzing. I lay on top of my sleeping bag, watching the stars, music blaring through the headphones. I started thinking about being alone, in Panama and in the midst of a great adventure. One thing was for sure; I was a rejuvenated man.

*

I made a big mistake the following day by looking at the map and deciding to chance reaching a town to refill on water and food. The town didn't exist and I was forced to keep going, another 20 miles. With all the hills and our experience of dodgy maps and road signs, I should have identified the danger but my eagerness got the better of me. Exhausted and seriously dehydrated I finally reached a lonely restaurant at the top of a massive hill and took sanctuary. I pushed my bike against a wall and collapsed on the ground, my body convulsing slightly and my head spinning so much so that I lost focus and everything went black. It was a perfect example of never knowing what was going to happen next. Not the next puncture or food break but finding the perfect campsite just when you least expect it; finding nowhere to camp when you are stuck on a mountain pass in Nicaragua; having food stolen in Alaska only for it to be replaced or finding an exact replacement of your derailleur in a dusty town in Mexico. Appropriate then that I happened upon a football pitch at the end of the day on the edge of a small village. These pitch sites were to die for, especially in Central America where dense jungle or thorny scrub left few options. Elated at my good fortune I rolled my bike across the playing surface to the far touchline and started setting up. The day had been blindingly hot but my two-day total stood at 184 miles and I was comforted in the knowledge of lots of food in the trailer. Quite suddenly a group of men and boys appeared from the trees and descended on the pitch for a quick game before sundown. Some of the younger lads came over to ask if I wanted to play but I was just too tired and instead applauded from the touchline, becoming an excuse for one or two to rest as they watched me fiddle with my bike or make sandwiches. At one point, this happened to be one of the goalkeepers! He stood there asking me a few questions, not hearing the screams of his team-mates who had lost possession and unfortunately our conversation cost his team the lead. It was hilarious! Once the game finished the children became fascinated with some of my gadgets especially the head torch and the music player and I indulged one of them by feeding Orbital through to him at full volume.

'¡Dejáme escuchar!' - 'Let me listen!' shouted his mates.

I was loving Panama. It had a different feel about it. Its underbelly of remote villages, emaciated cattle and the skinning of a horse by the roadside was in contrast with the odd section of dual carriageway and the proliferation of American fast food joints.

*

'Hola, ¿Como estás?' I began, reaching out to shake the teenager's hand.

'Bien, gracias.'

'I was wondering if I could camp the night on your lawn?' I said, continuing in Spanish. 'I'm looking for a safe place.'

'I don't know.'

'Are your parents here?'

'No but I'll ask my grandmother.'

The teenager wondered back a minute or two later with the good news so I thanked him and went to fetch my bike. Shortly afterwards the business of making camp became slightly ridiculous as he ordered me to set up next to some trees, a comfortable distance from the house, rather than on the well-kept lawn. I didn't care. I was more concerned with getting my flysheet up as it started to rain. It was only the second time I'd used it since California and it felt quite cosy to be inside listening to the raindrops as I ate my corn beef sandwiches. By the morning, relations improved dramatically because the mother of the household came over whilst I was packing up.

'Can I offer you some breakfast?' she enquired.

'That's very kind of you.'

I went inside and met the grandmother who I recognised from her spying on me whilst I washed under the garden hose. She and I made some small talk and then the mother came out of the kitchen with a delicious fried egg and ham sandwich. I brought them both up to speed with the trip, Paps's crash and the projects in El Salvador and in return they gave me some info on the road ahead.

"This might sting a little."

The house had a European flavour to it, decorated almost like a 1950's country cottage, with a wicker sofa and hardwood rocking chair. The papered walls were dressed with ornate landscape paintings and one or two black and white family photos and the table adorned with a white cloth and place mats. Both ladies seemed a bit star-struck to have a Westerner sat at their breakfast table spouting dubious Spanish and I could have stayed longer but thanked them and moved on, aware that time was ticking. Late on, without any water and on a fast dual carriageway filled with evening traffic, I began to worry.

I've got to get off this road. How far to the next junction? Please, come on…

A two-foot wide rumble strip was forcing me to cycle to the left of the white line. Each time a truck swept past it missed my left shoulder by about a foot. Then I got some divine intervention from a policeman out catching speeding motorists. We ended up exchanging a few laughs and jokes about the bike trip. He just kept saying, "No way!" in Spanish but when he told me it was 8kms to the nearest junction, I jumped back on the bike and pedalled like mad up the highway, motorists lighting my way. The officer's directions were spot on and I made it just in time to a suburb with a petrol station he had mentioned. Inside the station shop I explained my situation to the young cashier.

'I'll introduce you to Juan,' said the girl. 'He lives next to the Community Welfare Centre. Maybe you can camp there?'

'That sounds great!' I replied.

She called over her assistant to take charge of the till and then led me outside and around to meet Juan, who was indeed charitable enough to let me sleep on the porch. What is more, the Centre was protected by a fenced compound and there was a hosepipe to shower under. Panama City lay less than two hours' riding in the morning – a "roll-in" as we'd say - so I went back to the shop to thank the girl and stayed a while, enjoying a cold beer she gave me from the fridge.

'It's illegal for you to drink on the premises,' she said, as I sat on a beer crate perched next to the counter, enjoying her donation to our cause.

'Sorry. Do you want me to take the beer outside?'

'No, I want you to tell me about the trip!' she said excitedly. 'I can't believe it!'

Hoping she understood my Spanish, I filled her in on some of the more interesting aspects, the way we lived, some of the people we had met and of course, the projects. She and her assistant seemed to take a shine to me and I won myself another beer. Each time a local came into the shop, the girl introduced me as the crazy cyclist. I must have shaken hands with at least 10 Panamanians. For some reason I forgot to write the girl's name in my diary so her identity remains a mystery but I remember she had come to Panama a year ago to join her family after finishing university in Seoul. We kept chatting another half-hour before I retreated to my porch and slept off 14kms and two cans of "Panama". Happy days.

*

I'm here!...Entering Panama City! The end of the North American continent!
No highway linked the narrow isthmus of land between Panama and Colombia, so reaching Panama City signalled moving on by boat or plane. I wanted to share the moment with the boys. I had missed them. Suddenly my mind started wondering again, to pieces of road as I reflected on eight months of hard graft, frustration, joy and happiness. Gobbler's Knob, the Golden Gate Bridge, along Venice Beach in LA, the epic climb to Tepíc and the scorched landscape of Honduras. It was all coming back. Gobbler's knob was a different life, a golden time of innocence where naivety gave us a true sense of adventure. Now we were changed riders, changed men, hardened and oh-so slightly alone. I wanted the naivety back, to regain the feeling of originality but it was 8,000 miles back up the road, tied to the temperate weather, golden leaves and wet grass of Canada, where we operated in fleeces and waterproofs and warmed our bodies with flasks of hot tea as Paps started yet another campfire. I loved those days. I wanted to speak English again with the outside world. I wanted to see Brian, Karen, Ray and Joan, to listen to their stories and feel their support and guardianship. That was my "home", Canada and its snow-drenched peaks, rugged country and wholesome people. This was Panama; a far cry from Mexico yet a mental and physical no-man's-land where very shortly I would be facing the toughest decision of the trip.

'Hello, you must be James,' said Joost, arriving to find me dismantling my bike outside Plan's office an hour later.

'Yes, hi!'

'My name is Joost; like "toast" but with a "Y" sound,' he said.

The boys had failed to find room on a bus from Costa Rica so luckily for me, Melanie, the Regional Health Advisor, offered some accommodation at her place down the road and even arranged for her Dutch husband to come pick me up. Joost showed me to my room, how to use the computer's phone line and most importantly of all, where the peanut butter was kept. They and their two young children had just arrived in Panama after spending nine years in Brazil. As such, Joost was busy unpacking a mountain of boxes and constructing an eight-metre long book cabinet made from Amazonian wood so heavy that I nearly dropped one of the two-foot long shelves on my foot. Although I tried to keep busy eventually I traipsed upstairs and I found myself facing a computer screen with my personal details filled out on Copa Airlines' website. All that remained was clicking the "Confirm Purchase" icon and I was going to Colombia. My finger hovered over the mouse.

- I can't believe I am even considering this. Am I really going? Am I really prepared to do this?

- I don't know.

- Think about it, will you regret not going?

- Yes.

- Confirm your ticket then.
- Yeah, but once I've clicked then I'm going, the ticket is non-refundable.
- But you want to go, right?
- Yeah.
- So click the icon.
- But what if I get kidnapped?
- There's no one forcing you to go. Is it worth the risk?
- Probably not.
- So don't go. That's why Paps and Martin decided against it.
- But I know I'll really enjoy it.
- Stop messing about, go downstairs and make a coffee!

My anxiety had reached fever pitch after meeting Gabriela Bucher, a Regional Manager working for Plan in Panama. A Colombian, Gabriela implored me not to go once she learnt my intentions.

'Look, these are some of the people who've been kidnapped in the last ten years,' she had said, leafing through a book of photos several hundred pages thick. 'Most of them spent years in the jungle, some of them are still missing.'

'I know what you are saying but I really want to go,' I replied. 'I met a French couple in Nicaragua who just cycled through without problems and I've spoken to others who have done it. I want to see the country and meet the people, they're meant to be the friendliest in South America.'

'The people are fantastic. I love my country but I wouldn't even drive where you are going to be cycling. No one drives, everyone flies, it's just too dangerous. Don't go, I'm begging you,' she pleaded. 'Many Colombians will tell you that the country's problems are behind it, that the kidnappings are a thing of the past. In truth, it is a lot better than it used to be but there are still more than 2,000 kidnappings a year and they are only the reported figures.'

Back in front of the computer screen, coffee in hand, I continued my self-imposed deliberation.

- So, what am I going to do?
- It's clear you want to go otherwise you wouldn't have entered your credit card details.
- True.
- So, press click then.
- Really?
- YES!
- "Click."

There was no going back.

Chapter 14

Carlos and Alonso

'A timid person is frightened before a danger, a coward during the time, and a courageous person afterward.'
Jean Paul Ritcher
Born Germany, 1763

Start Point: Cartagena, Colombia. Mile: 8,825. 23rd March.

Why was I so stubborn? Why didn't I listen to Gabriela? I shouldn't be here, I really shouldn't be here.

Arriving into the Atlantic port city of Cartagena, all had begun well. I was met at the airport by "Plan's man in Colombia," Juan Carlos Rolong. JC's official title was Regional Support Unit Administrator on the Atlantic Coast, but as far as I was concerned he was simply my own personal bodyguard. JC was dark-skinned and of slight build, his radiant smile and laid-back manner putting me instantly at ease and his lack of English only serving to bring us together as we relied on my dodgy Spanish. His first task was checking me into a very swish hotel in the Old town, run by Geoff, a British expat who had sailed through thirteen years ago, decided he liked the place and married a Colombian. JC and I toured the beautifully preserved colonial buildings that make up the original settlement and then stood atop the military fortress built soon after to protect it against marauding pirates, like Sir Francis Drake. I replaced a fractured rear rim and I also found the time for some promotional work with a local paper but most important of all was the time spent discussing my proposed route through Colombia with JC and his colleagues.

'We think it's best you stay away from the eastern part of the country,' said JC, as four of us pored over the map on his desk. 'Although it's mountainous, by heading directly south you'll avoid the worst areas, where the guerrillas are most active. There are some problem areas that you can't avoid, especially next to the Ecuadorian border. Go toward Sincelejo and then on to Medellín.'

I had decided not to camp, opting instead for cheap family-run lodgings but I was still going to be spending 10 to 12 hours a day on ghostly mountain passes, advertising myself to all and sundry as a westerner who's only defence to the paramilitaries was pedal power. If someone wanted to "pick me up" it would be like taking candy from a baby and judging from the response within the office, Gabriela was right. Some Colombians seemed totally unmoved that I was about to cycle 1500kms through their problem-fraught country. Others were beside themselves in disbelief. The problem was, I didn't know which opinions to trust and as far as I was concerned, I was already in Colombia and my bike was built so it made little difference. JC did his best to reassure me that the roads were much safer than in the past and that with luck I would be fine but he was clearly worried. When he announced that he and his assistant, José, were going to follow me out of Cartagena for the first 40kms, I started fretting even more.

Blimey, is it really that bad? Am I going to be kidnapped in the first 100 metres?

Saying goodbye to them both was much more emotional and poignant than I ever imagined. Handshakes turned into hugs and a real sense of apprehension descended upon me. Suddenly there were no more chances to back out. Waving them off, my anxiety whipped up like wildfire. Forty kilometres done, a mere 1460kms to the relative safety of the Ecuadorian border and now I was on my own. Every bush camouflaged a would-be kidnapper and every passing motorist made the following phone call.

'Hey Carlos, it's Alonso.'

'Hi, Alonso. How are things?'

'Good mate, good. Anyway, you'll never guess what I've just seen on the road toward Sincelejo.'

'What?'

'A silly little gringo pedalling a bicycle and towing a trailer!'

'Christmas has come early my friend! I'll ring the boys and organise a pick up. Don't lose sight of him.'

These thoughts were still running through my mind 24 hours later as I continued across the hot plain south and entered Sinceléjo. A puncture in my trailer tyre only made things worse. Now I was properly shitting myself. I pulled over next to a line of restaurants fronting the highway and got to work as at least a dozen young men surrounded me. Opening up my Bert bag to retrieve the repair kit, questions started flying...

'Where are you from?' came a question behind my right ear.

'England,' I said, without turning around.

'Where are you going?'

'Quito.'

(Laughter)...'Why?'

'I am travelling from Alaska to Argentina.'

'From where?'

'From Canada.'

'Are you on your own?'

'Yes.'

'How much does your bike cost?'

'Not much, it's old.'

'How many gears has it got?'

'Twenty-seven.'

'I like your tyres.'

They are going to pull a knife and take my bike...they are going to do something...

The men were so close that their feet and legs were visible as I concentrated on fitting the patch. I could even hear them playing with the brakes and gears and talking about the 14,000 odd kilometres showing on the computer.

You idiot! You've split the tube. OK, calm down and think...

For weeks we had experienced problems inflating our trailer tyres due to incompatibility between our pumps and tubes. Tubes bought in Latin America had varying valve designs, none of which our pumps liked and only very careful, patient work enabled air to be driven in. Forcing the issue split the tube. I took out my only spare, fitted it into the tyre but still couldn't marry the pump to the valve. I was panicking.

'There's a car mechanic over the road,' suggested an onlooker, as I continued to sweat all over the pavement. 'They have air.'

'Thank you. That's a good idea.'

I gathered up my gear and pushed the bike over to the mechanic who set to work straightaway. In my haste I had also split the spare.

'Is there a bike shop around here?' I asked, stressing at the thought of going into town.

'Yeah, it's in town,' said the young mechanic.

'How far is that?'

'About two kilometres. Leave your bike here and take a moto-taxi.'

- Yeah and by the time I get back you'll have stripped the bike, sold all my gear and be nowhere to be seen. Fat chance.

- At some point you have got to start trusting people. They aren't all kidnappers and thieves you know. Besides, you have little choice. What do you want to do, push your bike 2kms through town, advertising the fact that your bike doesn't work? No. So, do what he suggests...come on, you are wasting valuable time here.

'Ok, will you look after my bike for me?' I asked, more in hope than anything.

'No problem. It'll be safe here.'

The mechanic put two fingers into his mouth and whistled the attention of a lad a hundred metres away who was straddling a motorbike at the side of the road and very soon we were speeding off into town. I couldn't help thinking that I'd signed away my whole trip and that I'd soon be making a phone call to JC, asking him to come pick me up.

'Phew! It's still there,' I said to myself, upon returning to the garage and seeing my bike and trailer. 'Ok, fit the tube and get the hell out of here...'

Five kilometres later the tyre was flat and my hopes dashed. I kept thinking some greater being was telling me to pull the plug and get out whilst I still had the chance. I wanted to scream with frustration. Luckily though, I was still on the outskirts of Sinceléjo and within reach of another mechanic.

'Who is that?' I asked incredulously, as he finished repairing my tyre.

'It's the President,' he said, gazing at all the flashing lights. 'He's visiting the area.'

A huge motorcade of blacked-out heavily armoured 4x4s zoomed by, led by about ten police motorcycle riders. Only then did I notice foot soldiers marking the junction and hear helicopters overhead. It was the stroke of luck I was looking for. For the next couple of hours I had my very own army as I followed the President's route south. Every 200 metres or so, stood a soldier with an M16 assault rifle slung over his shoulder, bored to tears studying the traffic or watching some cow digesting meadow grass in an adjacent field. I, on the other hand, loved every minute of it!

*

Considering the dangers, my plan for Colombia was to blast it even more than Panama. Yet that idea was at the mercy of the Andean mountain range. Its scale was like nothing we had seen before and my route would take me right along its spine, 1000 kilometres of mind-blowing climbs and endless descents. For me, Colombia was going to be the mountain capital of the world, a test to make the eyes water and the bottom smart with pain. That test began on day four. Until then, I had experienced little more than ranch land filled with cattle; parts flooded by rivers gorged with heavy Andean rainfall. At most, it had been a rolling landscape but now the mountains had arrived and they looked serious. Their rugged, buttressed flanks rippled down from above, coated in lush green vegetation. They were immense. Following the Rio Cauca upstream for forty odd kilometres, hemmed in on both sides, I crossed over the mud-rich river to the other side of the valley. Then the road left the riverbank and headed straight into the devil's throat. It went vertical.

Nerves and anxiety ebbed away to a gentle simmer as the effort ratcheted up. I forgot about the bandits in the bushes and started enjoying myself. That first climb was an unbroken 34km ascent to the top of the Alto de Ventanas pass. The road kept going, occasionally giving me a glimpse of what was to come. I'd bury my head and stare at the tarmac, all the while motivating myself with mind games and thoughts. Through the cloud base I went, shirt off, sweating furiously with visibility at less than 50ft. The fog swirled around me, covering me in a thin film of water droplets, leaving me to guess how I was doing. I kept panting upward, passing ghostly shadows walking down the mountain dressed in winter clothing, carrying their load of firewood or food. Little shacks marked the roadside and occasionally the sound of a barking dog or human voice broke the silence of the whiteout. On more than one occasion I stopped to regain my strength by sitting on the wet verge, topless, as the odd farmer with his horse and cart trundled by. I kept thinking how odd it felt saying hello like it were a normal occurrence for either one of us.

Finally, I topped out and started to read more than single figures on the bike computer. I donned a long-sleeve top and began falling, out of the clouds and back to the verdant green landscape, along a ridgeline that gave me an awe-inspiring view, several thousand feet deep off to my right.

No drive-through McDonalds up here. This is the boonies, Greg. It's so fresh, not a mosquito in sight, no burning sun, just lush green pastures and I have the road to myself!

I was ecstatic even to the point of feeling a little guilty.

- *Stop enjoying yourself so much, you could be in the back of Alonso's truck in five minutes. Just get the job done and concentrate.*

- *Yeah, yeah but look at this place! I'm so glad I decided to come. It's so bloody satisfying.*

Months of underlying angst and doubt were being washed away. I sucked in a deep lungful of fresh mountain air, watched a farmer milking a cow in the field below me and then carried on my way. Nothing could stop me. I was doing it; I was cycling through Colombia, against all the doubters! Maybe such potential peril made the experience all the more heartfelt but being in the highlands, feeling that cold air on my cheeks and seeing such untainted beauty was why I had come. I knew it would feel different, that it would have a sense of foreboding and I was right. I wanted to remember every blade of grass, every smell, the sound of the bell dangling from the cow's neck. It was too overwhelming.

Yarumal was a lowly town nestled 2,265m up in the highlands, the most spectacularly green landscape I had ever seen. No jungle or thick forest, just open pastures, clumps of trees and solitary farmsteads. I wanted to get off the bike and roll around in the lush grass like a madman but thought better of it and pressed on into town, pulling over at the first opportunity opposite a man leaning against the wall of a grocer's.

'Stay on this road,' he began. 'It turns into a one-way system but don't worry just stay straight and it'll take you to the town square. There's a nice cheap hotel on the corner.'

'That's great, thanks very much!'

'Where are you from?'

'England…'

This chance meeting with a thirty something Colombian man turned out to be one of my best experiences in Colombia and for that matter, the trip, for as I made my way down the vicious slope toward the hotel my Colombian friend reappeared alongside me on his motorbike. This time his wife was with him.

'We want to invite you to stay with us tonight,' he said, as I struggled to keep the bike under control.

'Really? That's very kind of you,' I replied, hoping I'd translated the Spanish correctly.

'We'd like to take care of you.'

Wilson and his wife, Marcela, were roughly my age and had a young son who moved into their room to give me some privacy. They washed my clothes, I used the shower and then we trooped off in trousers and fleeces to Marcela's grandparents for dinner. It was dark and the mountain air chilly as Wilson presented me to Granny and Grandad.

'This is James,' said Wilson, proudly. 'He's cycling to Argentina!'

'No!'

'And he started with two friends in Alaska back in August! They are waiting for him in Quito whilst he cycles through Colombia, on his own!'

Everyone centred their gaze on me, expecting some humorous response but all I could muster in Spanish was, 'It's crazy, right?' It seemed to go down well enough and I was immediately ushered forward to a table and chair on the patio, while Granny went off to the kitchen. A little while later, whilst tackling a second serving of sweet corn and cheese soup with a side plate of rice and answering more questions about the trip, Marcela's father came in. He must have been the fittest looking 50 year old I had ever seen.

'I run cross-country marathons around these parts,' he told me.

'You're kidding?'

'It's hard work you know,' he said, thumping his chest. 'There are plenty of hills.'

Everyone thought I was crazy to be cycling through Colombia, everyone that is, except Marcela's grandad who thought it was hilarious and all good fun.

'You have just come through a dodgy area, James,' explained Wilson, as a massive lightning storm lit up the ridgeline like a bank of paparazzi flashbulbs. 'There are many sympathizers of the guerrillas' cause living around here.'

'Even here in Yarumal?'

'For sure. Everyone has to be very careful what they say in public.'

'Is the road dangerous from here to Medellín, then?'

'It can be but once you are past Cali it's much safer until you get nearer the border. You must be very careful then.'

We finished dinner and walked down the hill so that Marcela could introduce me to her mother and sister and then to round off the night I offered to buy my hosts a couple of beers in a bar they knew in town. It had been a day to cherish, a day that had turned my view of Colombia upside down.

'Thank you so much for everything,' I said, packing away the Atlético Nacional team shirt Wilson gave me the following morning.

'This is for your son,' I said, presenting him with a Plan baseball cap JC had given me. 'You and your family have been very kind to me.'

'It was great to meet you, James,' said Wilson. 'Be careful and call me if you have any problems.'

'I will. Thanks again. Bye!'

'Bye!'

I was a tad forlorn as I clipped into my pedals. I'd been looked after so well, I didn't want to head back out into bandit country. Reluctantly, I waved goodbye and disappeared into the lush green hills.

'Wilson and his family as I say goodbye'

*

Coming down from Alto de Las Minas, a 3,500m high summit, I stopped at a roadside café to fill up my water bottles and was offered a coffee by two gentlemen in their forties, dressed in colourful Lycra, out enjoying a Sunday morning ride. They had just tackled the climb themselves, so we had much to talk about.

'That was hard work,' I commented.

'We climb this pass at least twice a month,' said one of them, bursting my bubble. 'This is the highest point on the Pan Americana in Colombia.'

'How long do I descend for now?' I asked.

'At least 40km!' came the reply. 'And then it stays flat.'

They were right. The descent down into the next valley was vast. I couldn't stop grinning although I did fret that my brake blocks might give way at any moment. As I squealed my way down the mountain, overtaking trucks and trying to keep the speed under 40kmph, I kept spotting opportunistic kids heading in the other direction, clinging to the back of trucks that were growling their way up.

Cheeky buggers…Ingenious! Wow, there goes another one! And another!

I kept spotting them, one hand on the truck the other on the handle bar. Their ingenuity reminded me of a woman we had seen in Nicaragua cycling with one child wrapped around her neck, one child on the crossbar and another sat on the handlebar.

I love this place! I love it!

*

Getting lost in Santiago de Cali, one of Colombia's most notorious cities, wasn't the brightest thing I'd ever done. In fact, I soon found out that I'd been cycling down the wrong road for 10kms. The shantytown on both sides of me was an obvious concern but I was more annoyed at the lost time. My mistake had cost me an hour and it was all the more significant today as I was aiming for Popayán some 750m above Cali and 140kms away. I swung the bike around and hit overdrive. My map told me nothing of what lay in between because I was using a few pages ripped out of a tourist guide, so it was a case of just cycling like a madman. Like usual I kept calculating and recalculating my progress, stopping only to periodically chomp down some food. With Popayán still 30kms away and the light failing, I was extremely fortuitous to stumble across Piendamó, a tiny mountain village with no more than a shop, bakery and most importantly of all, a basic hostel. It was a close call and I lambasted myself for it. My arse was also complaining. Apparently, it didn't like the blisters and sores that had started to blemish it's otherwise conditioned form. Indeed, the only way of shutting it up was to lie on the bed with my legs bent at the knee.

Me: Now, is that better?
My arse: Much better thank you. Have you got any cream to take the edge off?
Me: I'm afraid not.
My arse: Can you go and buy some?
Me: Have you seen where we are staying tonight? There's nothing here.
My arse: You could at least go and have a look!
Me: Do you want to be kidnapped?
My arse: Maybe. At least I'll get a rest from that bloody saddle!
Me: Yeah, whatever!
My arse: Yeah, bothered!

My arse had a point. The size and sheer number of climbs for so many days on end were taking their toll. So many times I wanted to explode, to rant, to scream and throw a tantrum at the sight of yet another 25km brute but without an audience, what was the point? Very quickly I just put the desperation to one side and got on with it.

Luckily, I persuaded my arse to cycle with me to Popayán the next morning and I treated it to a hotel in the centre of town. The cool mountain air and a stroll around the whitewashed colonial architecture gave me plenty of time to consider the final leg of the journey. I was nearing the border. Ecuador was a mere 340kms away yet those kilometres accounted for the most dangerous section. I sat in the main square, sipping a coffee and reflected on what had passed. I hadn't seen a single foreigner since leaving Cartagena and felt privileged to have passed through such a devastatingly beautiful country. Colombia felt special, because of its problems. I was drawn to it, captivated by the generosity and warmth of its people, yet, when my front tyre punctured midway through the next day I became acutely aware of my vulnerability and started panicking like I had done after leaving JC and José. The road was ghostly quiet, too quiet. Ferreting around for my repair kit, two men suddenly appeared out of the scrub a hundred yards away, one of them holding a huge machete. My heart skipped a beat, then another when they turned and saw me working on the tyre. Carlos and Alonso finally had their chance. They started walking toward me and my stomach began twisting and turning. I felt sick. My mind raced at a hundred miles an hour but I thought of nothing. They were close enough to be heard. I had nowhere to turn, nothing to offer.

- *What do I do?*
- *You've got one tyre off and your trailer's detached, you're screwed.*
- *Shit. What shall I say?*
- *Does it matter?*
- *No.*

'Hola, Como estás?' asked one of them, enthusiastically.

'I'm fine thanks,' I blurted, half inclined to start whimpering like a spaniel.

'Where are you travelling to?'

'To Quito.'

'It must be heavy, your trailer,' said one of them, pointing to my 20 kilos of gear.

'It makes things harder.'

I was waiting for one of them to get serious and tie my wrists together but it never came. 'Would you like some food? We have some jalabe. Here, try,' he said.

I took a gooey block of something off the end of his razor sharp machete and started chewing. It was sun dried sugarcane syrup, incredibly sweet but pleasing nonetheless. 'It's nice!' I said, predictably.

'Take some with you,' he replied, opening a plastic bag and dumping in several large pieces.

So much for my prejudice. These guys had no intention of harming me whatsoever. All they wanted to do was quiz the random foreigner during a break from the toil of the fields and they even had the kindness to pass on a little goodwill. My heightened state was clouding my judgement and I'll tell you why. As well as listening to the opinions of people like Gabriela, before coming to Colombia I had spent many hours reading posts given on travel forums over the internet. One of them came in response to a claim that travellers can have a trouble-free experience in Colombia. My clarifications appear in non-italics. Gomezman5 writes...

Why would you even consider risking your life in a country that is at the top of the list for civilian kidnappings? 40% of the landmass is not even controlled by the legitimate Colombian government but is in fact controlled by the FARC, Colombia's largest and oldest guerilla/terrorist organisation. I was born in Colombia and I have family in Colombia yet, I cannot, will not pretend that all is well. Cali is no place for a foreigner to live. While the central area of the city is reasonably safe, if you drive only 45 minutes outside to towns like Florida, Buga (I cycled through Buga blissfully unaware of who might be watching), *and Yumbo, you are entering territory completely controlled by the FARC. In other words, you cannot rely on any local, legitimately established government authority to protect you from the guerilla threat. If you are there more than a few hours, you will be identified by locals and reported to kidnappers. Everyone from the initial informant to the local kidnappers (who sell you to the guerilla kidnappers) will be paid. If you don't have family* (in Colombia), *you don't have a compelling need to go there.*

What was different about cycling through Colombia was not the petty crime, robberies or corruption within the police or security services (which were just as likely if not greater in parts of Mexico and Central America) but the kidnap risk. During some of the quieter moments when the road was empty, I thought I had applied to the following job advertisement.

"Terrorist/Paramilitary guerrilla organisation seeks well-mannered pale-skinned western traveller, preferably without any existing medical conditions to cycle a fully-loaded bicycle and trailer along ghostly quiet mountain passes for the purposes of kidnap training. Please note: This is a one off event. Those candidates who feel they fit the above role need not apply, as we'll find you! Benefits include chauffeur-driven 4x4 transfer to your secluded post-kidnap jungle hideaway."

This is the reason why I respected so much Martin and Paps's decision not to go. Notwithstanding my humble western status, targets don't come much easier than me. So, deep down why did I go and why did I continue cycling on day two when a nappy would have been more useful than a bicycle? Because I kept thinking back to a pair of French cyclists we had met in Honduras and how utterly relaxed they seemed about their experience in Colombia. That, and the feedback I'd got from one or two cyclists I'd contacted over the net. It was they that had given me the faith, not the travellers who'd written, "Loved it and couldn't work out what all the fuss was about."

I was lucky, Colombia had treated me well. In fact, the closest I'd come to any real harm was sticking my finger in a ceiling fan whilst getting dressed one morning. Instead, a sack full of incredible experiences were mine to cherish. JC and José, Geoff at Casa La Fe, Wilson and his family, the three young lads who insisted on filling my water bottles one lunchtime or the father and daughter who pulled over to buy me a cold drink and give me US$1, Colombia had done its utmost to look after me. Soaked to the skin and freezing cold as I stood waiting to be stamped into Ecuador the emotion of it all just hit me like a freight train. I wanted a hug from one of the boys. I wanted one of them to look after me, to push my bike into an awaiting hostel and tell me that the trip was over, that we had reached the end of the line. Only later, when sat on the end of my bed did the full weight of the last 16 days boil over. I broke down and sobbed like a child, wiping away tears with my towel. They kept flowing and flowing until my face was red and my eyes bloodshot. Solo cycling was a different game. Now and only now was I beginning to understand the loneliness but incredible sense of achievement felt by cyclists such as Jason. Colombia had been an overwhelming experience.

*

'Is Anthony here, Claus?' I asked.

'No, he left two days ago.'

Claus had half the hostel under renovation so it was virtually empty, giving us the opportunity to sit on the back patio in the last of the afternoon sun. We took a moment to saviour the view, beer in hand. Quito looked resplendent, a dash of white against a dark green Andean bowl of mountains that encircled us in all directions.

'So are you going to chase after Anthony?' asked Claus, now aware of my predicament.

'I'm not sure. Maybe I'll stay and help you paint the breakfast room!' I replied.

'I could do with some help.'

'Either that or fly to Buenos Aires.'

And that's precisely what I did.

Chapter 15

Chicken and Rice

'Nothing amuses me more than the easy manner with which everybody settles the abundance of those who have a great deal less than themselves.'
Jane Austen
Born England, 1775

Start Point: Quito, Ecuador. Mile: 9,970. 21st April.

I followed the hostel assistant at Casa Helbling up the stairs to meet someone I recognised.
'Hello mate!' I said, breaking into a smile.
'Hello old chap!' replied Martin.
'Long time no see!' I continued, as we gave each other a hug.
'Too bloody long mate!'
'How are you then?' I asked. 'Ready to let it rip?'
'You have no idea. Let's get this trip done.'
After finally getting to Panama City, Martin and Paps had parted company, Paps flying to Quito whilst Martin toured around Panama and then met Sam in Miami when she flew in with work. I, meanwhile, had cycled through Colombia and flown to Buenos Aires to see Carolina for a week. Time off the bike reminded us there was more to life than living in a tent and following a white line like some crazed maniacs. We wanted the trip done.
'It was so depressing getting on that plane to come back,' I admitted. 'I need to move on with my life.'
'The way I see it, if we go for it we'll be done in three months.'
The next day we began that quest and started chasing down Paps's twelve-day head start. Cycling out of Quito and south through some impressive mountain scenery, we spotted the peak of Volcán Cotopaxi and then negotiated a nasty 10km climb before plunging off the Andean shelf. The 80km descent took us from a cool 15°C through the cloud forest to sea level and 35°C with 90° humidity. Jungle now flanked us on both sides.
'Two hours that took us!' Martin screamed. 'That was awesome!'
I crossed over the road to where a number of people were selling fruit from some poorly-made wooden stalls and returned with a huge bunch of bananas.
'How are we going to eat all of those?' laughed Martin. 'You must have at least twenty there!'
'But they only cost me 25 cents!'
Southern Ecuador turned out to be a mixed bag. Our route took us through mile after mile of banana plantations, broken only by the odd piece of ranch land. Roadside workers wielded huge machetes to keep the jungle at bay and

dogs risked their lives by snoozing on the hot tarmac. We slept in a recreation ground and then on a football field, before taking the advice of some locals the third night by moving into the local police station. At first it seemed like a good decision as we were given an empty shell facing the highway and access to an extremely basic and filthy toilet block. Two lads appeared, wanting help with their English homework but then things turned sour as our room transformed itself into a torture chamber. We lay on top of our thermarests, sweating like we were at some beach resort, listening to lorries' engine braking for the police road check 30 feet away. By 1am we resorted to moving outside behind the building, preferring to take our chances with the bugs and snakes. As if on cue, some dogs started barking in the adjoining property.

How does anyone get any sleep around here with this racket going on? Martin, stop pretending to be asleep, I know you're not asleep.

'Pisst, are you awake mate?'

'Of course I am,' said Martin, glumly.

'Ahh! What time is it?'

'1.45am.'

'We are gonna be tired tomorrow.'

'Yep.'

'I wonder what time the cockerels will start?'

'Don't joke about that.'

Sure enough they started at 6am, giving us no option but to saddle up half an hour later with less than four hours sleep under our belts. Our change in mindset didn't falter. Despite the punishing heat and humidity, the flat road gave us all the encouragement we needed and the miles just flew by. In the first 5 days from Quito we covered 425 of them and got over the Peruvian border. Gone were the banana plants, now we rode along open stretches of an increasingly scorched landscape as the humidity was replaced by a dry heat, courtesy of the Humboldt Current, a cold Pacific Ocean current that deprives the entire length of the Peruvian coast, as well as much of Chile's northern coast, of any precipitation. The result is a 2,500-mile long coastal desert, where sand dunes and bare rock plunged straight into the ocean. We were going to cycle every mile of it.

'Peru reminds of Mexico you know,' I remarked a few days later as we cycled side by side.

'Why?'

'It's hot, poor. Rubbish is strewn everywhere and there are stray dogs shagging each other.'

'True but at least people don't "pisst" you like they did in Mexico.'

'That was so annoying!'

'I take it you are not that fond of Peru then?'

'When we came over the border I quite liked it, I thought all the tooting we got from the drivers was good fun but it's wearing thin now. A truck blowing its horn in your ear doesn't grab me. No one seems to take pride in anything.'

'I know what you mean.'

I had been to Peru before when I was in Bolivia. On those occasions I was backpacking my way around, sitting on buses and spending most of my time in quaint colonial mountain towns such as Cúzco and Arequípa. Being on the bike was something completely different though. We were seeing the forgotten places up close and personal, not the ones promoted in the tour brochures. Travelling by bicycle also gave us the sights, smells and first hand interaction with local life that just passes you by on a coach. The environment made it seem all the more real. In truth, some parts seemed wholly unreal as mile after mile, day after day, white, pink, purple, grey and black rock melted together in a kaleidoscope of colour to form a haunting theatre for cycling. We climbed and descended through valleys and across open plains, the wind stinging our arms and legs with sand. We'd stop to marvel at Mother Nature's splendour only to cycle into the next village and see rubbish lining the highway and half-built mud houses crumbling back to dust.

*

'What the hell are we doing out here?' I asked Martin.

'I have been asking myself that for nine months!'

'Seriously, this wind is bloody crazy. We've had days of this and there are 500 miles before we get to Lima!'

A headwind each afternoon was grinding us down. It was especially severe in the more exposed sections where it slammed into our chests and faces, slowing us to less than 10kmph. I wanted to give up. I wanted to sit at the roadside and treat the wind like a petulant child, turn my back on it and wait for it to stop screaming at me. Why should I have to put up with this? Was it not hard enough? I thought of Paps, of his personal struggle and it galvanised me to make it to Chiclayo, another oasis town where field workers lined the highway with bricks of mud, cut and laid to dry in the sunshine. No sooner had we left the shelter than the wind start up again. As was normal, we took out our trailer flags and bitched.

'This is going to be fun,' I said, with a huge amount of sarcasm.

'It's completely open by the looks of it,' said Martin, noting the arrow straight road ahead of us.

'Let's just see how many miles we can get.'

I led off into the wind, the sun low in the sky over our right shoulders turning the desert a deep red. We were alone again, head down, battling our invisible nemesis.

'Flags out as the wind whips up'

I'm sure it's even stronger than yesterday and we've only done 2km since we took the flags out. I've had enough of this. Fuck the desert. Fuck Peru. I hate this fucking wind, my fucking diarrhoea.

Martin was a few hundred metres back, head down. We kept going another five tortuous kilometres before pulling over, exhausted and dizzy with the effort.

'Where are we going to camp, mate?' I asked, with an air of desperation.

Martin and I scanned the featureless desert on both sides. 'It doesn't look good does it?' he said. 'And the sun is going down fast.'

'Looks like there's a hut further down on the left. Do you see it?' I said, pointing into the distance. 'Let's check it out.'

Even before arriving we knew the news was bad. The hut was the gatehouse to a landfill site that covered the desert for hundreds and hundreds of metres in human and domestic waste. Yet we went to investigate nonetheless.

'Oh, dear,' said Martin.

I joined him at the gatehouse and stood in silence, reeling from the stench of urine. 'We won't be staying here.'

The mud floor was full of empty beer crates and infested with flies so we returned to the roadside and scanned the desert once more, hoping for a miracle. For some reason Martin and I had rather unwisely decided against a map for Northern Peru so we had no idea of what lay ahead but the road continued for as far as the eye could see. It was all but featureless.

'They say this is Air Force bombing land and to beware of mines,' I remarked, translating some signs planted a few metres off to the right of the highway. 'How about we tuck in behind those small dunes over there?' I suggested, pointing out beyond the signs.

'You're kidding right? You just said there might be mines. I don't fancy it, mate.'

Martin was right, I just couldn't contemplate cycling back toward Chiclayo. We were out of daylight, needed protection from the wind and there was nothing but a fly-infested hut, a 1000-hectare rubbish tip or a minefield to choose from. Eventually we succumbed, turned the bikes around and accelerated up to 40kmph, courtesy of the instant tailwind. I was gutted. We kept going 8kms until we got back to a petrol station and took refuge behind a wall, a few metres upwind of a noisy and foul-smelling diesel generator that powered the forecourt lights. This was the best we could hope for. Stars filled the night sky and Chiclayo glowed in the distance a few kilometres away. It was the 1st May and Paps's 30th birthday. Our hunger for miles had cut his lead to around five days.

'What a day,' commented Martin.

'People don't understand,' I opened up.

'They can't possibly. How do you explain the day we have just had? You can't.'

'If Paps has cycled this I have got so much respect for him. I couldn't imagine doing this solo.'

'Do you think he cycled it or got the bus?'

'I'd be sorely tempted to get the bus, at least to Trujillo.'

'Me too.'

'Sometimes I think he cycled it and then the wind blows and I think, it's just too soul-destroying.'

Paps's recounts his time on the road to Lima…

The decision to cycle alone had been decided for me by the other two. It amuses me that at the time I didn't twig cycling alone through one of the toughest places on the planet signified a huge personal challenge. Yet, whilst I was on my own, it was precisely that sentiment that kept me going.

"Don't give up. Don't stop, no matter how slow you're going. Fight the isolation, fight the heat, fight the wind. Use your Spanish. What would Martin do? What would Wils do? Don't be afraid. Don't give up…Don't stop,"

I literally spent whole days repeating these sentiments to myself in a continuous effort to keep moving. Then there were the nights; where to camp to remain hidden and not be spotted when leaving the road; trying to sleep with every noise magnifying my constant paranoia. Your job is to imagine that each day is long, hard and tiring. You are dirty, hungry and fed up with the cards you've been dealt. You have no one to bounce ideas off or to rely on when the weather takes a turn for the worse or the map doesn't show the fork in the road you have just encountered. Now start repeating all those feelings in your mind, the ones of being alone, isolated and often a little afraid; day after day after day. If you manage all that, then you may be on the way to being in my shoes.

Five days later our love-hate relationship with the desert hadn't changed one bit. We were failing to gain more than a few kilometres at a time before resting and my spirits couldn't even be lifted by our never-ending supply of biscuits. Today, I had other things on my mind. Pulling up for another break Martin got straight to the point.

'What's the matter, mate?' he asked, 'You have been stewing all day about something.'

'I can't stop thinking about the wedding.'

'That's not good.'

'I just can't let it go. I'm still so angry about it. They have no idea how hurt I am. I mean, look at where we are! Stuck on a 10km hill in the Peruvian desert, sweating like a pig. It sickens me.'

'You have got to let it go, mate.'

'I can't.'

'It's you that is suffering not them. Like you said a few days' ago, you can't expect anyone to understand what we are going through out here. It's not their fault.'

'It's not about that. Mum and Ted said they would support my decision not to return. They didn't. It's as simple as that.'

'It's over mate.'

'Exactly, it's forgotten about, like it didn't happen. They just go back to their lives. I thought they supported me, that they were really proud of what I was doing. This trip took two years to plan for Christ's sake. I quit my job. Doesn't that register with them?' Martin remained silent as I kept ranting above the thundering trucks. 'Obviously I would want to go to my sister's wedding under normal circumstances but this is not a normal year! I set out to complete something seriously special…'

'And you are going to,' said Martin, interjecting.

'Hopefully I will but the uniqueness, the special integrity has gone now. It's been destroyed. I am on a completely different trip and feel very alone. I feel cheated. That's why I went to Buenos Aires, because the integrity just isn't there anymore. You weren't back in England being polite to people who haven't got a fucking clue what they are talking about or understand what we are trying to achieve or how we had been living for five months. I didn't belong there.'

'You need to find a way of dealing with it mate because it is tearing you apart.'

My barny on that hillside was an explosion of frustration, something I had revisited a number of times. The anger rose during harder times perhaps when we were rationing food, when the wind blew or after two or three days of climbing. Downtrodden, my mind would wander back to the pressure that had been placed on me to return. Underneath the "We understand but do it for your sister" comments, one message came through. "Say what you want, you have to be there."

'I'm sorry you had to hear all that again. I feel a lot better now,' I said.

'That's what I'm here for.'

'Shall we get going?'

We were one day's ride from Lima, where Paps awaited. Our self-inflicted schedule had created an alarming appetite. The following is what we *each* put away on the 129km day into Lima;

4 Jam rolls (breakfast)
2 Ham rolls (post breakfast)
4 Rolls filled with chicken, ham, cheese or fritter (morning rations)
1 Plate of chicken and rice served with chips (1st lunch)
1 Plate of chicken, rice and vegetables (2nd lunch)
36 Biscuits
2 Bananas
4 Tangerines
1 Bowl of soup with roll
1 Portion of chips
1 Bowl of ice cream
6 Chocolate cakes
(Oh, and a bottle of rum between us)

When we didn't eat well, life became much harder. We had completed the 1,200-mile journey from Quito in 17 days. Eating worked.

'A rare smile during our struggle along the Peruvian coast'

*

'I've got so much respect for you,' I remarked to Paps, as soon as I saw him. 'Martin and I were bitching like hell, you should have heard us! The wind!'

'Don't worry, I was swearing constantly!' grinned Paps. 'The section between Trujillo and Chimbote was horrific!'

'It's great to see you though!' I said, slapping him on the arm.

'And you.'

Seeing Paps was the injection I needed. His road-rash and injuries had healed well, so too my feelings of anger. I couldn't escape the feeling of responsibility for what he had endured by getting to Lima but there was a freshness and sparkle to our banter and he too was desperate to finish the trip. Rebuilding our relationship again started by filing out of Lima, the first time together since the morning of Paps's crash, eight weeks and 2,700 miles back up the road. We posted 88 miles and followed that up with 101 miles. Our exuberance continued as we past the thousand foot high sand dunes at Ica and onwards through the Nazca Lines where we lost 2,000ft of elevation by returning to the coast. Then the dreaded wind hit and voices started whispering at me from within.

- I don't believe this, I am at the front, again. Again! They are chatting and I am killing myself. I am sick of it. Martin hasn't been at the front for days! Right, that's it, I'm slowing down, fuck them…Why should I do all the work?

Less than a minute later Martin's shadow drew past me. 'I'll lead for a bit mate,' he said. 'It must be hard work in this wind.'

- I take it all back. I feel better already.

I rode at the back for a while, tucked in behind Martin and Paps, enjoying the lull in effort. Occasionally, I could even afford to freewheel and take in the blue and white surf breaking only a hundred metres to our right. Then I started feeling sorry for Martin.

- Poor chap, he looks to be really struggling. Go on, do the right thing, go to the front and give him a break.

I hit the gas, went past Paps who was struggling with his knee and pulled in front of Martin. 'I'll take over for a while, mate,' I said, as I felt the full force of the headwind.

'Thanks,' came the reply.

Before long Nice Wils had disappeared and Evil Wils was again cursing the faceless shadows of my riding partners. This pattern of riding, one where I led, Paps sat in the middle and Martin brought up the rear had been set in stone even before entering Canada. I can't explain why but for 70% of the journey we rode like this. It wasn't because I was the strongest rider and it wasn't because Martin was lazy. Indeed, sometimes I never led all day or perhaps for only 10 miles, and any one of us could be found at the front cranking up the pace. Martin was especially famous for it. On more than one occasion, Paps and I found ourselves clinging on to the back of his trailer wheel – out of pride – when the computer read Distance: 70+ miles, Speed: 20+ mph, yet, the habit of me leading had become so ingrained that most mornings I instinctively pushed my bike to the front, the boys took up their positions and off we went. I felt quite happy there when the wind wasn't blowing. It meant I had a clean road in front of me and I didn't have to worry as much as the back marker when on tight narrow roads filled with fast moving traffic. I could dictate the pace, where we stopped and I liked getting the miles done. Paps commented that having me at the front ensured a modicum of progress because although I wasn't fast, crucially I didn't dawdle.

*

'I feel dizzy, I need to eat something,' said Martin, pulling up next to me.

'OK, I'll open that tin of tuna and make a sandwich' I offered, adding, 'Yauca is only a couple of kilometres away now.'

'I am shattered.'

Yauca was a small town stuck in the middle of the desert, our reward for four nights under the stars and a total of 576kms on the clock. It was a place to rest up for a day, get a hot shower, watch cable TV and eat plenty of junk food. Well, that's what we thought. In nine months of riding, Yauca was easily our biggest disappointment and let me assure you, we had stayed in some frightful places. The owner of the town's only hostel was a guy in his seventies who promptly turfed out his children and all their kids to make space for us and our cash. We each got a room or more accurately a cell furnished with a bed and a bedside table. That was it. No fan. No curtains. No nail to hang clothes on. No lamp. No TV. No plug points to recharge our electronics, just a bare light bulb hanging from the ceiling and a barred window to stare through. The cold-water shower worked but hadn't been cleaned in months. Strangely though, there was hardly a murmur from anyone. Resigned to our fate we just got on with it.

'Snaking our way through the desert'

On the roof was the laundry, where buckets and a sink filled with water sat in a small wooden shack. The view told the real story though. To all intents and purposes we were in a medieval town. Half-built houses made of baked mud, scraps of wood and plastic sheeting gave way to lifeless desert. Only one street was paved and children ran around shoeless. Dogs barked, people sat in doorways and clouds of dust and litter danced through the streets on gusts of wind. This was Yauca.

The poverty we had ridden through since December had reduced my mind to a pulp of constant resignation every time another example hit me square between the eyes. Peru, certainly coastal Peru, was the epitome of poverty. "What *is* this place?" I thought to myself from the rooftop laundry. After six months I had reached saturation point. The miles, the constant tiredness and stress, combined with my cotton wool upbringing meant I could stomach no more. I wanted out. The thing was, Peru had plenty more in store for us yet.

Chapter 16

"Pull your shorts down"

'Happiness is nothing more than good health and a bad memory.'
Albert Schweitzer
Born German, 1875

Start Point: Yauca, Peru. Mile: 11,490. 18th May.

Getting to Chile's northern most city was an act of desperation. At least one of us had been ill for the previous ten days with varying degrees of diarrhoea, nausea and fever as we tried frantically to get out of Peru. The latest attack had had a massive effect on me as my appetite and strength disappeared and I spent every food break squatting behind a rock with my roll of toilet paper. To make matters worse, we had chosen to take what we'd been told was a well-maintained gravel road along the coast in an attempt to cut the distance to the border and avoid some massive climbs on the Pan Americana to the north. Yet the road was abysmal. We should have guessed that 'well-maintained' meant 'it existed' and nothing more. We took an almighty battering as we made our way at a snail's pace along the 80km section in a day and a half. 100kms short of the border and with me unable to retain any liquids, a decision was made to get me to the nearest point of decent medical aid - Arica.

'Struggling to Arica; after 139kms we prepare for a desert camp without food or water'

For a short while all seemed to go swimmingly as I successfully obtained the services of a minivan driver. We loaded on the bikes and trailers, squeezed in and set off all be it in the opposite direction to a mud hut where a chap poured in a few litres of fuel from a watering can as the driver kept the engine running.

Come on, let's just get out of here…

We set off again, this time heading toward the border with the window down and a cool breeze flooding my lungs. As I started to dream of fresh sheets and the magic of modern day drugs, incredibly, (well it would have been incredible had we been anywhere apart from Peru or possibly Mexico) we got lost. Our man had lived his whole life 100kms from the Chilean border and forged a living as a *taxi driver* but didn't have a clue where he was! At one point, he flagged down an oncoming truck to ask for directions and was told abruptly to turn around and take a road we had past several miles back. I was too ill to care. In the spirit of all things Peruvian though, once on the right road and obviously bored, our driver decided a shortcut was in order. 'It takes 20kms off the journey,' he assured me. Suddenly we were on a gravel road full of ruts, potholes and off camber bends and my stomach was doing cartwheels.

Why can't he just drive on the paved road? Now we are doing 30kmph instead of 100kmph. Why does every Peruvian we meet want to either rip us off or just be fucking stupid? What is it with these people?

For a brief moment I considered the merits of throwing him out of the car and continuing on ourselves. We continued on another forty-five minutes, all the while my stomach and head bracing themselves for the next pothole. Then Paps woke from his siesta.

'Where the hell is this guy taking us, Wils?'

'I can see the main highway now,' I commented.

We approached the junction only for the driver to hit me with, 'The border is only ten kilometres in that direction. I'll leave you here.'

I'll leave you here? What the hell is he on about?

This wasn't a favour he was doing us out of the kindness of his little Peruvian heart. We had agreed the drop point and the cost, a princely sum for this guy, plus he knew that at least one of us needed medical attention. 'The price was to take us to the border,' I said.

'Yes but it's downhill all the way from here.'

There was no way we were parting company but all the same I was lost for words. I frantically searched my brain and quickly remembered some grammar I had learnt whilst in Buenos Aires back in April. 'Por favor, no seas Peruano.' 'Please, don't be Peruvian.' The driver seemed to get the message and drove on. I stared out of the window, daydreaming empty thoughts as the vast expanse of the desert rushed by. 'Hang in there, not long now,' I said to myself. Peru had given us the full treatment, maybe more so than Mexico. I stared at the rust on the inside of the door for a while and then noticed a gigantic Chilean flag fluttering in the distance. 'We are here, we are here.'

The look of shear disbelief and then indifference on my face when the driver asked for a tip was enough to make him turn around, get back in his car and drive off. His antics were then replaced by an over elaborate border crossing procedure which began by getting a form from, of all people, another taxi driver. Eventually we got through, prepared the bikes for the 20km ride and I made use of the toilets, again.

'It's so good to be out of that shit-hole,' I offered, with what I thought was the appropriate level of blue language. 'Get me to a hospital.'

'Have you noticed that the cars don't toot and no one is whistling at us?' remarked Martin.

'It's absolutely brilliant.'

'Only one more border crossing to the bottom lads!'

*

There was complete chaos at the A&E registration desk. Indeed for a brief moment I thought I'd stepped back over the border. The wannabe patients had decided against an orderly queuing system in favour of an all out scrum.

God this hospital must be really good.

Slowly but surely I got to the front. Disappointingly though, the clerk just took my details and told me to wait my turn. Before I knew it an hour had slipped by as I watched Chileans watch me, their curiosity heightened by the fact that I was still in my cycling gear and my hair matted from three days in the desert.

'Wisun!' shouted a nurse.

I was ushered through a set of doors I had been monitoring and put in front of a nurse who took my heart rate and blood pressure. Three minutes later I was back at my chair in the waiting room.

This could be a long night. I bet Martin and Paps are eating. They'll at least be clean and have their kit organised. I wonder what food they are lining up? I feel like shit. I bet our taxi driver is clean. I know he is rich. Why does that chap with no front teeth keep staring? Please, I need a doctor.

It wasn't long before I got my wish and I had one examining me in what appeared to be a corridor in the staff's gossip quarters. All manner of people whizzed back and forth, dressed in different coloured uniforms, carrying charts and reports. After I gave another run down of my symptoms the Doc began peering into my mouth and prodding my belly. Then he disappeared and came back ten minutes later with a colleague, who did no more than look at me and continue listening to the opinion of his associate. I had stopped trying to translate by this point but once my doctor was addressing just me, I perked up. All I could decipher from the first pass of his unbelievably fast Chilean Spanish was that they were going to run some tests on me. The quizzical look on my face triggered him to repeat what he had just said but on the second pass I only upgraded 'test' to 'getting a sample.' Then he gesticulated with his hands in a way that needed no translation whatsoever.

Oh bloody hell; they are going to stick something up my bottom. Is this really necessary? I mean, I've been ill before but no one needed to venture anywhere near that region.

The Doc told me to relax, wait for the nurse, and then promptly disappeared.

- *They wouldn't be doing the test if it wasn't necessary.*

- *Yeah, right. That's why all those nurses have suddenly started laughing. The joke's on you!*

A nurse appeared and although I detected no response to my, "Hello, how are you?" I continued to presume she was kind-hearted and was going to treat me gently. She muttered something about an injection and then came over to administer it. I looked away, felt the sharp jab and then relaxed as she left me in peace. I felt dreadful and wanted some painkillers for my stomach and head but fifteen minutes passed by before the nurse reappeared and got straight to the point.

'Turn and lie down on the bed please.'

'OK,' I said, trying to make eye contact.

'No. Lie on your front.'

Oh god, this is it. She looks terrifying, look at the size of her forearms!

'Pull your shorts down....that's it.'

Losing a bit of pride was the least of my worries, yet every nurse in the bloody building was getting a look at my freckled tan line and white bottom. Why on earth couldn't she shut the door? On went a pair of surgical gloves and out came a pair of cotton buds. Peru was getting the last laugh.

'Argghh!' I yelped, as the nurse used her powerful forearms to forage away with the cotton bud.

Shit that hurt. Go easy love, I've had a long day too. I hope the kids in El Salvador appreciate this!

'Argghh!'

The second bud hit its mark. I winced at the thought of further action but was told to pull up my shorts and sit upright on the bed, something I found very difficult. My dignity had reached an all time low. Not even squatting behind a tree trunk as wide as a cricket stump or a bush with no leaves was as bad as this. It was the trip. Just like getting forced off the road by dubious driving skills, being offered women or armed protection, sleeping on restaurant floors or squatting in full view of two young lads tending to their herd of goats. It was what the trip was.

My next dose of treatment involved being hooked up to an IV drip and pushed through the corridors in a wheelchair to join three other patients fighting their own private battles. The orderly placed me on a bed opposite an elderly gentleman breathing erratically with the aid of an oxygen mask. Upon my arrival he gave me the thumbs up and a broad smile, which then morphed into a coughing fit and sizeable production of phlegm. Dribbling his mouthful of mucus into a receptacle and replacing the mask he started talking to me.

Poor man, you look like I feel. I haven't got a clue what you are saying, sorry.

I raised a smile and nodded nonetheless, which was enough to make him stick his thumbs up again. Across the room to my right was a middle-aged woman, slumped in a chair being treated for what I deemed had been a loss of consciousness. The woman looked flushed and completely sapped of energy but wasn't producing any phlegm and neither was the young teenage girl sat in the far corner waiting patiently with her mother.

Ok, the worst is over now. I just need to be patient and I'll be feeling like a million dollars by the end of the night. God, it's 9pm already. I wish my new friend would stop coughing his guts up. Where is his wife or family? I wonder if anyone is going to charge me for all this?

The plan had been to get to Arica, get well and get back out into the desert as soon as possible. Although we were still 3,500 miles from Tierra del Fuego, it felt like we were within touching distance of the end. Potential freedom from the bike tasted good and everyone wanted to crack out some big miles through the Atacama Desert and south toward Santiago, Chile's capital. Initially, we thought it would take just a couple of days to repair the damage Peru had inflicted but it didn't pan out that way. After my stint being re-hydrated and then given a prescription for antibiotics, I returned to the hostel and endured three days of eating soup, toast and water biscuits in between trips to the bathroom. Frustratingly, I didn't seem to be getting any better and although the boys were fit enough to ride, they were still suffering with lesser bouts of dysentery themselves. Life became one long lie in. When I wasn't on the loo, I was sipping water and staring at the TV, clocking up unimaginable numbers of films. Martin and Paps took trips to the internet café or the call centre, or the cinema. One of their other ways of killing time was eating chocolate covered ice cream at MacDonald's.

'How are you doing mate?' I asked, as Martin came into my room from another meaningless walk around town.

'Fine, you know,' he said, shrugging his shoulders. 'Put it this way, I've just been researching campervan conversions on the internet for the last three hours.'

'That bad?'

'I'm afraid so.'

'Any luck with finding vans for hire in Argentina?'

'They are all so expensive. How are you feeling?'

'A bit better thanks. I'm not going to the toilet as much now. Maybe after tomorrow we'll be able to ship out? Are you going to allow me some peanut butter on toast?'

My test results confirmed I was on the right medicine but the whole hostel was now one big hospital ward. Paps was struck down again, along with a young Dutch couple and the hostel owner's daughter. The only person with any semblance of energy and fitness was Martin.

29th May, Rest Day, Arica, Chile. Still not riding. Martin and I go on the hunt for trailer wheel bearings and eventually find and fit them. Paps a bit better and starting to eat. Two visits to MacDonald's for ice cream. Nice steak and mashed potato dinner.

Out into the Atacama Desert we eventually rode, a haunting graveyard of a place. The road took us inland, away from the coast and through a region that hadn't seen rainfall for 400 years. Open plateaux of Martian-like rock gave rise to 10km long straights. Then a 15km climb would make us sweat for a couple of hours before we descended down the other side. The entire place was lifeless, save for the odd human driving a vehicle or sat at a table in a roadside café. We'd stop to fill up on Paila; a delicious concoction of fried eggs and bacon served to you in its very own frying pan and then head out again into nothingness. The region was once Bolivian until a border dispute with Chile resulted from the discovery of nitrate, silver and copper deposits in the area. It culminated in the War of the Pacific in 1874. Six years later, Chile had secured the Atacama corridor, the province of Antofagasta and the Peruvian province of Tarapacá, thereby turning Bolivia into a landlocked state. Mining operations littered the landscape, most notably steel plants left to rot once operations became economically unviable by the mid 1900's. One or two were later put to sinister use by Augusto Pinochet, the military General who came to power in the overthrow of Chile's government in 1973. He used Chacabuco Camp to hold hundreds of political prisoners who were considered a threat to the newly-formed dictatorship. Many were doctors, lawyers, teachers and professionals. The isolation and terror must have been inconceivable. We past another one of these abandoned nitrate plants - Oficina Anita – and I noticed Martin up the pace as we bore down on the small village of Bacquedano. Looking across at Paps - who seemed to be coping much better than me with the outlandish pace - just long enough for us to make eye contact, we had a conversation without moving our lips.

Wils:	Are you enjoying this?
Paps:	No. Are you?
Wils:	No. Why is Martin doing 25mph when it's the end of the day and we've done 75 miles?
Paps:	I have no idea. Why are *we* doing 25mph?
Wils:	I have no idea. Pride maybe?
Paps:	Probably. I'm knackered.
Wils:	Me too. Shall we slow down then and let him go?
Paps:	I will if you will.
Wils:	No, I will if you will!

We kept going, Martin ratcheting up to a mind-blowing 27. It was the price we paid for him enjoying the "burn" as he put it. We could barely stay with him during these times, despite benefiting from the slipstreaming effect. Luckily, "The Machine" eased down into Bacquedano so as not to melt his tyres, allowing Paps and I to go in search of bottled oxygen. "The Machine" was just one of a string of nicknames Martin had earned himself since leaving Prudhoe.

If they weren't allied to his prowess on the bike then they were linked to his hair which had only been cut once. On days off when The Machine had shampooed and gone walking around town in the sun, his hair buffoned to such proportions that it took on its own gravitational pull. Lion-O, Hasselhoff and Donadoni (after the Italian midfield dynamo of the early '90s) were just a smattering of other names Paps and I came up with to amuse ourselves. Other, less complimentary monikers, allied to his methane production or lack of deodorant use also cropped up from time to time. Trust me; in Canada when our diet consisted mainly of beans, it wasn't advisable to be tucked in behind The Machine.

Anyway, back in Bacquedano we weren't the only ones looking for a bed for the night. So too was a young German lad by the name of Claudius, a good-natured traveller loaded with gear. Claudius was out for a 3-week blast around Bolivia and northern Chile and was the first cyclist I'd seen since northern Peru. All four of us split up to quiz the locals, finally getting lucky with a couple who owned a diner at the end of a block of buildings fronting the main highway.

'Hello. I've been told you might have a place where we can stay the night?' I asked, directing my question at an overweight lady sat at a table at the back of the bar.

'How many of you?' she asked, with barely a scrap of interest.

'There are four of us.'

The screaming of some indiscernible Spanish resulted in the rapid appearance of her husband, who then led us off to a bunkhouse at the back of the village. Claudius loved cycling but even he was bemused by the scale of what we were doing. We though, had started to relax about it all. Peru was now long gone and so was the frustration of being held up for a week in Arica. We were making great progress and getting on well. What is more, with a change in climate came a change in perspective. Mornings were cold, warranting a hat, gloves and several layers when starting out. The sun became hot but not truly searing like Peru, meaning the months of bitching about the heat were over, soon to be replaced by the cold but that meant the end, and that meant freedom from the routine, the bike and the never-ending white line.

*

'270kms to the red carpet treatment! Ron!' cried a voice behind me.

Our destruction of the Atacama was all but complete. Cycling along, enjoying the Martian landscape, only a couple of days stood between us and Carol Davies, a family friend who'd been kind enough to offer us sanctuary when we reached her place north of Santiago. Anticipation of home cooked meals, hot showers and plenty of western style comforts, meant everyone was in an extremely buoyant mood and when that happened, Ron appeared.

Ron had become an institution on the trip. Normally, he'd pop up during times of good fortune, perhaps when a 10 mile downhill suddenly presented itself.

'Look at that!' someone would say, spotting the road plummet into the distance.

'Let's carve it up, Ron!'

'Don't have to pedal for 10 miles, Ron!'

During such times Ron littered the conversation. Like a call to arms, he would galvanize the group, forge a spirit of optimism, be a rallying cry if you like. He took on endless forms, enough to fill a library. There was Ron, Rahan, Rrrrrrnnnn, Rrrrraaaaaaaaaannn and every possibility in-between. Yes, we had become delirious and were short of new conversation but Ron wasn't - at least I hope not – a product of dementia. He was a means of conveying support or pleasure at a comment made by one of your friends. At other times Ron was used to exaggerate or identify with a certain experience or underlying thought.

Paps: 'These hills are killing me, Rrrrrrrrn!'

Wils: 'I'm sweating like a pig, Rahan, need to stop in a minute, Rrrrrn!'

Martin: 'Let's ditch the bikes and buy an RV, Rrrrrhhaaaan!'

Ron gave us the ability to mock the heat, the poverty and the wind without introducing negativity. Many, many times, when the situation was dire, Ron came to the rescue and we rode out the other side intact. He was our very own superhero.

*

'Where are you going to cross the Andes?' enquired Carol's husband, Cristían.

'The pass between Los Andes and Mendoza,' I ventured.

'You should make sure it's open. It was closed last week because of snow.'

Our 2,500-mile desert odyssey was over and Cristían and their teenage son Pablo had come to pick us up from a service station on the edge of town. Mountainous snowfalls in the upper reaches of the pass had buried the road, leaving 2,000 trucks on the Chilean side waiting to get through. None of us fancied the alternative, another pass, much lower in altitude but also further south that meant crossing via a windswept gravel track into the frigid waste of the Argentine interior where temperatures on the bike and in the tent would be unthinkable. Patagonia was entering the full grip of winter and the only way of avoiding the inconceivable cold – for now at least - was to traverse from here, across to the Atlantic coast where ocean currents would keep us relatively protected.

Our stay with Carol was awesome. A party was organised in our honour by the expat community and attended by 15 or more working at the three world-class observatories located in the mountains to the east. Surprisingly, there was very little talk of stellar constellations or supernovas, it was just a good old knees-up.

'Are you shirking the beer?' I enquired, smirking at Paps' empty bottle.

'I've had four and I'm wasted already!' he laughed.

'Me too!'

'I'm lying in all day tomorrow.'

'Right then, let's grab a couple more. It's fill ya boots time!'

Chapter 17

A touch of stardom

'Insanity: doing the same thing over and over again and expecting different results.'
Albert Einstein
Born Germany, 1879

Start Point: Coquimbo, Chile. Mile: 12,905. 13th June.

'This is it boys!' said The Machine, smiling with delight.

A nauseous feeling swept through the pit of my stomach as I saddled up and stared at the snow-covered Andean mountain range. Today was a massive day. Our target was Argentina and although only 40 miles away, reaching it meant conquering the dreaded 3,200-metre high pass. We knew the road was probably clear but the altitude and cold were sure to be brutal. I kept thinking back to my time in the mountains of Colombia, trying to remember the size of the obstacle that lay in front of us and how we might fare. I'd done several passes the size of this one but it had been in a temperate environment. Now a bitterly cold wind and icy road meant facing a night in the snow if we failed to make it to the Argentine side. A seriousness took hold and no one messed about.

I led out at a brisk space in the sunshine, the boys pushing me along. The fertile, vineyard-covered slopes did nothing to soothe my nerves. As I kept the wheels turning, a niggling urgency had me calculating and recalculating our imaginary progress. Like a bothersome spot or piece of peeling skin I couldn't leave them alone. Then within the space of a few miles we became engulfed on all sides by bare contorted black and red rock. The last great climb of the trip was upon us. As the valley sides went vertical and our pace slowed, I found myself recalculating on an almost permanent basis.

'Is it time to stop yet?' interrupted Martin.

'I'm pulling over,' I confirmed, nodding ahead.

We stood around, nailing bananas, biscuits, chocolate and loading up on water. 'Time to put on another layer and some gloves,' I said, as the mountain wind ripped through my sweat-soaked jersey.

We pushed on higher and higher into an ever-narrowing valley, through box tunnels built to protect motorists from avalanche-prone slopes. When we stopped again, I became aware that all traces of vegetation had disappeared. We were higher than I thought and the air was truly bitter.

'It looks like the road swings left into that valley,' said Martin, as we waited for Paps.

'It can't be long until the switchback section,' I remarked, giving away my anxiety.

'I'm going to keep going. I don't want to get cold.'

I zipped up my jacket, broke open another packet of biscuits and watched Martin continue to the apex of the valley, trying to kill time. My growing concern caused me to wonder across the road, kicking it clear of stray stones. I wanted to be with Martin but more than that, I wanted to gauge Paps's mood. This would be the biggest test all of us had faced in eleven months but Paps's knee threw in the unknown. I popped the sixth and final biscuit into my mouth as the fourth and fifth still clung to my teeth. Slowly but surely Paps trundled in.

'How you doin' mate?' I asked, aware that I was now cold.

'Not bad,' he said, pensively. 'I can't press hard as my knee is hurting already.'

'There's plenty of time,' I said, knowing Paps would spot my lie straight away. 'We just have to tick over and we'll get there.'

'Well I hope so,' he responded, playing along.

'Do you want some of my tea?'

Paps's attitude seemed spot on. He had given up trying to cling to The Machine or I in favour of ticking over at a pace his knee could tolerate so I left him to it and headed on. Within a minute the valley had opened up and the full majesty of the climb was towering above me. The same feelings of nerves and excitement that I'd had that day on the Atigun Pass rushed back. It had been our first major obstacle and this climb, the "Paso Cristo Redentor," signified our last. If we could get over this, an 800-mile wide plain was ours for the taking. Then we would turn right and be pointing straight at Tierra del Fuego.

'Half way up the first set of switchbacks'

Throughout the year I'd never been able to dismiss any climb, no matter how small. A half-mile ascent gave me the same jitters as a 40km Colombian monster. It was weird. Deep down I knew I'd get to the top but somehow each time I saw the road steepen it left me questioning my ability. In response to the crescendo of nerves, I would concentrate like hell and start talking to myself. This climb was no different. The huge, overwhelming set of switchbacks loomed above me, perhaps numbering more than thirty. Buses and trucks snaked their way down the mountainside toward me, tiny splurges of colour against the grey, ashen rock. I found an even lower gear and spotted Martin, powering away on the third switchback, reminiscent of his lead up the Atigun.

This is it Ron!

The scale was breathtaking, the panorama improving with every turn of the wheel. I forced myself to break with tradition and look beyond my front wheel to find Martin two curves away, my view of him made possible by the terracing effect of the road. It also meant I could see Paps entering the switchback section, some six to eight curves below. We were all in our own worlds, fighting our own demons, just like hundreds of times before. Passing drivers tooted their horns and shook their fists until forty-five minutes later I was on the back of Martin's trailer wheel. We pulled over straight away, both exhausted.

'My arse is on fire!' he commented. 'I wanted to stop about half an hour ago.'

'This is big!' I declared, knowing it would lead to a rally of banter.

We spent a few minutes gulping down water and talking it up. I was relishing every minute of it. Climbing in these conditions was something completely new. It felt extreme, almost obscene to be out here. After thousands of miles in the saddle it still felt weird to be so exposed and we all knew how much colder it would surely get before the day was out. I tore myself away from Martin and Keith and ploughed on up through the snowline, as more passengers leaned out of windows to snap us.

At the top of the thirty-third switchback, sweating despite the cold, I realised we were far from done. A snowfield perhaps a mile wide separated me from a second set equal in stature. My heart sank and I began to wonder if we would make it.

Ok, keep going, keep it slow and don't look at the switchbacks. Don't look at them. God, my feet are like blocks of ice.

I crossed the snowfield at an awful pace slipping on the ice and turned the corner to begin the next set. Neither of my fellow riders had appeared and my extremities were starting to freeze. I was still only wearing a pair of woollen gloves, shorts and a cycle jersey under a long sleeve t-shirt. I kept riding for a whole hour ignoring the cold until the road opened up again and I found myself surrounded by defunct ski lifts.

I stopped alongside a metre-high drift, stood the bike to attention and raced to find my jacket and waterproof trousers as the wind sliced through me. One or two sheds stood flanking the road perhaps half a mile away. My eyes welled up and ice-cold tears started streaming down my face. Then I noticed the road.

Oh no…please no, not more of this. My head is killing me, where's my hat? I need another pair of gloves…

I set off again, the wind stinging my face and my fingers frozen to the handlebar. I couldn't feel my feet or hands but a mere ten minutes later I was opposite the entrance to a ski resort. Snow lay in drifts two metres high on each side of the road. Only the occasional 4x4 pulled in or out as I waited to see if Martin or Paps were going to appear. After fifteen minutes I wimped out and went to investigate the chances of getting some hot food and liquid from the resort hotel. When I returned, Martin was stood at the side of the road, togged up to the nines with layer upon layer of clothing.

'Hi mate,' I said, squinting into the freezing wind.

'You alright?'

'Tired and cold. You?'

'I feel ok.'

'There's a buffet style restaurant at the hotel.'

'Nice one. I'm not sure we are going to make Argentina today. It's getting late.'

'It's another few kilometres apparently. The road keeps going, look,' I said pointing away to my left. 'How far back is Paps?'

'I'm not sure. I stopped to wait for him but got too cold, I had to keep going.'

Twenty minutes passed by and we had started to contemplate heading down to find him when Paps arrived. It had been *the* climb of the trip and a massive strain on his knees. The last time I had spoken to him was 6,000ft further down the mountain. What an effort.

'I can't go on without a rest, guys,' he said, calmly.

'That's fine, mate,' Martin replied, noting how exhausted he looked. 'Wils says they're serving hot food in the hotel and I think we are out of time.'

What I didn't know at the time was that Paps had sensibly necked four cans of energy drink before setting out. He only came clean much later when he and I laughed and joked about his famed "cycling master class" back up in Canada. On that occasion, the day into Pemberton where we camped in front of the police station, Paps had led from start to finish and I, the supposed climber in the group, couldn't get anywhere near him. At the time, I had put it down to Paps having a better than usual day but such was his fear of failure on a day of expected mammoth climbs, Paps had resorted to other measures. There's nothing wrong with drinking cans of energy drink, after all, it's just one step further than eating two plates of chicken and rice for lunch, yet, keeping it secret pointed to the pressure he was feeling, a pressure to keep up on the hills. Paps couldn't risk the appearance of inferiority, of failure and he didn't want to be all alone. I cannot believe how completely out of touch I was with what was happening to him.

Retreating into the hotel, I went off to investigate the price of a room, stepping over all the guests' ski gear.

'It costs US$210 for a bunk room but we get breakfast thrown in,' I said, reporting back.

'I knew it wouldn't be cheap,' said Martin.

'That's bloody crazy!' said Paps.

'I'll see if we can sleep in the maintenance shed or that restaurant over the road.'

I needn't have bothered as both the restaurateur and the maintenance guys refused to give us space to lay out our sleeping bags.

'It looks like we'll have to stay here,' commented Paps.

'Maybe the manager will give us a discount,' I remarked.

I was directed to the manager's office and waited a while whilst his secretary finished her phone call. 'Yes. Can I help you?' she eventually asked.

I explained the situation, one where I forewent mentioning the absurd rate and gave the charity angle instead in an effort to win her over. For added good measure I then lied a little by saying Paps had an injury, which he had agreed to fake. After all this effort she merely told me to come back in half an hour to which I duly obliged. She picked up the phone, rang her boss and I heard her explain our request.

'You can have a room in the bunkhouse for US$105. That includes breakfast.'

The climb had been serious. None of us, not even I, who had been over the pass in a bus 18 months previous, expected the second huge set of switchbacks. The higher we got, the colder it had become and the less oxygen there was to keep going. We were now 2,850 metres up, an altitude where we got 27% less oxygen than we would from one breath at sea level. (Climbers on the summit of Everest receive 68% less oxygen per breath).

*

'Es la cumbre?' I enquired, as a bearded man strolled out of a building built into the rock face at the side of the road.

'Yes, this is the top!' he replied, enthusiastically in Spanish. 'You can't cycle through the tunnel so I'll take you in the truck.'

'I am waiting for my friends.'

'No problem. Do you want a cup of tea?'

'I have some thanks.'

'Where are you from?'

'England.'

'Ah, David Beckham!'

A sign to the side of the tunnel entrance read, "3,200 msmn." The boys arrived and our friend went off to start up the truck. As he did, Martin started filming.

'Have you got anything to say, Paps?' he asked.

'It's a good jam roll!' he joked, taking the first bite of his sandwich. 'No, it's spectacular isn't it. I mean, it was a bit of an effort getting here! I'll never come here again and if I ever ride to this height again I should be shot!'

We loaded on the bikes and trailers, jumped into the warm cab and set off through the tunnel. At the other end, bright sunshine lit our entrance to the fourteenth and final country.

'Argentina gentlemen!' remarked Martin.

'There's a sign back there about the Falklands belonging to Argentina. I don't think so!' stated Paps, his exuberance overflowing.

'Ah!' laughed Martin.

I came in to give the boys a big hug. 'Last country, last country!' rejoiced Paps.

'We made it fellas!'

The final chapters on our adventure were being written right before us in a rare moment of true togetherness. Everyone embraced beneath a fluttering Argentine flag. The desert had gone and South America was almost in the bag. Everyone donned plenty of layers for the freezing descent.

'Let's rip it up Rrrrrrannnn!'

'Gonna put my foot down Rrrrrrhnnn!'

Despite the headwind and icy road we didn't hang around. Peaks blanketed in snow gave way to pink, orange and purple rock as we lost height on an alarmingly fast road. Up to our left loomed Cerro Aconcagua, the highest peak in South America. A lump developed in my throat.

I just can't believe it. This isn't real. We're in Argentina!

Our descent out of the Andean range continued well into the next day, passing vineyard after vineyard, the single-track highway changing to a fast running dual carriageway where we experienced our first taste of Argentine driving skills.

'Screeecccccchhhhhh!'

Holy shit!

In total fear, I nervously glanced a few feet to my left and saw a guy at the wheel of his Fiat, facing the wrong way, heading backwards across the highway toward the central reservation. He looked as terrified as me.

'Holy shit!' I screamed, this time engaging my mouth.

*

A touch of stardom

'The first sign showing the Holy Grail, "Ushuaia"'

'It's completely collapsed,' said Martin, hunched over, studying his pedal.
'It doesn't look good,' I confirmed.
'I won't be cycling anywhere on that, I'm afraid.'
'We are getting a lift then. Let's flag down a bus.'

Things had begun well on the Pampa. This vast open grassland was like nothing we had seen before. Forget the never-ending straight roads of Canada, Peru or Chile. On the Pampa the road would stay straight for two hours and then some. It became a test of mind-over-matter as mile after mile the arrow straight white line disappeared into the distance. There was nothing to look at save for an occasional hawk sat on a fencepost or a few million head of cattle on each side of the road. Now that Martin's left pedal had shattered, boredom was replaced by frustration and anger. To explain, I need to take you back to Tijuana.

Since arriving in Latin America, I had paid a price for being the Spanish speaker. In the early stages it meant being in charge of nearly everything when conversing with the outside world. Food purchases, accommodation arrangements, laundry, phone calls, directions, fuel for Steve or buying bike parts. As the boys studied hard and picked up confidence they started pitching in, yet even in Argentina, seven months later, there was still the appearance of the "Let Wils sort it" attitude. This attitude angered me more than the mosquitoes on the North Slope. Fair enough when things get complicated, like at the Ski resort but tell me; how hard is it to stick your thumb up for a lift?

  - *The pedal is broken Martin. Taking it apart at the side of the road is not going to get us to San Luis. Why are you messing with it? Why are you not thumbing a lift? You can waste as much time as you want, I am not thumbing a lift when you are perfectly capable of doing it yourself. And Paps, why are you pretending to adjust something on your trailer?*

  - *Stop being so damn stubborn. This is really childish, thumb a lift you prat!*

  - *No. Screw them.*

- You want to have a hot shower and a day off tomorrow, right?
- Yeah.
- Well, don't play games. Get your thumb up and get on with it!
- Shit! This is totally out of order.

I got up and stuck my thumb out as Martin continued to study the tiny pieces of his broken pedal. The voices in my head, born and bred on the deafly quiet roads of northern Canada, were continuing to play havoc with my psyche. The only reason they grew so powerful was that voicing them out loud resulted in catastrophic consequences, as seen at Bullards Beach, in El Salvador and in Costa Rica. Keeping many of them private always seemed sensible because they were pathetic most of the time and ten minutes or two hours later the storm in a teacup had invariably blown over. The same applied here. With a fresh pedal on Martin's left cog arm, three hours later we rode out of San Luis toward Villa Mercedes and the hope of a hostel for the night.

'Why didn't he start thumbing a lift?' I said to Paps, with Martin some 300 metres off the pace.

'I'm not sure,' said Paps, with a wry smile on his face. He had seen this coming and knew full well what was going through my mind. 'Mate, nothing gets done unless you sort it, you know that,' said Paps, in reference to the language. 'I mean, what did I do? You got the lift, the directions to the bike shop, the directions to the ATM, found the supermarket and then bought the food!'

'Yeah but it wasn't your pedal that collapsed, it was Martin's. He had zero urgency to do anything! It should have been him that was sorting it out, or at least *trying* to do it. If I hadn't done something we'd still be in San Luis right now, moping about!'

'Don't take it personally, it's your character to get things done. That's why you lead on the road all the time. Martin prefers to do it a different way and if I had my way, I'd sleep in 'til eleven every morning!'

We both laughed. Evil Wils was back in his cage. The little annoyances that build over the course of weeks on the road suddenly become the biggest issues in the world. Without warning, you'd find yourself annoyed with how one of your friends ate a sandwich or how he put all the guy ropes up when there wasn't a breath of wind. You convince yourself that you don't like it and that's it, it's inside your mind and you can't let it go, all because of the bubble we were living in. Martin was probably trying to magic a repair job, something he did on many occasions but I was convinced he was stalling to avoid speaking Spanish to a bus driver. He certainly meant no malice by his actions. My irritation had been magnified by the need to reach Villa Mercedes and secure a day off. Days off were gospel, hostel rooms a reprieve from the daily grind where we could watch mindless TV and eat junk food for a while. Within minutes of arrival our gear would cover every inch of the room and the air rancid enough to make the maid gag when she came in with the towels. Every single time we approached a day off "hostel talk" would take over like nothing else mattered, the precise reason why Yauca had been such a kick in the teeth.

*

'The lady is getting the local TV to come and do an interview with us,' said Paps.

'You're joking?' I said.

'Maybe you should go and check?'

I went back into the grocers and ran straight into the assistant. 'Don't go anywhere; I've just called my friend who works for the TV station,' she told me. 'He wants to do an interview.'

'OK but we don't have much time,' I replied, fretting with nerves.

'He'll be here in two minutes.'

Within seconds a battered car older than me pulled up and out jumped two guys, one holding a camera and the other a big fat microphone. A couple of grinning faces melted into the background and I was left to do the interview alone. 'Please speak slowly otherwise I will not understand you,' I said, warning my interviewer.

At least this isn't going out live!

'I am here in town with three cyclists, from England, I think?' he began, turning to face me.

'Yes, that's right,' I confirmed.

'And tell us about your journey.'

'We started in Alaska last August and we are travelling down to Ushuaia.'

'That's fantastic. How is it going?'

'Really well,' I lied. 'No major problems but we are glad to be nearly finished.'

'And what do you think of Argentina? Do you like it?'

'Yeah the people are friendly and the food is much better than Peru!'

'Ah! I can see that you are carrying quite a lot of equipment,' he said pointing to our trailers.

'We have everything with us; tents, sleeping bags, clothes, spare parts...'

The interview went on another couple of minutes before I was spared any more embarrassment. Then we headed off to find lunch where our infamy caught up with us once more. Settling down for a big plate of meat and salad on the edge of town, a chap came into the restaurant holding a microphone. I didn't wait for him to spot us; I just waved, got up and went outside to do the interview as the boys continued watching a World Cup game. This time it was for the local radio. The format was similar but my interviewer was much more animated.

'I am stood outside a local Parrilla at the side of Ruta 35 with a young Englishman who is cycling to Ushuaia with two friends. Hello, how are you?'

'We are very well thank you, just having some lunch. Then we go toward Santa Rosa.'

'Very good. How long will it take you to get there?'

'We hope to be there tomorrow night.'

'That's great. I must say you're not wearing much, just a long sleeve T-shirt and a pair of shorts. Are you not cold?'

'Well, it's hard work on the bike you know!'

'Ah, yes, well I hope you are prepared for the cold down south.'

'Everyone is warning us about that!'

'And so what is the plan after the trip has finished?'

'My friends return to England and I am off to Buenos Aires. My girlfriend lives there.'

'Oh really? Is she Argentine?'

'Yes.'

'Lucky you!'

The chef, who was meant to be tending his huge grill of meat, was instead doubled over laughing at the deterioration of the interview. 'And how did you meet her?'

'Whilst I was in Buenos Aires learning some Spanish last year.'

'That's fantastic.'

Then there was a little pause as a question came in from the studio. 'I've just been asked if you have anything to say about Argentina's favourite son, Diego Maradona?'

I remained silent, smirking at my interviewer's line of questioning as the chef again started weeping in the background. 'The Hand of God?' he pressed.

'I'd prefer not to talk about that!'

'Ah, yes, probably best!'

Chapter 18

Patagonia

'Character builds slowly but it can be torn down within incredible swiftness.'
Faith Baldwin
Born America, 1893

Start Point: Huinca Reñanco, Argentina. Mile: 13,725. 27th June.

Carrying the bikes and trailers over the thorny scrub we placed them beneath a large tree and started kicking away leaves and twigs in preparation for our tents. It had been our biggest day ever; 165kms, aided by a massive tailwind. Everyone was in a good mood and what is more we were now pointing due South. A few days later all that harmony had vanished.

'I can't go on like this, I can't handle it anymore,' I said to Martin, as we rode past a sign indicating a petrol station in 3kms. 'All my feelings of Mexico and Central America have come flooding back.'

'If he wants to get a bus then let him,' said Martin. 'I'm not playing these games any more. He took me for a ride in Guatemala. I know it's selfish but I just don't care.'

'I'm going to talk to him,' I responded.

'Yeah?'

'Yeah, otherwise this is going to end in disaster. You go ahead and we'll stop at the YPF, yeah?' I said, referring to the petrol station.

The previous day an argument had broken out at the side of the road over how much time we should spend in Trelew. Paps wanted two days to rest his knee, Martin and I wanted one day. In truth, Martin was so focused on getting to Ushuaia that he didn't want to stop in Trelew at all but I had managed to convince him otherwise. Arguing over one day seems petty but after eleven months on the road no one was willing to give any ground.

Ever since Lima, the race to the bottom had been planned and continually updated to the smallest detail by Martin. Each night he gave us an update on the mileage remaining to the next break, the distance to Ushuaia, all of it based on a very simple strategy. Choose a target which pushes you to the limit for four or five days, take a day's rest and then repeat. Lima to Yauca, 4 days, 576kms; Arica to Bacquedano, 5 days, 651kms; Villa Mercedes to Rio Colorado, 5 days, 696kms. Yet this strategy, one which we had all signed up to, made us tired from sunrise to sunset, day after day. During rest days we rushed to keep the bikes working, ate, slept and then off we went again, chasing place names and dreaming of a hot shower.

Back in Rio Colorado Paps advised me that he was "so fucking bored" and couldn't "…be arsed to talk," so I was expecting a bust up at some point. When the subject of Trelew was brought up, it was a bomb waiting to go off. Everyone fought their corner tooth and nail and afterwards, without anything resolved and another day of fair weather spoilt, I again considered riding off on my own just to escape the pressure. The crux of the argument had centred on Paps's frustration that the "strategy" couldn't spare one extra day in Trelew to rest his knee. Martin and I thought Paps just fancied an extra day off. That night I wrote,

4th July, 145 kms to rough camp. Problems today; Paps's two-day mood/mardy transpires as knee and tiredness problems. He wants two days in Trelew to rest. Martin and I don't believe him. I think he is fed up and bored, as he has told me he can't be bothered to chat or converse. Great attitude. Good to see he is consistent though. I am at the end of my tether with yet another lovely day of weather and conditions ruined. A man and his wife stopped and showed me photos of their house in Ushuaia covered in snow.

Leaving Martin, I slowed my pace right down so that Paps, who was some way back, was forced to come up along side me. We were out of earshot by now and spread across the road, two abreast.

'Come on then, let's have it,' I said, my heart thumping with adrenaline.

'What?'

'I can't go on like this, not now we are so close to finishing. I want us to talk about yesterday. I can't stand this bad atmosphere any longer.'

'Yeah? Me neither mate but honestly, I couldn't believe what I was hearing,' said Paps, readying himself. 'I am stood there telling two of my closest mates that I can't keep riding, that I am in serious pain and that my only option is to get a bus to Trelew so that I can rest properly and what do I get? "Do whatever you need to, mate." There was no concern for my state of health, nothing! I'm sorry but my opinion of you and Martin went down a lot yesterday.'

I sensed a repeat of Bullards Beach. 'Mate, it was the way you said it. Why make flat out statements like that after not talking for two days? It was like you were looking for a reaction. Why not say, "Guys, can we adjust the schedule cos my knee is really painful and I'm struggling." Instead, all we got was "When we get to Sierra Grande I am getting a bus." What are we meant to say to that?'

'Maybe I went about it the wrong way but you guys only seem to care about the schedule.'

'I am disappointed in how I acted. I was angry and should have approached it differently. We are all experiencing a lot of stress right now, big miles and the end of the trip, so close yet so far and all that. Come on, let's hold it together,' I said.

'I know.'

'We had big problems up in Mexico and Central America and we took care of them. Believe me mate; I don't want to be cycling with anyone when the mood is this bad. Yesterday we had a superb tailwind, it was sunny and the day was ruined because of that argument. I don't care what Martin says about "so much for the non-existent Patagonian winds" or "winter" or whatever. The wind is going to kick our arses at some point and we need to be together as a group. We can't afford to be fighting each other, we have come too far. I mean, it's less than 1,800kms now.'

We neared the entrance to the Petrol Station. 'Fair enough,' said Paps.

'Let's talk about Trelew and see what happens. If you can't ride then we'll have to adjust.'

'OK, I'll try. Thanks for the chat, mate.'

Paps and I managed to clear the air but our chat was no more permanent than placing a band-aid over a shark bite. The thing was, we didn't need surgery, we just needed the band-aid to hold for a while. Just a few weeks and it would all be over. 90% of the trip was done. How had we survived? How had we each made it this far? I'm not sure any us of really knew. We talked about it a bit when in the mood but were never able to come up with a definitive answer. Determination, grit and down right stubbornness were all mentioned but something else accounted for getting out of the sleeping bag at 5.30am, cycling 80 miles and washing with a flannel, only to repeat it, time and time again. There seemed to be a hidden factor, an energy source if you like that we automatically plugged into when times were tough. What that was I still have no idea. I mentioned to the boys that I felt we cycled inside a bubble, a bubble that protected us, provided security, gave us a sense of invincibility, like no one could hurt us (apart from Colombia). It's a feeling that remains with me now but it's still incredibly hard to describe. It was as if we were being watched by a greater being. Not by a god but rather a TV producer stuck in a far away studio watching our every move via a bank of screens. That's it, a Truman Show scenario, where the whole world tuned in to follow three cyclists along an endless white line. In Mexico, Martin nicknamed us 'The Muppet Show', in reference to how people stood and gawped in disbelief each time we entered a town. It even became vogue to sing or whistle the theme tune as we past by the next group of bewildered hecklers.

"It's time to play the music, it's time to light the lights, it's time to meet the Muppets on the Muppet Show tonight!"

We were a comedy show half the time. Why? Because anyone who leaves behind responsibilities to family, girlfriend or work can't possibly be taken seriously. It went further. Surely someone riding by bicycle so far from home had been forced to do so, presumably through dishonouring their family in some way or because they couldn't afford to travel by bus or car. After all, why would someone choose to live like that, to carry all their belongings, live off the street, sleep in fields and wash in rivers? Being laughed at, pointed and jeered at just made us plug into the energy source or sit in the bubble. Maybe the bubble only existed in my world but we all seemed to have a hidden factor.

The man with by far the biggest hidden factor was undoubtedly Paps. I'm still unsure how he made it to Argentina. Here was a guy, who like his two cycling partners, had signed up for a stupid idea. Like his two cycling partners, he had zero touring experience or even cycling passion. Like his two cycling partners, he had never attempted anything remotely as demanding but unlike his two cycling partners he was carrying an injury. That was the key, discriminating factor. I think it's fair to say he failed to control his emotions from time to time and that's why he acted how he did and said what he said but let's get one thing straight here. From time to time we all slagged each other off. We all bitched and we all cut corners. Paps's emotions were undoubtedly born out of the added burden of an injury. It didn't matter that the pain came and went sporadically. Indeed, perhaps the uncertainty made it all the more frustrating? Two weeks of painless riding (apart from the bottom I must stress) followed by four consecutive days of pain every time he planted his right foot. How would I have felt? How would I have reacted under those circumstances? To wake each morning unsure if I was destined to spend all day at the back as my riding partners disappeared into the distance. How would that have made my feel? Bitter maybe? Resentful? Lonely? Inferior? (Hence the secret energy drinks). Damn right it would. How would I feel knowing it might continue for a year? How would I feel when there was nothing I could do about it? Lost maybe? Helpless? Angry? Yep. There's no saying how I might have acted had I known that I was almost certainly doing myself permanent damage. Knowing that each time I felt that sharp twinge of pain it was doing further harm to an already pre-diagnosed condition. Would I ask myself; What am I trying to prove? And to whom? And for what purpose? For sure I would. And when these episodes of pain occurred would I want to be joyful, cheery? Would I want to join in and crack jokes? No. And that brings me back to the hidden factor, the energy source. Paps had it in riches. Why else would he be cycling next to me in Argentina? I can only appreciate that now, after the pressure has gone. On the bike, my own stress, combined with a reaction to his behaviour, blinded me. I was unable to grasp what was happening right in front of my own eyes. Paps was cycling with two friends but to all intents and purposes he felt alone. That's why his achievement is all the more impressive, all the more inspiring. But it doesn't end there. Forget my solo ride through Colombia. Imagine this; You are threatened with being dumped by at least one of your riding partners and are left with two choices. 1. Agree to cycle solo from at least Quito to Lima or face riding 5,500 miles solo to Ushuaia. 2. Go home. Why? Because your friends don't recognise, understand and account for your injury. An injury that was diagnosed before the trip began and one that had been carried ever since. Now imagine how hard it is to firstly go along with the ultimatum, secondly have the will power to ride solo to Lima and thirdly then rejoin the same people and ride a further 4,000 miles to the bottom, all the while thinking, "…they just aren't getting it."

I can see it all now, I have a more balanced view but it's too late. I wasn't there for him. I wasn't able to see past the causal factors and help my friend overcome his suffering. Yes, I was patient and I was concerned and yes, I did try to manage what was happening but clearly I didn't do enough. Had Martin or I been more adept at encouraging a stronger emphasis on Paps's knee being a team problem we would have all benefited. Of that I am sure. Wherever you might be right now Anthony, take a bow.

*

Rejuvenated from taking a room each we spent only one day in Trelew and set our sights on Comodoro Rivadavia, a sizeable port town lying 340kms to the south. Things started well with a massive 158kms. It took our average in Argentina to a startling 136kms (84 miles) on riding days, almost double that of Canada. Paps's knee was holding. As expected, the road south was a different animal. There were no services, absolutely nowhere to top up our food supply or protect it by eating a cooked meal at a truck stop. In order to play-safe we had four days' supply to cover a distance that would take us two and a half. Or so we thought. Once the Patagonian wind announced its intentions the second day out from Trelew our progress dropped significantly and eating levels went through the roof. The four-day supply was virtually gone. It meant rising on day three, still 90kms short of Comodoro and any form of salvation. The night had been cold and wet, where we fought our hunger and waited for the tents to disintegrate in the wind. Cycling out was a hellish effort, long wispy clouds hanging low in the blue sky, signalling the trouble that lay ahead. Twice we huddled at the side of the road debating what to do whilst eating our last bit of food.

'It's still 70kms to Comodoro,' said Martin.

'We aren't going to get there,' I said. 'We are out of food, it's bloody freezing and we can't go quicker than 10kmph. We need a lift.'

'Yeah but no one is stopping,' asserted Paps.

'Well, what the hell are we going do then?' I asked, irritated by the lack of options.

We tried thumbing a lift for over an hour without success, watching the clouds move in. Off we set again aware that if it started to rain the temperature would be unbearable. A few miles later, bunched up together we spotted a white outline on the horizon.

'That could be Punta Salamanca!' shouted Martin, above the wind.

'It looks like a service station!' I replied.

We battled on, my eyes filling with water and tears streaming down my cheeks as the wind whistled between my face and glasses.

Please be a service station, please. Or a café, I don't care, just something.

Martin was correct; the two or three white buildings did indeed constitute Punta Salamanca. Unfortunately, it seemed that no one had lived there for at least 10 years. The place was completely abandoned. All that was missing was a creaking sign, some tumbleweed and perhaps a poncho-wearing Clint Eastwood. The former café was boarded up and covered with graffiti. Rusting tin cans littered the ground and plastic bags fluttered in nearby bushes.

'I don't fucking believe it,' I said, my frustration boiling over.

'Shit,' said Martin. 'We have to get a lift otherwise we are in real trouble.'
'I know.'
'Having a van out here to break the wind wouldn't have made a scrap of difference, you know.'
'I know. The wind is just too powerful. We'd need a bloody lorry.'

Back in Chile and in preparation for entering Patagonia during winter, we had considered hiring a van for a few weeks in order to overcome the power of the wind, the idea being for one person to drive whilst two cycled right behind. It would also mean we could carry as much food and water as we needed and even sleep in the van if the wind was too powerful or night temperatures too cold. After researching our options however, the cost of doing so was prohibitively expensive.

'I am feeling dizzy,' I said, staring blankly at the abandoned buildings. 'I need to eat.'
'I think there are one or two biscuits if you want?'
'Let's wait for Paps to get here and then try to get a lift. I'm going to the loo,' I said, walking off with my roll of paper.

The best spot I could find to do my business was behind a three-foot high pile of gravel set back a hundred yards or so from the buildings. Peering over the top of the gravel I watched Paps gesticulate what I presumed was his frustration to Martin. Then to my amazement, a lorry heading to Comodoro seemed to be slowing on approach.

It's stopping! It's stopping!

The wind was so ferocious that for a frightening moment neither Paps nor Martin heard the lorry's engine and I couldn't risk moving without soiling my underwear. With their backs turned they had no idea that a potential lift to Comodoro was waiting a hundred yards away. I watched the driver jump out of the cab and start striking his tyres with a wooden baton. I scrambled for the loo roll but then Martin came into view, running toward the driver.

Yes! Good lad, come on Martin!

*

'It's still pitch black out there,' said Paps. 'And you should see the wind, it's incredible.'

Fearing the worst I left my half-packed trailer bag and went out into the street. The wind was whistling through town, attacking anything in its path. Illuminated by the streetlights, trees strained as the wind tugged violently at their leaves and branches.

'Are we seriously thinking of riding in that?' I asked, once back in the hostel.
'Looks like it,' said Paps.

We all continued loading the bikes but I sensed everyone knew how futile the gesture was. Out of town and now fully exposed to a constant blast of air, cycling was rapidly becoming the world's most dangerous pastime. Without warning, gusts slammed into us pushing us two to three feet into the middle of the road. It was suicide. We survived one or two close misses but when another sudden screech of tyres forced me off the road in terror, I broke into tears. I was at meltdown.

'What the fuck are we doing?' I screamed.

'Take it easy mate,' said Paps.

'I can't cycle like this, it's fucking suicide!'

Paps came over to put his arm around me 'OK, OK. Take it easy.' I walked away, returning only once I had regained my composure. 'Do you want to head back, mate?'

'I just can't see the value in being out here,' I said, rubbing my eyes. 'Maybe it'll be better once we are on the open road? I'm happy to go on if you two want to keep riding.'

Unbeknown to us at the time, the maximum-recorded wind speed for that day was 54mph. The only way I can describe that power is to say that it's strong enough to knock you off your feet should you not lean into the wind. We went on, out of stubbornness until Paps was forced off the road by a truck that came within a whisker of killing him. It was too much.

'Guys, we need to make a decision here otherwise one of us is going to get killed,' said Paps, with a remarkable air of calm about him.

I had already made up my mind. 'Let's turn around and get the hell out of here.'

The worst-case scenario was that this wind was with us until the bottom and that we might have just cycled our last miles. The only option was getting a bus to San Julian, the next principal settlement to the south in an effort to leapfrog the current weather system. It was a ghostly place, devoid of any noise and hardly any streetlights. Exiting the bus the cold was staggering. Ice covered the ground and I started fretting about night-time temperatures. By the morning everyone was togged up with a laughable amount of clothing, hoping that the calm conditions would prevail. Little vegetation covered the ground now apart from a beautiful carpet of hardy yellow grass that so characterises southern Patagonia. At the edge of town we past an airfield used by the Argentine Air Force to attack British forces during the Falklands War in 1982 and then snaked our way through open country, the road becoming extremely exposed and hillier than I imagined. There was no sign of life for mile after mile. It was just us, one or two Rhea (an ostrich like animal native to Patagonia and the Andean Plateau) and the odd passing car, bus or truck. The remoteness reminded me of the North Slope but here we were riding in winter toward the source of all the cold air; Antarctica. By midmorning our worst nightmare was realised as it started to blow and blow hard. We continued, praying it would relent but by 4pm and with the light fading we agreed it was time to stop. We had managed just 62kms in eight hours. I found it hard to get the tent up as the temperature dropped like a stone and my fingers froze. Later I made the effort to nip out for a pee before quickly clambering back into my tent and zipping up, my breath rising through the beam of torch light as I scrambled to find my pair of thermal gloves. I was already wearing two pairs of socks, thermal long johns, a pair of trousers, thermal long sleeve top, three t-shirts, two long sleeve t-shirts, a fleece, a waterproof jacket, a neck buff and my thermal hat. I was also benefiting from a silk liner which increased the rating of my 3-season sleeping bag by half a season but I was still cold.

'The thermometer is reading -3°C,' said Paps.

'What time is it?' I asked him.

'Half past six.'

'Blimey, it's gonna be cold.'

'I'm cold now and I'm already wearing nearly every piece of clothing I've got!'

The night was polar, made worse by my mattress deflating every couple of hours because of a puncture I'd failed to locate since California. Each time it deflated the frozen ground woke me up and left me shivering inside my bag listening to the wind slamming into the side of my tent. Every few seconds a blast of ice-cold air entered and I cursed the helplessness of our situation. Peering out through the tiny hole of my sleeping bag I could see my half-full water bottle lying a few inches from my face, frozen solid.

'Is anyone awake?' I ventured, once it had been light for a while.

'Yep,' came Martin's voice.

'I don't think it's worth going anywhere in this, is it?' I asked, referring to the wind.

'No. Let's sit tight and see what it's like in an hour shall we?'

'I'm not going anywhere!' shouted Paps.

'I am so bloody cold!' I yelled, seizing the opportunity to moan.

'At five o'clock this morning the thermometer was reading minus five!'

Unbeknown to Paps and I, Martin was in the midst of recording a diary entry on Keith. It read...

It's nine o'clock in the morning...the wind is blowing pretty dramatically and it's been a pretty cold night too. Paps's thermometer read about minus one at five o'clock yesterday evening and it got substantially colder than that during the night. My water bottle is inside my tent and is frozen...I'm in my sleeping bag, three layers including my fleece, a pair of shorts, pair of trousers, two pairs of socks both of which are thermal, pair of gloves, a neck buff and a hat! I just shouted to Wils and he agrees that we're not going to be riding yet.

Yesterday we got about thirty miles on the same amount of food we were doing 90 miles...so we are eating the same amount of food to do a third of the distance...and this is why in the next couple of days there is gonna be some pretty big decisions made. It's looking bad news actually...it's looking like we might not be able to get to the bottom on the bikes and we've obviously got a lot of southward to do, so its only going to get colder. The problem being we can't carry enough food to get between supplies. After Piedra Buena, Rio Gallegos is about 250kms and if we are only doing 60kms a day we can't carry enough food to allow us to do that, purely because the wind is so bad and the nights are so cold. Yeah, some big decisions in the next few days...see if the wind drops and allows us to ride. So there you go, Thursday

13th July, 31 years old, wrapped up in a tent in southern Patagonia thinking what the bloody hell I am doing here. I won't be for much longer by the looks of things!

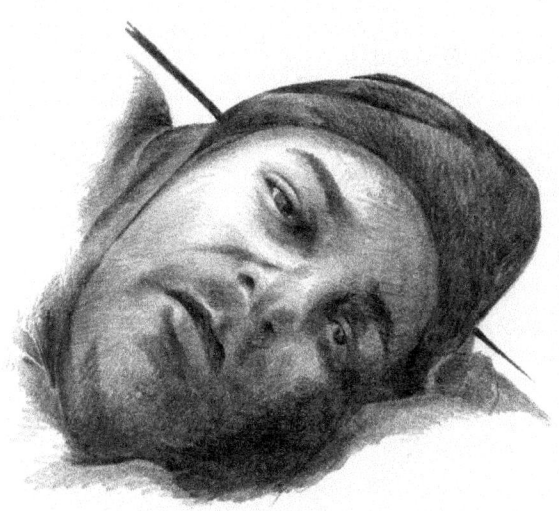

'Martin records his feelings to Keith'

An hour later we broke camp in an apparent lull yet our faith in the weather was misplaced. Within minutes the wind was pounding into our chests and faces. With the temperature hovering around zero, the wind chill made it feel like -8°C on the bike and such was its ferocity I had to turn my head in order to breathe.

This is it. We can't ride in this. We need to make a decision.

I looked over my shoulder to see the boys half a kilometre apart following my lead. I kept going, ignoring the inevitable, the wind buffeting and pushing me into the road. It was all futile and after half an hour I succumbed. I dismounted to be pushed to the ground by the wind, collapsing behind the bike. I was a beaten man. The wind was so strong I couldn't think straight. It whistled through the wheels of the bike, stabbing me in the back like an annoying classmate. I wanted the teacher to send it to stand in the corner. It was roaring at me, eroding all my resolve. Slumped against the trailer, zombie-like, I studied the approaching shapes of Martin and Paps in the featureless distance. I thought about what to say to them, to end this madness. I wanted to cry. I wanted to be swept away from that cold hell. A long while passed, empty thoughts passing through me.

'This is crazy,' I said, as Martin pulled in.

'It's a little pointless,' he agreed. 'How far have we come?'

'Twelve kilometres in two hours.'

'Shit. That means it's 48 to Piedra Buena.'

'There's no way we are gonna do that in this,' I said, referring to the wind.

'I know.'

A few minutes later Paps also pulled in, silent. A sense of desperation was taking hold within all of us and eventually it boiled over into words. 'This is totally pointless! I am knackered and we've only done 12K. How far to Piedra Buena, Martin?' asked Paps, above the noise of the wind.

'At least 48.'

'Well we aren't going to do that are we. The wind is getting worse!'

'Shall we put a tent up and wait it out?' I offered, without thinking.

'The wind will rip a tent to shreds, it's too powerful. Also, we've got hardly any food. Let's try to get a lift,' said Paps.

'But there is no traffic, plus it's too cold to just sit out here,' said Martin. 'I think we need to carry on or head back.'

'If you and Wils want to carry on that's fine but I'm not cycling any further,' said Paps.

No one spoke. The faces of my fellow riders mirrored exactly how I felt. This was it. This was the end, the final throes. Eleven and a half months' cycling had come down to this. Paps piped up again.

'Guys, if you want to keep going, then go for it.'

'There's no way I am leaving you at the side of the road, mate,' I said, looking at him. 'We stay together, it's way too dangerous to leave anyone out here.'

'I don't want to call the shots,' continued Paps. 'I want you and Martin to keep cycling, if that's what you want to do. Don't give in cos I am. You know how I feel, we have been battling this wind for days. There's no way we'll make Piedra Buena.'

'We have to stick together.'

'I agree,' said Martin.

'Well what are we going to do then?' reiterated Paps.

I wanted to scream, to have a real tantrum. We deserved more than this. 'This is bullshit!'

For a long while nobody said anything. 'Come on,' confirmed Martin. 'I think we've all decided that we're heading back to San Julian.'

*

The city of Rio Gallegos was shrouded in darkness when we arrived six hours later. Unloading the bikes, everyone put their front wheel back on, reset the brakes, straightened the handlebars and attached the trailer. Then we rode into town. Later that day, we looked up the next six days' weather forecast in an internet cafe. Outside it was blowing 34mph from the south and the computer screen in front of me predicted no let up. I was mortified. Martin recalls…

By the time we reached Rio Gallegos and saw that the weather system had not changed, we were at our wits' end. Sometimes reality strikes and a critical decision must be made. We had been forced to take alternate forms of transport before; the pick-up in Canada that ferried us through some road works or the articulated lorry when my rear wheel collapsed in Chile. The decision to go to Rio Grande by bus was just another one of these critical decisions.

In total we had stolen 600 miles on the bus between Comodoro Rivadavia and Rio Grande. All that stood between us and Ushuaia now were 220 frozen kilometres across Tierra de Fuego. Would the wind blow again or would we get through? Would we have to retreat and be obliged to take a humiliating bus ride to the finishing point? None of us could stomach the thought of not making it. It would be unthinkable. We rode out of Rio Grande, pensive, not daring to tempt fate. Around the estuary we went, and out along the Atlantic coast spotting plenty of wildfowl and birdlife as the conditions remained calm. Then the road took us inland through a stunted forest, past frozen lakes where we saw some opportunistic huntsmen bag an unlucky beaver resting atop the ice. The temperature was bitter but there was still no wind. We stumbled upon a lodge on the shores of Lake Fagnano and three Englishmen went to sleep with an impossible expectation.

'This is it boys!' said The Machine, as we broke out the following morning.

I took in a huge breath of air and hooked in to the straps of my right pedal. The day had finally arrived, the day where reaching Ushuaia – just a name, a make-believe place until now – was within touching distance. 'Please let us through,' I said to myself.

Just 60 miles separated us from our goal. My biggest fear was that the wind would blow or the road would become buried with snow. We climbed away from the lake, up along a mountain road, through a gorge and up the flank of a valley. A generous layer of snow became a permanent fixture with the road covered in ice. What few vehicles there were trundled past on snow chains as we went over the pass and down into another snow covered valley. Martin and Paps led the way. Only the sound of my tyres crunching through the powder and my heavy breathing could be heard through the deafening voices in my head.

What a spectacular goodbye from life on the road. We have made it...it can't be. We were nobodies. There were so many doubters, so many false promises but look at us now, veterans of the road about to cross the finish line together. It's too much...

We were close; thirty kilometres then twenty then ten. At times I freewheeled with one leg outstretched on the ice, searching for more grip. My heart thumped hard with excitement, like it had done on that infamous day out of Prudhoe. Something we had planned, dreamt and lived for three years was about to end. In a strange way I didn't want to get there. No matter the problems of the past twelve months, right now I wanted the experience to last a little longer. Our way of life was all but over. Breathing heavily, tears streaming as the ice-cold air blew against my face, I looked forward to see my two friends, several hundred metres ahead, guiding me in to the finish. I started daydreaming about the two of them; Martin and his difficulty in being away from Sam, his hatred of cycling. Ahead of him was Paps who had beaten the self-doubt, come through his break up with Naomi and most incredibly the pain and frustration of his knees. Seeing him at the front seemed to fit the script. On we went, each kilometre feeling like five as the anticipation became unbearable. Underneath a ski lift and along the gently rolling valley we rode, trees lining the way. There wasn't a breath of wind, just the crunching snow and our thoughts. Even the sight of both of them losing grip on the icy road couldn't stave off the expectancy of seeing the welcome sign.

Where is the sign? We must be so close. Where is it?

The white line had taken us to the edge of reason, along a biscuit highway filled with madness and despair that had arrived in Oregon and swelled to extraordinary portions over the following 11,000 miles. Yet now the madness had vanished, replaced by a wellbeing soaked in ecstasy, overflowing in emotion, a fantasyland that knew no boundary. Quite suddenly we were at the end of the rainbow.

'Is that it? That's it! That's it, that's the sign! We're here boys!' screamed Paps.

I looked down at the computer. It read 23,828kms (14,812 miles). A broad smile broke out across my face as I concentrated on not stacking it in the final few yards.

I'll be damned, Paps is right, that's it, that's the sign!

My memory of what happened next is a bit sketchy. All I know is that we pulled up, got off the bikes, hugged and then started taking photos. I have no recollection of who did or said what, until a police officer wondered over for some casual banter. 'Can you take a photo of us please?' I asked him, amid the commotion.

'Sure. Where have you come from?'

'Alaska.'

'Yeah? When did you leave?'

'August.'

The officer paused to digest what he had just heard. 'Not bad!'

'How far is it into town?' asked Paps, after the all-important photo was secured.

'3,000 kilometres,' joked the officer.

Epilogue

As I write this, the trip ended nearly two years ago. Believably, perhaps, everything came to an abrupt end and there was no team celebration in Ushuaia. Put simply, no one had the energy or inclination to fake an atmosphere that simply didn't exist. Instead we each sat back and reflected on what had come and gone.

Over the following couple of days we hung out, called home and visited a neighbouring National Park. Paps and I stripped our rides of what we wanted and passed the rest to Martin, who salvaged as much as he could. The morning of Paps's and my departure we all convened in a coffee shop with Keith to record 45 minutes of our feelings. On the tape we look subdued; a few jokes, a few stories but more than anything we were shot to pieces. Most incredible was how casually we said goodbye to each other. My farewell to Martin was played out on the high street.

'So this is it,' I offered, feeling rather unsure about what to say or do.

'Yep,' replied Martin, stepping forward to hug me.

'Thanks for looking after me,' I said, his embrace causing me to force back the tears.

'Make sure you stay in touch, OK?'

'Absolutely, bye mate.'

'Bye.'

It was that simple. Paps and I flew to Buenos Aires where I was met at the airport by Carolina. Stepping outside the terminal building our goodbye was similarly brief.

'Mate, why don't you take this taxi and we'll catch the next one?' I offered.

'It's fine, I know where I'm going,' said Paps. 'You get out of here.'

'Many thanks for everything,' I said, leaning in to wrap my arms around him.

'Same to you mate, same to you.'

Some six months later, Carolina and I saw the band, Coldplay, play live in Buenos Aires. When they played "Politik", I quite unexpectedly broke down in tears, unable to hold back the memories that the song induced within me. I had played it in my tent one frozen night in southern Patagonia when I was shivering with cold and the tent was shaking violently from the wind. Hearing it resonate around the concert hall overwhelmed me, engulfed me. I couldn't escape the tent, the cold, the effort of that year and the physical distance we had cycled. I could feel the pain of my frozen feet and fingers, how it felt for my body to be shaking uncontrollably. I could see the glow of my head torch and visualise the remoteness of our location, the utter loneliness that 11 months riding had left inside me. Stood in that concert hall, my body was finally releasing the pain and emotion it had collected. As tears rolled down my face I thought about Paps and Martin and it was then that the level of the challenge hit me like a tidal wave. We had produced something very special that year, something to indeed hang my hat on.

James Wilson.

Plan International

A few days after visiting the projects in El Salvador we received the following email.

Date: *Thu, 2nd Mar.*

Dear Anthony, James and Martin,

I figure by the time you read this, you probably have already left Salvadoran territory. I just wanted to reiterate that I very much enjoyed meeting you as much as everyone else in Plan El Salvador. No words will ever be enough to express our admiration and gratitude for the support you are providing to the education of countless Salvadoran children.

…Good luck and take care! Han.

Han Dijsselbloem, Country Director, Plan El Salvador.
Registered Charity No. 276035. www.plan-international.org

Statistics

Distance cycled:	14,812 miles (23,838kms).
Time:	347 days.
Average including days off:	42.7 miles per day (68.7kms per day).
Average excluding days off:	61.2 miles per day (98.5kms per day).
Longest Country:	Mexico. 2,750 miles. (4,430kms)
Shortest Country:	Honduras. 60 miles. (96kms)
Greatest distance in a single day:	102 miles. (165kms) 29th June. La Pampa, Argentina.
Shortest distance in a single day:	2 miles. (3kms) 12th February. Santa Cruz, Mexico.
Highest number of consecutive days in the saddle:	14. Newport Beach, USA to Santa Rosalía, Mexico.
Highest total in a calendar week:	527 miles (849kms) 26th June to 2nd July. Argentina.
Highest total in calendar month:	1,880 miles (3,018kms) June.
Highest altitude reached:	3,500 m. Alto de las Minas Pass, Colombia.

Kit List

Bikes:	Dawes Sardar with strengthened rims and butterfly handlebars.
Original Saddles:	Specialized body geometry.
Suspension:	Cane Creek Thudbuster seat posts.
Original Tyres:	26x1.75 (or 1.5) Schwalbe Marathon.
Transmission:	9 Speed Shimano Deore.
Trailers:	BOB special anniversary edition with waterproof hardwearing trailer bag.
Tents:	2-man Vango Microlite 200.
Mattresses:	Thermarest self inflating.
Sleeping Bags:	2 Vango and 1 Nanok, all 3 season with separate silk liners.
Water Filter:	MSR Miox.
Stove: Stu & Steve.	MSR Dragonfly with 2 no. ¾ Litre fuel bottles powered by regular petrol. (Hexiburner back up stove).
Cooking set:	Pots, plates, bowls, cutlery, washing kit.
Principal cycling gear (each):	Foska cycling tops, long sleeve ADS top, fleece, waterproofs, cycling underwear, shorts, trousers, hat, gloves, neck buff, helmet, thermal socks, SPD's, sunglasses.
Additional kit:	Thermal underwear, socks, pants, walking shoes, sandals, wash kits, towels, water bottles, tool set with spare spokes, bottom brackets, jockey wheels, tyres, inner tubes, gear and brake cables, derailleur, oil; head torches, first aid kit, lipsil, whistle, mosquito repellent, anti scratch clicker, mosquito head nets; repair kits for tents, mattresses, tyres; tape, 2 digital cameras, 1 video camera with associated discs, batteries and chargers; bungee cords, stuff sacks, washing powder, glasses, contact lenses.
Miscellaneous:	Diaries, pens, novels, dictionary, IPODs, Passports, Money.

Route & Chapter Guide

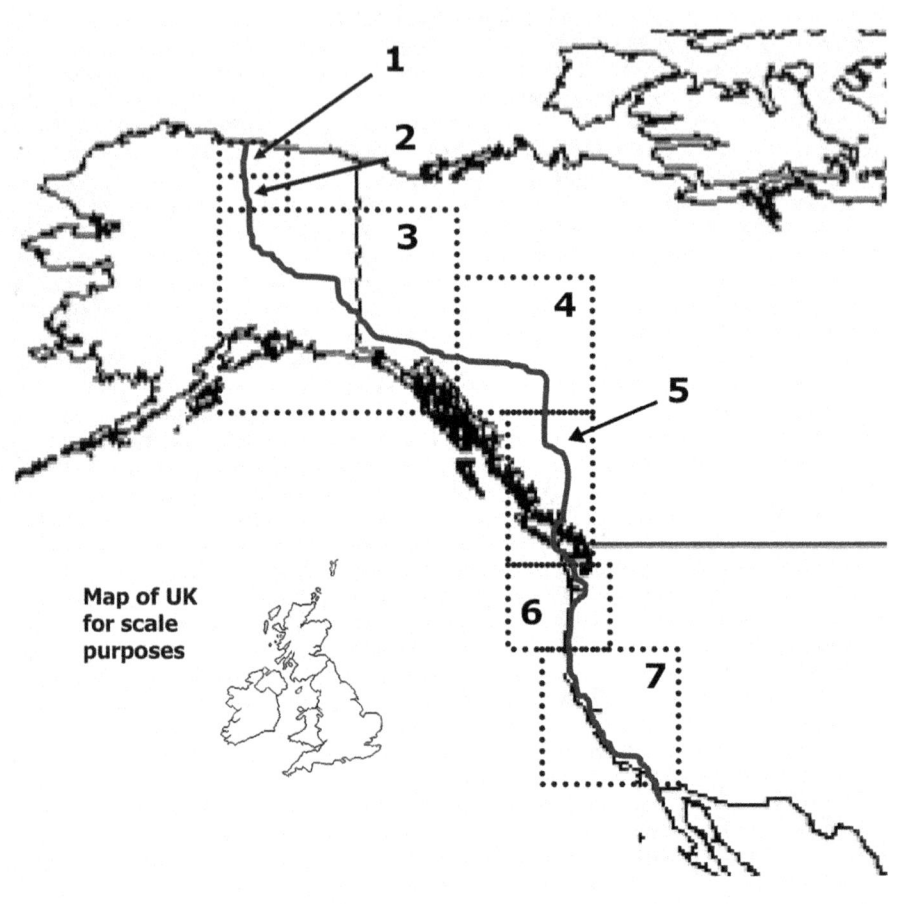

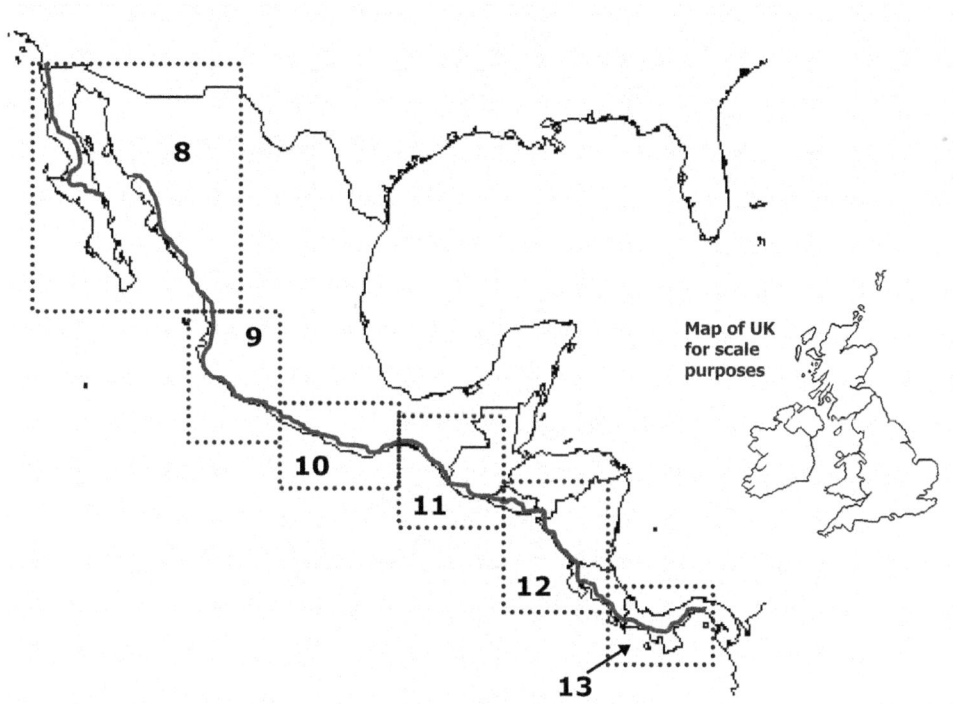

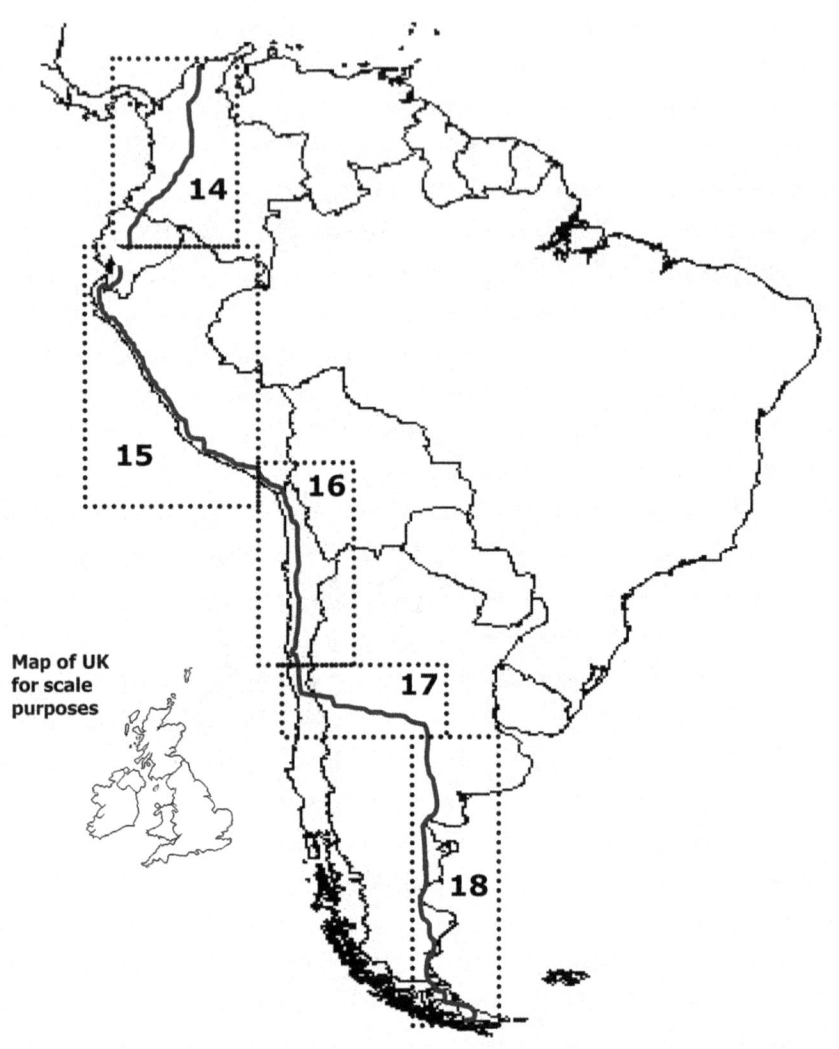

www.ingramcontent.com/pod-product-compliance
Lightning Source LLC
Chambersburg PA
CBHW062210080426
42734CB00010B/1862